NOTES FROM THE
NEW UNDERGROUND

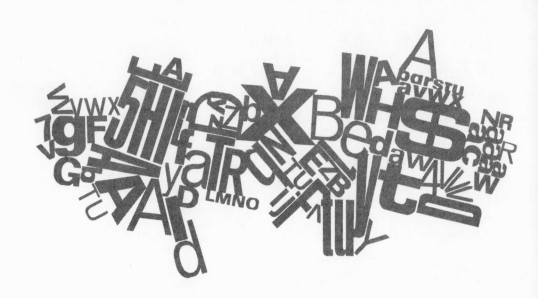

Notes from the New Underground

AN ANTHOLOGY

EDITED BY JESSE KORNBLUTH

NEW YORK / THE VIKING PRESS

FOR MY PARENTS, AND
CHANDLER BROSSARD

CONTENTS

viii / Contents

III. The Nature of the Revolt   119

IV. The Hippies: Flowering of a Nonmovement   199

V. The Ascendancy of Agape and Its Abuses   245

2 NY PATROLMEN SHOT IN AUTO MELEE

NEW YORK—Two patrolmen were shot and wounded when a gun battle erupted Tuesday night among three off-duty policemen following an automobile mishap on the Cross-Bronx Expressway.

The injured were identified as probationary patrolman Nicolo J. Danisi, 24, in critical condition with a head wound, and patrolman John Dalton, 41, in serious condition with a chest wound. Both are in Jacobi Hospital.

All three were dressed in civilian clothes and driving their own cars when the incident began.

—*Boston Globe,* July 10, 1968

Introduction

On a warm May day twenty-two years after the defeat of Nazi Germany, members of the police attacked a crowd of several hundred people in New York City. Arbitrarily ordered by a policeman to move off the park grass, they had refused; before the afternoon was over, seventy policemen had roughed up an obviously pregnant woman, sent three people to the hospital, and arrested thirty-six more on a "noise complaint." One man, hysterical and bloody, screamed as he was being led away: "My God, my God. Where is this happening? Is this America?"

The question was rhetorical—the incident occurred in New York's Tompkins Square Park. Those who were arrested were hippies, which seemed the most relevant fact to the press. "HIPPIES CLASH WITH POLICE," *The New York Times* headline claimed; it ran over a story by a former police commissioner. Only in the last few paragraphs did the reporter suggest that the police had provoked the incident. "What could we write?" he explained to a reporter from *The East Village Other*. "The hippies did clash with the police. We couldn't say the police attacked them. I did the best I could."

Anger at the injustice of it all is superfluous; city officials recognized their *gaffe*—it is simply bad public relations to beat white kids in daylight—and the mayor made sure the cops didn't stage a rerun. And in the end, if you tried hard enough, you could develop a rationale for the event; in the argot of the moment, everyone was doing his thing. Is everybody happy? Then shut up and do your thing.

But "doing your thing" proved less acceptable if you belonged to a deviate subculture like that of the hippies, and to the general delight, the problem of equal social justice for the hippies seemed irrelevant. It was agreed that dealing with protesters was more popularly approved than harassing people who seemed to want to be left alone. You could argue rationally against protest while our fighting men were overseas, but it was hard to criticize the hippies without descending to their level of irrationality.

Yet that kind of irrationality tells us more about the *status quo* than a dozen peace vigils. For the moment someone stops talking about change and just begins to enact it, we generally find a defender of the public morals rising to the occasion with the usual question: "What right do you have to criticize if you can't do better?" It's an old argument, and Samuel Johnson thought he'd settled it two hundred years ago ("You may scold a carpenter who has made you a bad table . . . It is not your trade to make tables"), but it doesn't much matter. The question hangs, the silence makes it an accusation, the stammered reply is the admission of guilt. What hippie could run the country better than General Motors? And if he could, why would he want to?

So the hippies and all they represented were judged no better than anyone else; they understood, some say, at least as well as the Republican Party what was wrong with the country, but the vulnerability of their life style finally did them in. Because few listened seriously to the chants of antiwar demonstrators, the triumph of official irrationality was virtually insured. Knowledge, as a pre-McLuhanite once insisted, is power, and there are those who remember when there used to be some truth in that statement. Now the idea seems laughable.

With the power structure opposed mostly by those even less cohesive than the hippies, contemporary history will read more and more like bad Pinter: something went radically wrong during those years; what was it? Politics, of course, for one. Stripped of gentlemanly niceties, the kindest statement about the period is that the decline of political values from sordid to simply disgusting was gradual enough to prevent mass lunacy. When Robert McNamara, then in favor with the Johnson Administration, let it be known his favorite poet was Yeats ("Things fall apart; the center cannot hold"), we might have guessed about future developments. For the failure of liberalism, with all its noble resolve and corporate savvy, necessarily ushers in the forces of repression; if the people don't appreciate what is being done for them, then let them see what can be done to them. Read skeptically, President Johnson's voice is enough to frighten even Berkeley leftists: "The overriding rule which I want to affirm is that our foreign policy must always be an extension of our domestic policy. Our safest guide to what we do abroad is always what we do at home."

But it doesn't stop with politics. Just to keep things lively, the pill put the screws on conventional morality, while drug use soared beyond Dr.

Leary's wildest hallucinations. But the mass audience had its own opiates; the movies surpassed their own norms of triviality to plumb new levels of myopic profundity, while television managed to make Negro violence look small time.

And then there was the ubiquitous war: the war that dislocated all sensibilities (even if you liked it, you wanted to win and get out), the war that caused Navy pilots to carry plastic baby bottles on bombing missions (to relieve "a terrible dryness in the mouth"), the war that saw 1500 tons of napalm dropped each month on soldiers and civilians (although an American commission of physicians reported in *The New York Times* that "most burn cases . . . had been caused by the improper use of gasoline as a cooking and lighting fuel").

There was little sense to any of it, but the adults seemed able to cope; in late '67, seventy-five per cent of those consulted in the Harris poll felt that militant protests hurt the cause of peace. But many of the young— who weren't asked for their tax dollars, merely for their lives—could smell a cop-out, and as we became able to see trends, we began to realize that we were being had. And in the grand style of P. T. Barnum.

We thought, and I say this with some embarrassment for my naïveté, that adults really meant what they said, that when Presidents speak of peace they don't mean war, that when terms like democracy are bandied about they don't mean the totalitarianism of the center. It is honestly very difficult to understand words these days; my old school motto— "Dare to be true"—seemed to make sense for two centuries, but "flower power," which some thought had about the same meaning, was lucky to last a year.

But the disillusionment of the young quickly becomes cliché; one forgets too easily that a runaway is a child who forsakes his home for the streets. These breathing, confused organisms who take their lives in their own hands are looking for some meaning to it all; how many of them, one wonders, find anything to live for? Meaning is among the rarest of our country's commodities in these days when no one gives an honest answer. Adults lie; there's no other way to phrase it, and what's worse, they seem to do it most in the little issues. Drinking heavily, disregarding the warning on cigarette packages, they condemn marijuana, tell you to cut your hair, turn down the music. One remembers all too well the article in the *Times* by a child psychiatrist who warned parents to be suspicious of drug use if the child spoke of God, love, or peace. It is well known among college students that school psychologists generally cooperate with the deans, and the deans seem glad to oblige the federal authorities.

So while it must seem like the blind leading the blind, there's a bit of self-preservation in the refusal of adolescents to speak openly with anyone but their peers. And because only the young seem interested in rock music, youth culture reinforces itself, a process that explains the popularity of the "underground press."

Although underground newspapers are hardly serious literature, they do seem to have a few preoccupations with the truth; at least, they tell us what we are predisposed to hear. In any other area of American life, this might be taken as one more example of rampant hucksterism, but in the case of these newspapers it is simply a matter of the audience and the editors being approximately the same age. Quite simply, an underground paper is generally written by the alienated for the alienated.

What is perhaps most exciting about these papers, from the adolescent viewpoint, is that adults seem to abhor them. Judges mutter about possible censorship when advertisers promote intriguing sexual devices; the underground press is a grab bag of the *verboten*. Taken in quantity, the papers' ritualized reports of drug busts, radical politics, and third-rate astrology are about as dull as the stock-market quotations. No matter; readers will flip through all of it until they learn who's to be trusted, who's to be ignored.

Only two years ago, one could easily ignore the entire spectrum of underground papers; at that time the word "underground" applied mostly to moviemakers. Then came the Underground Press Syndicate, formed to capitalize on the implications of subversion contained in that title and to trade articles of interest so that they could reach a wider audience. Twenty-five papers appeared haphazardly before public attention was focused on the so-called hippie communities, and although membership in the Syndicate skyrocketed to fifty papers in a few months, it was generally assumed, even by the editors of some of the papers, that the decline of the hippies would bring about a corresponding slump in the number of newspapers. No one had counted on JohnsonHumphrey.

The continuation of the war in Vietnam and the attacks on both responsible and militant dissent kept the papers alive, and the general trend in world politics encouraged others to join the UPS brigade. High school students, prohibited from criticizing their education in the official papers, started mimeographed newssheets to generate controversy. Membership climbed to one hundred, and requests for associate status doubled. While tightrope finances failed to sustain some, efficiently managed newspapers were able to expand, often to the dissatisfaction of local officials. In Cambridge, Massachusetts, the *Avatar*—perhaps the most professional of all the biweeklies—was removed from newsstands by an overzealous mayor; when its editors applied for a street permit, they were told *Avatar* was a commodity, not a newspaper, and the free-speech issue was void. Forty arrests later, *Avatar* was still without a street permit and still in operation.

But *Avatar* is the exception to the general pattern of official displeasure. Editors of many papers have visited their local jails, and in a number of cities, extreme pressure has caused papers to fold. Should this opposition to a minority press frighten other papers away from political subjects, the value of such journals will be further diminished.

For the moment, however, the underground represents more than a loose configuration of biweekly journals; it is also an attempt to legitimize dissenting reporting, to develop a constituency for radical politics, and, of course, to titillate an audience too well versed in political and cultural affairs to enjoy the mindlessness of mass journalism.

Honesty is no cure for the banal, however, and the present collection includes perhaps even more of the folly of this generation than of its wisdom. Both have been hard bought, but even after several years of publication, most papers still have not developed a coherent view of the contemporary American experience. From this occasionally incoherent plea for understanding and reform one hopes for some more profound realization of our dilemma. For the age-old argument about the follies of youth could not be more inapplicable here; the issues are serious, the alternatives few, and the potential for genuine rebellion is omnipresent. *Forsan et haec olim meminisse iuvabit*, as Virgil wrote; someday, we may look back on these times and laugh. And then again, we may not.

—JESSE KORNBLUTH

January, 1968
Cambridge, Massachusetts

NOTES FROM THE
NEW UNDERGROUND

I. The Contemporary American Juggernaut, and Beyond

If you are a young man, scheduled to be drafted to defend an abstract freedom, you cultivate a desperate appreciation of the absurd. If you are a young girl, receiving a superior education in preparation for a job as a secretary, your sense of the ironies of life increases untempered by the resignation that supposedly accompanies maturity. We have little in common with our parents, who suffered during the Depression only to resolve that the elimination of personal poverty was their primary aim in life. Now, on the whole, they have succeeded, but history is not rich in free lunches, and their overemphasis of raw Protestant ethic is counterbalanced by our antimaterialist commitments.

The moral bankruptcy of a nation that prides itself mostly on its seventy million television sets and its yearly bonanza of overpowered cars is apparent to most people of any sensitivity; when a country's primary value is production, efficacy becomes paramount and human values are shunted aside. Adults are caught in this trap. For a middle-aged man, bound by the reinforcing obligations of parenthood and marriage, escape is limited to fantasy or to the intellectual oblivion of sports, sex, and liquor. But the young do not have these responsibilities, and it is only natural, then, that they do not rush to fill minor niches in our country's corporations. "Business can be creative," the ads blare, but even the most casual encounter with American industries leads one to believe that the concept of creativity has been strangely redefined.

If we refuse to succumb to traditional aspirations, it is because we see too well what success has done to our elders. Politically powerless, morally confused, and spiritually afraid, they would have us believe that time and the liberal tradition will set things right. We recognize our impotence and admit to chaos, and that not only makes possible a tentative groping for a way out, but also is the starting point for all discussion about the chasm between the generations.

If the underground press is confident about nothing else, it is sure it knows what ails America. Allen Katzman, a poet and an editor of New York's East Village Other, *examines the distorted values of middle-class society and suggests one method of exposing its hypocrisy.*

I Read the News Today, Oh Boy

ALLEN KATZMAN

FADE IN: A man's face flashes on a nineteen-inch screen. As a child's smile starts to invade the lower corners of his cheeks, he holds up to the center of the picture a conventional image of a time bomb, black and round with a fuse on its topmost portion. The words TIME BOMB are written on its frontal surface to eliminate any other conclusion. Below these words appear a thirty-second register of time with, of course, only a second hand. He pushes down on the fuse engaging it and it begins to tick away. His objective is to throw the bomb to someone else before the clock reaches thirty and the fuse pops up. He throws it to a child on his left who in turn throws it to another child on his left and so on until it lands back in the man's hands. The fuse pops up as he grabs it and the children yell out "you lose." FADE OUT.

The above is an actual description of a commercial for a new toy game called Time Bomb, which appears on TV every evening at around eight o'clock. It is not only a game for children but adults as well. It gives us a peek into where America is at or going and what games are being played on our consciousness every day at around eight o'clock. The irony would be complete if the game caught on and sold like hotcakes. It would make the Parker Brothers game of Monopoly appear to be more than mere imagination. And who's to say it's not? Who's to say it's not more real than what appears on TV or for that matter in the newspapers?

When we reach across to twist the dials of our set or touch the black encrustation of alphabet soup called words that appear daily on cheap paper, how can we say where we end and it begins? When we bite into that first morning's bit of toasted bread and stare at our everyday reality of digestible events, who's to say we are not more addicted to this mental

The East Village Other, December 15, 1967

5

feast than we are to breakfast? And who's to say that the thing being devoured and the devourer are not one and the same, that we are not fodder for a greater feast called Media?

The credibility gap has allowed the incredible to take place. Most reporting of news events takes on a ludicrous effect because of what and how much is reported. When District Attorney Garrison states that "the People who killed President Kennedy are those who had the most to gain from his death and we all know who they are," and it's reported in the media along with other strange facts about UFO sightings, the Hippies, the Runaways, the Anti-war people, the War people, what's doing on the planet earth, what's doing outside the planet earth, and who put the clam in Mrs. Murphy's chowder, the news takes on a strange discoloration all its own. Even in a clear moment of sanity or total inebriation, one can honestly mistake it for something else like just another rerun from the TV show "The Man from U.N.C.L.E."

It's all a game, the mulberry bush of the frantic fact, and we go round and round until we are hypnotized by the dynamics of it all or fall to the ground in a heap of exhaustion.

What the technocrats would term "overload input" occurs when we try to control or break the conditioning. What the psychiatrists call "schizophrenia" becomes our reality when the conditioning begins to crumble. How many people do we know who are strong enough to resist it all and come up smelling like roses?

Of course the news is not the only game that takes place every day and which people readily accept as *real*. In the next couple of months and so on until Election Day, our minds will be inundated with the oldest game of all—Politics. Men with real flesh and bone will don the costume of Candidate. They will kiss babies, come to your neighborhood to shake hands with you and listen to your problems. They will appear on radio and TV, in debates and interviews. They will take on character, shape, and size and we will fill in all their words and actions of what they will do if nominated or elected with all our own meaningful frustrations, hopes, and desires. Each one of them will become a Specter of our own making without a possible trace of the most banal of human functions: a ghost who has solved the problem of elimination. They will be packaged and presented to the public in all possible ways—taped, live, or in the flesh—but always synthetic.

And then will come the National Conventions to nominate a Party Candidate, which will take on the proportions of the largest spectator sport in history. We will be there as it is made, manufactured, or programmed into us for some future time. And after the nominations, more speeches, more words, more live and taped interviews and debates until the final day when the whole game is absolved by our own simple yes or no. We will enter the sport at the last possible moment, run home to watch it happen on TV as the election returns come pouring in, to see how our one moment of active participation fared, and all brought to us live by the makers of who, what—Reality?

About a year ago the media reported the interesting fact that Our President did quite a bit of the People's business while on the toilet; an appropriate throne for any king. It was one of the few times in the history of communication that a fact was more than pseudo. What Our President was doing and thinking became, in a rare instance of reality, reconciled.

What is real and what is not remains a mystery to us. For those of us who know, and they are few, the game is just that—unreal—and will remain so unless we ourselves catch these specters off camera, away from the game struct called media, in a private moment of nakedness where what they mean is what they say, and maybe then it will all be real.

What it all boils down to is one large pseudo-event, you might term it, the hype of the year. It is our inheritance as children of the media, the TV teener and boppers, and it is an inheritance we are learning to use at a faster rate than do our parents who spawned it.

In the next few months and so on to election day of '68 the Underground Press, in cooperation with the 125 college newspapers of the liberation news service, will hold its own pseudo-event. We shall elect our own man to rule over the Underground States of America, who will also double as the spiritual ambassador to Washington, D.C., Capital of the United States of America. We shall form our own conventions with our own rules and our own brand of politics. We shall report it in our media using our own publicity resources, the 185 newspapers and radio stations across the nation, thereby drawing away publicity from the "other" election.

When the establishment press reports how the campaign of Nixon (if he is nominated) is going in Hoschkoch, we shall report how our candidate, the High and Mighty SH (Spiritual Head), is doing in Paduck. When the establishment press reports on what Nixon or Johnson or whoever believes in, we will report how our candidate loves, lives, and breathes.

The media has placed a time bomb in our hands called politics—a game which we will play to the hilt, and when the fuse goes off it will be the children of the printed page and dotted image who will yell out "you lose."

Paul Goodman was battling the Establishment before many of us were born. Political essayist, Utopian planner, and poet, he combines the anger and energy of the young with the breadth of vision of the mature. The events he predicts for the 1980s are becoming the realities of the 1960s.

The Diggers in 1984

PAUL GOODMAN

I. Socio-Psychological Factors

There were two main movements toward rural reconstruction in the early '70s. The first was the social decision to stop harassing the radical young, and rather to treat them kindly like Indians and underwrite their reservations. This humane policy—instead of raids of Treasury agents on the colleges, horrendous sentences for draft card burning, cracking children's skulls on the Sunset Strip—was the idea of social engineer Donald Michael, of the Institute for Policy Studies. Michael argued that, if the serious aim of society was to increase the GNP, it was more efficient to treat the non-conformists like Indians. Naturally, this was difficult when their reservations were in the middle of metropolitan areas, like the Haight-Ashbury or East Greenwich Village, or on the big university campuses. But this plan became much more feasible when an inventive tribe, the Diggers, suddenly remembered the peasant and Taoist origins of their ideology and began to forage in the country.

The second wave of ruralism was the amazing multiplication of hermits and monks who began to set up places in the depopulated areas for their meditations and services to mankind. There had always been individuals who felt that the mechanized urban areas were ugly and unhygienic and who therefore fled to the country, at first only for the summers. (I remember a nest of these in the '50s around Wardsboro, members of the Congress for Cultural Freedom supported by the CIA.) But it was not until the early '70s that humanists began to realize that society had indeed reverted to Byzantine or Late Imperial times, and who therefore withdrew to save their souls.

These two kinds of emigration sufficiently explain, I think, the present

Ramparts, September, 1967

patchquilt of settlement in Vermont. On the one hand, where the Diggers settled, there are square-dance communes with their unauthentic mountain music and the extraordinary effort to develop a late-frost hemp, something like the inept taro culture in Micronesia. The Diggers have been called lawless, but their simple code—(1) Live and Let Live, and (2) the Golden Rule—is probably adequate for their simple lives. Except for the ceremonial hemp, their agriculture is strictly for subsistence; many of them live like pigs anyway. On the other hand, the hermits and the religious, with their synods according to Roberts' "Rules of Order" and their Finnish-style wooden architecture, perform social services by running Summerhill-type schools and rest homes for the retired. And their beautiful intensive and glasshouse farming, copied from the Dutch, provides the only tasty urban food now available. Besides these, there are the gurus like Goodman, who lives across the Connecticut and is terribly old.

The two distinct types coexist peaceably and of course are peaceable people. Indeed, it was during the Vietnam troubles that society first began to encourage their exodus, to get them out of the Pentagon's hair. It happened this way: Diggers and many other youths were burning draft cards in embarrassing numbers. In desperation, to get them away from settled places, the *agents provocateurs* began to schedule the be-ins and T-groups further and further out in the sticks, with transportation paid by the CIA. To the government's surprise, this caught on. The urban young suddenly decided it was groovy to dig up carrots right from the ground, to shake down apples, and to fuck the sheep; they began to camp out, and then to squat and settle. They also imagined they would grow hemp. Many professors, meantime, after signing several hundred anti-war protests in the *Times* (for which, by some slip-up, they could *not* get a CIA subsidy), finally became conscience-stricken about working for M.I.T., Columbia, and Berkeley, and quit and set up little colleges in the hills. The rest is history. But it was not until the Kennedy-Wallace Administration that the official policy of land grants and rural subsidies began. (As we shall see, this was after the Seven Plagues.)

At present there is plenty of mixing between Digger types and professor types, though at the beginning they hardly communicated. When some authentic music comes to Vermont, from Tanzania or Cambodia, it is common to find beatniks with their matted hair and lice sprawled on a professor's maple floor; and there is intermarriage. I do not mean to imply that Diggers are unattractive. Some are unkempt in a becoming way, some are diamonds in the rough, a few are real barbaric dandies. On the whole, they are sweet and serviceable people, are glad to serve as school aides, pull weeds, etc. The professors, in turn, are democratic and would like to teach them something, but unfortunately there was the break in the cultural tradition that occurred at the time of "Don't trust anybody over thirty." Since the young wouldn't trust anybody— justifiably—they couldn't learn anything. And now their own children have an unbreakable apperceptive block, impervious to Head Start programs.

Common elements in the Vermont culture are fresh food, good hi-fi and much playing of musical instruments, jalopies of all vintages, disregard of moral legislation, and low taxes. At some level, all are good citizens. Public services are cheap, roads are good enough, because everybody pitches in. It is touching to see Diggers who won't wash their faces carefully depositing their beer cans in litterbaskets. Another common element is, of course, Senator Aiken, who is now one hundred.

II. Ecological and Economic Factors

Generally speaking, emigration and rural reconstruction were unexpected consequences of the Great Enclosure policy, which was supposed to get most people *off* the land and speed up urbanization. This is another example of the rule that, if people survive, inept social engineering will produce a contrary effect.

The American Enclosure of the twentieth century consisted of subsidizing chain grocers and agrindustrial plantations, giving high profits to processors and packagers, befuddling the public with brand names, destroying fertile land for suburban sprawl and aircraft companies, destroying water supplies and importing expensive water, preventing rural cooperation by monopoly tactics, destroying country schools, farmers' markets and small food stores by urban renewal, destroying villages by highways and supermarkets. By the '60s only six per cent of the population was rural. Vast beautiful areas had been depopulated and were returning to swamp, as in the later Roman empire.

Meantime there were obvious signs of urban over-population. Urban costs mounted geometrically, for utilities, sanitation, policing, housing, schooling, welfare, transit, etc. To live in a densely populated area, in however degraded a condition, was itself a luxury; yet the inhabitants were becoming poorer and poorer. The middle classes, who had options, fled to the periphery to avoid taxes and the lower classes. Despite the agricultural technology, the price of food did not diminish, since the economics scale went to the middlemen; and once the possibility of small competition was destroyed, the chains went to town. One could no longer buy an edible tomato. When southern sharecropping was destroyed by mechanization, no effort was made to give subsistence to the Negroes; they were forced to come to northern urban areas, even though the worst public housing cost twenty thousand dollars a dwelling unit to provide. (I say "urban areas" because there were no longer such things as "cities." I say "dwelling unit" because there were no longer such things as "homes.") A psychiatric survey of midtown New York in the '6os showed that seventy-five per cent of the people were neurotic and twenty-five per cent needed immediate treatment. There were seventy thousand heroin addicts in New York.

Since the structure was economically unviable, there were frequent riots, school boycotts, rent strikes, and strikes of municipal services. To these, the government responded with noble speech, confused programs, and enough actual money to finance several reports by sociologists. Departments of urban affairs were opened at several universities. In 1966, the mayor of New York said that it would cost fifty billion dollars to make New York City alone "livable."

Thus, the Summer of Seven Plagues was entirely predictable, and was indeed predicted. It is still not clear, however, how many of the disasters occurred in a chain reaction, and how many were just "bad luck." It started with a transit strike in one of the big urban areas. For a couple of weeks many people couldn't get to work, and every available motor vehicle in the region crammed the streets. Then finally occurred what we had been expecting for years: the traffic got so thick that it did not move at all. Unfortunately, instead of just giving up and abandoning the cars for a time, the drivers kept edging back and forth to extricate themselves. And during this crisis there occurred a serious temperature inversion and a wind from the factories to the west. That night, forty thousand people died from the smog. The shock of this tragedy ended the transit strike. But unluckily, on the next night occurred the power failure that lasted two days and cost two billion dollars, more than the cost of a month of the Vietnam war. This seems to have had some connection with the previous troubles. Some double agents paid by the CIA to do studies in sabotage had decided that it was a bully time for fun and games. This was one of the CIA's bigger booboos.

All spring and summer there had been a drought, and now a week after the blackout came the climax of the water famine, when the outmoded pipes sprang some fatal leaks that were not patched up in time. In an urban area of ten million people, this caused untold suffering and perhaps another twenty thousand deaths. And this in turn led directly to the great riot, for it *was* a long hot summer. And a few days later the new SST, returning from its maiden voyage, overshot and plunged into the skyscrapers. But this too had been in the cards and had been foretold. It is now more than a decade since the Seven Plagues, yet we still cannot calculate the mental breakdowns.

It was at this time that one of the junkies among the Diggers was heard to say, "Zap! This urban area has put the whammies on me!" "But man," said his friend, "like how you gonna score up there in that mountain where a stream runs?" "Zap! I say Zap!" A coed said, "I am tired of having premarital intercourse in urban areas. Who loves to lie with me under the greenwood tree, come hither! come hither!" As in a dream, an economist remembered Borsodi's "Prosperity and Security," which he had read as a boy. And a humanist wrote a paper pointing out that Michelangelo's Florence numbered one hundred thousand and Goethe's Weimar perhaps twenty-five thousand.

A finite number of years later, after several million people had already emigrated to the land, Lurleen Wallace—Bobby had had the usual Kennedy luck—signed the Land Grant and Rural Subsistence Act. Mildred Loomis, the grand lady of the Green Revolution, was named administrator; but since she was a kind of Henry George anarchist, her phone was bugged.

III. Rural Reconstruction

The tendency of efficient technology since 1900—electrification, automobiles, power tools, distant communication—was toward dispersal and decentralization. Only promoters and self-aggrandizers had pushed the urbanization. Thus some kind of rural reconstruction was bound to occur. When cybernation made possible the absolute concentration of a whole industry in a small area with a small labor force, the vast agglomerations of factory towns became obsolete; and there was no technical reason why decentralized teams of designers and programmers should not tend their gardens or go fishing. Nevertheless, it has been a gradual process, full of serendipity and hang-ups, for rural life to find its present shape.

The present rural reconstruction, such as it is, is not "pastoral" withdrawal. The Diggers and the humanist professors wanted to get out of the urban areas, but they certainly did not intend to quit the mainstream of social problems; if anything, both groups were more socially committed than the average, though they did not have the "politics" of liberal reformers. In any case, they created a framework of social service, and the immense number who have come since the Plagues and the government grants have fitted into it. It is a peculiar post-urban kind of ruralism.

(As of 1983, the "rural" population was twelve per cent, and the United States as a whole was already more livable. Perhaps most important, there has been a lively revival of regional towns, instead of the idiotic "new towns" and dormitory towns conceived during the '6os.)

The Diggers and professors were pacifists. They took ecological problems seriously and were, of course, the chief agents, as workers, pressure group, and by nonviolent resistance, in cleaning the rivers, diminishing the insecticides, stopping the despoiling and the motels. And finally, they adopted the principle, each group in its own competence, to use the country to help solve urban problems that were insoluble or too difficult or expensive in urban settings. Following this principle, they were able to channel back to the country a portion of the enormous urban budget, e.g., for education, welfare, and psychiatry. Let me give a few examples.

Back in the '6os, it had become not uncommon for Diggers and other young people to go insane and be hospitalized for a short spell, whether because of LSD or just life in America. This brought them in contact with the appalling reality of harmless loonies rotting away in asylums. Now, when they took to the country, they prevailed on the doctors to release many such people to their own easy-going custody; and this resulted in the spectacular increase in remissions that has revolutionized therapy. A similar process occurred with tens of thousands of runaway adolescents who used to end up in reformatories. And also, a surprising number of adult derelicts managed to settle down among the Diggers and begin to farm and feed themselves. That is, just as the Students for a Democratic Society developed into a kind of Franciscans among the urban poor, many of the Diggers soon came to be running Catholic Worker type farms in the country.

Ironically, when the professors, using institutional and political means, tried to initiate similar programs, they met with far less success. For instance, they proposed country schooling and farm life for a certain number of slum children, in order to open their minds and give them some options. Likewise, they tried to encourage people on welfare to get out of the urban areas to where they would get more for their money. These proposals required administrative changes so that the urban money could be allotted to the country, and naturally the urban administrators resisted. But astoundingly, the poor also resisted, saying, "You're sending us back to the sticks!"—they were thinking of their own parents in Mississippi. It was not until 1978, when the government finally came around to the Guaranteed Income, that the poor could make rational choices because they could make their own choices. And almost at once ten thousand Negro families came to Vermont, took the land grant, and bought jalopies like everybody else.

As a cultural force, the hermits and monks were more adept. During the middle of the century, of course, the universities became totally corrupted by the industrial-military; apparently Western culture was done for. But yang and yin, just at this moment the humanists reappeared in the woods, to Xerox the manuscripts and carry on the tradition. And soon came hordes of eager students, apparently from nowhere, since they had lain low during the brainwashing. Indeed, it is only now, in the last terrible year or two, that we can begin to appreciate what a tremendous brain drain from society their defection has been. A vastly disproportionate share of the imaginative emigrated to the country. The dull were left behind to manage things. But since the social machine was mainly run by computer, its ineptitude did not show up, until . . .

But to end on a merrier note, let me mention the beginnings of specialist farming, where I happen to know the inside story, entirely typical of our human arrangements, alas. M., the mayor of a rather large urban area in the middle west, was the brother-in-law of L., who owned one of the hotels. L. thought he could steal a march on his competitors if he could revive the novelty of edible food. He got M. re-elected and M. rammed through the quixotic re-establishment of a farmers' market, where L. signed the prime contracts. But to everybody's consternation, this tipped off the national fad of Quality that boomed in the middle '70s. Luckily it happened overnight. By the time the chain grocers tried to have fresh food banned under the Food and Drug law, it was too late.

IV. 1984

And now?

"God moves in a mysterious way His wonders to perform." But He's not a skillful mechanic. A man drives over a cliff and "by a miracle" he only breaks his back. It would be more divine if he were a better driver and stayed on the road.

An H-bomb "accidentally" fell on Akron, wiped it out, and blasted or poisoned two million people. To be sure, it was the fourth "accident," though two of the bombs exploded at sea and one killed only a few score Eskimos.

What stupid fuck-ups men are! No, they are probably not stupid by nature. By working in rigid institutions with crooked purposes even an intelligent animal must make a moron of himself. McNamara set the standard for them all.

What *is* miraculous, however, is that even the Americans have now joined the universal revulsion. It looks as though the industrial-military is finished. But of course, then, the entire fabric of society is in shreds, since they have no other method of organization. It isn't even a "revolutionary situation." With the fall of the CIA, every left group has lost a third of its members and one hundred per cent of its funds. And since the Air Force couldn't get a ship off the ground today, every right group is impotent. I suppose the universities will have to close. What will become of the CIA? What will become of the National Merit Scholarships?

It is already clear that we here in Vermont are going to be inundated. These people are running back and forth like chickens without heads, and naturally a lot of them run to us, since we have developed some kind of rudimentary structure of community. But what? In the country at large, a rural-urban ratio of twenty to eighty per cent or even thirty to seventy per cent is thinkable, it even makes sense. But this present flood is chaos.

Well, we'll do our duty as we always have. We're braced for it and—thank God—at whatever cost—is there *really* a possibility of peace? Can we *live* without the nightmare of those bombs always in the back of our minds, or will we all flip?

More notorious than most playwrights of his age, Michael McClure is the author of The Beard, *a play featuring a sexual act on stage, which on one occasion caused the arrest of the performers by the San Francisco Police. Insofar as there are spokesmen for the San Francisco underground community, McClure can be considered among the most prominent.*

Poisoned Wheat

MICHAEL McCLURE

OH, BLUE GRAY GREEN PALE GRAHHR!
TRANQUIL POURING ROSE LION SALT!

There is death in Viet Nam!
There is death in Viet Nam!
There is death in Viet Nam!
And our bodies are mad with the forgotten
memory that we are creatures!

Blue-black skull rose lust boot!

Citizens of the United States
are in the hands of traitors
who ignore their will and force
them into silent acceptance
of needless and undesired warfare.

EACH MAN, WOMAN, CHILD

is innocent
and not responsible
for the atrocities committed by any
government. Mistakes, hypocrisies, crimes
that result in the present
FASCISM

are made in the past in
HISTORY.
Structural mechanisms of Society
create guilt in the individual.
((Now it is worst when man is at the edge.
He may be freed of his
carnivore past—and is on the verge
of becoming a singer and glorious creature
borne free through the universe.
Soon no lamb or man
may be eaten
save
with the smile of sacrifice!))

It is our nature to explore
that which is called Evil
by the hater of matter
and pleasure. But GUILT
is untenable! Guilt is not
inheritable. Acceptance of guilt
for a Capitalist heritage creates fear.

NO ONE IS CULPABLE FOR THESE CRIMES!

We are flowers capable of creating the seeds
and fruit of new liberty.
Like beautiful flowers the profits of Capitalist
society are the blossoming
of the agonized labor and starvation
of the world's masses.
THAT I AM A FLOWER DOES NOT MEAN
THAT I AM RESPONSIBLE
FOR THE AGONY OF THE ROOTS!
But, as a man, I am conscious of the agony,
labor, pain. And murders take place
for Society!

Acceptance of guilt for the acts of
entrepreneurs, capitalists and imperialists
smothers, tricks, and stupefies

the free creature! He will, is, driven
to fear, racism, and inaction!

If I forget, for a prolonged moment,
the mammal, sensory pleasure of which
I am capable
I must toil to over-ride
the creeping guilt that destroys
me spiritually!

I AM NOT GUILTY!

I AM A LIVING CREATURE!

I AM NOT RESPONSIBLE FOR THE TRAITOROUS
FASCISM AND TOTALITARIANISM THAT SURROUNDS me!!!

((The definitions of *fascism* and *totalitarianism*
must be reviewed in light of the new media developed
by technology. The nature of the human
mammal is being remade and it is time for
redefinitions . . .))

I AM NOT RESPONSIBLE
FOR THOSE WHO HAVE CREATED
AND/OR CAPTURED the CONTROL DEVICES
OF THE SOCIETY THAT SURROUNDS ME!
I despise Society that creates
bundles of individual cruelties
and presses them en masse
against the helpless.

CAPITALISM IS FAILURE!
It creates overpopulation, slavery,
and starvation.

Whether I be in Soviet Russia, Red China, or Imperialist
England or France, or Capitalist United States,

I am not responsible for the fascist
or totalitarian crimes
that are whitewashed
under the title *Modern History*.
I AM INNOCENT AND FREE!
I AM A MAMMAL!
I AM A WARM BLOODED SENSORY CREATURE
CAPABLE OF LOVE AND HATE AND ACTION AND INACTION!
CAPABLE OF GUILT AND CAPABLE
OF SPEECH AND STRIVING!

—I am sickened by the thought
(and photographs)
of cruel and vicious executions
and tortures of Asian
and Algerian soldiers.

I AM SICKENED
by the oncoming MASS STARVATION
and the concomitant revolting degree
of overpopulation, and the accompanying
production of incredible numbers
of useless physical objects
whose raw materials demand
a destruction of those parts of nature
I have come to think of as beautiful!
—THOUGH I REJOICE IN THE FOREST
AND CAVES OF THE FUTURE!

BEING SICKENED IS A LUXURY
that I cannot afford without loss
of spirit, gradually
becoming irreparable! I am a man!
Sickness *and* guilt must be cast off!
Guilt is a luxury.
Being sickened is meaningless.
CAPITALISM AND COMMUNISM ARE A POLITICAL CONFRONTATION!
I have escaped politics. I disavow
the meeting whether it is a means to
war or co-existence!
The meanings of Marxism and laissez faire
are extinct.

The population of the United States will double
by the year 2000. Certain South American
nations double each eighteen and twenty years.
There is no answer
but a multiplicity of answers created by men.
A large proportion of men are on the verge
OF STARVATION!
When density of creature to creature reaches
a certain degree
the ultra-crowded condition is a
biological sink.
Rats in overpopulation experiments
become insane in predictable types . . .
perverts, cannibals, hoods, criminals, and semi-
catatonics. When crowding reaches a certain
point the animals respond by more need
and desire
for crowding!
SAN FRANCISCO, TOKYO, LONDON, MOSCOW, PEKING!

The human being is the commonest object!

Each human being must be responded to.
There are too many for the nervous system.
Man evolved as a social creature
and rare animal. He is now
the commonest large animal
—and threatens all other creatures with extinction.

((In the Neolithic, men made both plants and animals
subject to his appetites through cultivation
and domestication—the stress
of this guilt began a genetic change in his
being. He mutated himself—population
began.
Now he is capable of freeing himself
from the Neolithic Revolution
and must choose betwen
song and suicide!))

Cynicism and escapism are the shapes

of reaction to the torture and slaughter
of Asians, Asians placed
in overpopulation and starvation.

I AM INNOCENT! In my innocence I may act creatively
and *not* fulfill a pre-prescribed pattern
of guilt leading to escapism and cynicism.

COMMUNISM WILL NOT WORK!
Communism will not create food in quantities
necessary for man's survival.
By European and American imperialism,
by outright conquest and introduction
of technology into non-technological nations,
colonial nations are directed to produce
products desired by the West.
They are trained as consumers
of Western material artifacts.
They are given Western medicine which lowers
the mortality rate.

If an American accepts these facts he must assume
guilt and responsibility!
THIS IS NOT SO! Society will have
the individual feel guilty so that he will fly
from the possibility of action.
SOCIETY WILL THEN PERPETUATE THE STATUS QUO OF SOCIETY!
But this is not factual for Society is insane.
A status quo is not being perpetuated.
Society is masochistic.
It deludes itself that a status quo is
maintained. It is driving for its destruction.
WESTERN SOCIETY HAS ALREADY DESTROYED ITSELF!
The Culture is extinct! The last sentry
at the gate has pressed the muzzle to his
forehead and pulled the trigger!
The new civilization will not be communism!
POLITICS ARE AS DEAD AS THE CULTURE
they supported!
Politics are theories regarding the speculated
laws of power—their applications

have never touched men except in shapes
of repression!
NEW SOCIETY WILL BE BIOLOGICAL!

HISTORY IS INVALID BECAUSE WE ARE ESCAPED
FROM HISTORY. As individuals we inhabit
a plateau where civilization is perpetuated
by the mechanisms of a rapidly dying and masochistic
Society. We are supported by traitors
and barbarians who operate war
utilizing the business principles of this Society.

THOSE WHO CAN SEE AND FEEL ARE IN HIDING. THEY HOPE
for a few years of life before the holocaust.
They are caught up in the forms of evangelism
that are hysterical reaction
to population density. They hope
for a miracle. The thrill of the beauty
of the new music and entertainment media—as well
as religion—are evangelism.
It is beautiful that even hysteria can be made
to give assurance and pleasure and some means
of satisfaction.
—BUT IT IS A LAST DITCH BIOLOGICAL REACTION.

The small hope for salvation by means of utilization
of hysteria is pathetic!!!!!
The bombing of Asian fishing villages can be equated
to the new music
save that one is beautiful
and one is not. The witness of the new intellectuals
testifies to the beauty of both!

Beauty IS hideous!
Mussolini spoke of the beauty of bombing
villages as the ss cherished the pleasure
of executing Jews! ((What INSANITY
to have Israel as thorn to the Arabs!))

The human mammal is not capable of receiving pleasure
from the tortured deaths of his own kind
without previous acceptance of insanity

or the development of insanity
within himself!
The masses of planes that fly over

ARE NOT PASSENGER SHIPS

but are bombers flying to Asia!

STOP UP THE EARS—it is true!

AND WHO IS FLYING THEM?

What name for those who accept authority
and enter the cockpits?
No doubt as in the bombing of Guernica!

What name for the voice of authority that tells
the pilots to enter the ships?

THE ACCEPTANCE OF THE IMPOSSIBLE IS CYNICISM!
To admire or be silent about pain and death
IS CYNICISM!
To enact a role when Society is a corpse
IS CYNICISM!

Whether the corpse be a young Soviet or Chinese or an old
U.S. corpse!

WITHDRAWAL FROM INFORMATION IS ESCAPISM!
Escape from the ears that hear the bombers pass?
Evangelism—whether it be of art or religion
is escapism.
There must be a milieu for action.
Barbarism,
Atrocities,
Bombings,
Poisonings
of wheat in Cambodia,
Secret Government agencies,

and all manifestations of political hysteria

LEAD TO GENOCIDE! OR MASS STARVATION
and such Hell that death would be better!

FREEDOM FROM GUILT AND RESPONSIBILITY
is necessary to the individual so he may
receive the normal pleasures of body and life
—whether it be the pleasures of a Congo tribesman
or a city dweller in a European or American city!

IDEALISM IS EASY FOR THE MOST WEALTHY AND THE MOST
IMPOVERISHED!

POLITICS IS DEAD AND BIOLOGY IS HERE!

FEAR AND GUILT MUST BE CAST ASIDE LIKE A DIRTY ROBE!

CYNICISM AND ESCAPISM MUST BE PUT ASIDE INSTANTLY!

The 'traitors directing the barbarism must have power taken
from them!

There is no single answer to the new biological confrontation!
There must be a multitude of solutions!
They must be arrived at by thought and action.
Neither is possible without energy and information!

Society and Government smother both energy and information!
The majority of the citizens are against the war!
War creates guilt that causes blindness!

Blindness means hysteria and flight!

An arena must be cleared for new thought and action
that is not national in scope
but incorporates all human creatures . . .
and all creatures to come!
—All who will move to the stars to investigate
the possibilities of infinite freedoms.

EACH MAN IS INNOCENT!
The point of life is not rest but action.
DEATH IS REST

—everyone will have enough rest for eternity!
NOW IS THE TIME FOR ACTION.
THE WAR MUST BE STOPPED—THE WORLD SEEN CLEARLY!

THE UNIVERSE IS MESSIAH!

WHAT IS THIS SMOKE?

The neon napalm flash is filth and death!

GRAHH!   **BLESS!**

Eben Given, staff artist for the Boston Avatar *and the Daumier of the underground, lives on Roxbury's Fort Hill with most of the paper's editors. A year of this arrangement, combined with the unrelenting harassment of the Cambridge and Boston Police Departments, has given the* Avatar *folk the missionary zeal of Roman Catholic converts, and that sense of purpose sets their writing apart from the more common paranoia of these papers.*

The Wakening of the People

EBEN GIVEN

"Polarity, or action and reaction, we meet in every part of nature—to empty here, you must condense there. An inevitable dualism bisects nature, so that each thing is a half and suggests another to make it whole; as spirit, matter; man, woman; odd, even; motion, rest." That is Emerson's voice on compensation.

Now in these times—in the sheets of these newspapers is an extreme example of a compensating force and these times cry out for extremes. For only through awareness of opposition—of polarity, can that center be found, the point of balance which takes from both sides and increases itself.

This paper has got a single point from which it is united, both within its own structure and to the larger structure of the united underground, or Free Press. It is that the meaning of true purpose and Liberty can no longer be found and maintained in outward circumstances—neither in conformity or attachment to causes—but in inner awakening. An awakening not of the senses merely but of the *Purpose* behind the senses.

In this world there is a roaring and a grinding of gears. We are walking in a cyclone of sounds and smells and colors. We cannot escape it, no Himalayan hut is high enough. Be it without—or within us. We can't escape it any more than we can escape our own mind or finally our own feelings. We can't escape it because we've created it. We're not here by any accident of Fate. We're here only inheriting what is ours. And it *is*

Avatar, September 1, 1967

ours and some of us will want to run away and some of us will run away, but it will follow you through the years and the days into the far corners of space and scream at you in forty languages at once and wave its fingers in your face and there you'll be at last with your back up against the wall.

Nor can we stay in this world either. For it's a world of sleepwalkers. Beings completely turned off to the underlying meaning of the trial and drudgery of their existence. Defenseless in the deluges of sensations that fall on their heads like snow and bury them under so that they can no longer stand upright but only crawl like moles beneath the surface of the swirling drifts holding each other's tails in their teeth. The blind leading the blind.

Now our people are being waked. Like a man who dreams that he is being strangled and wakes to discover hands about his throat.

In this time the great structure is beginning to be seized by some and shaken so that it is no longer seen as an impenetrable wall. And others, having eyes, will see the fissures in the wall and will understand. A few now, but behind those few is a power of destiny, the terrific force of compensation.

We are in the world and understand the lessons of the world. We are of the western world. And that world is creating us at this time. Because the western world is the world of material values, wealth and power, it is become the center of the world's chaos and danger. It has created a material structure that has grown so disproportionate, the true values and ideals that formed and fired it have been concealed and other later causes have been found to explain and justify it. We have gotten so immersed in the building, the original concept has been forgotten— the reason *for* the building.

Because we have become a land of sleepwalkers, the compensating force must bring about balance. And not many are going to awaken but those who will awaken will awaken *fully* and one man awake and centered to the *needs* of his time and the needs of man, stands in the balance to ten million of those who are sleeping.

We will awaken here and come together here—for no other nation has equal power of opposition to create us. A great force *always* creates its opposite. The greatest force in America is confusion, of blindness, of forgetfulness, of untruth.

The force that it must necessarily create will be a force of self-reliance, of vision and recall, a force of truth.

It will be self-reliant. Its security will not be how much of the material world it must have, but with how much it can do without.

It will seek out only the material tools that can add to and further its message from one man to another. It will recall the message from one man to another. It will recall the message, that it is not a new message—that it is the first of all messages and it will proclaim that message from its source—which is that place from which all innovations fall and all leaders and inspirers of men. Knowing the truth and living it—it will expose the heavy calculation of ignorance.

The overwhelming power in America is confusion, and it will not let up but will become greater.

Leaders will arise and one will be on the one side and one upon another, and third sides will appear and contend with the other two and the order will get too heavy to hold any longer and it will fall into many pieces. All this is to come.

Now there are some who are preparing. Knowing that they are the balance that is forming and coming together they are collecting the strong tools of the world and digging in. For they know how strong a foundation must be set down. How firm in the earth they must become to withstand the storms that *will* arise. And they are building a language and a communications that will not be swayed and cannot be suppressed.

Because it is the word of opposition—created solely *by* opposition—opposition will only increase its strength. Now these words do not constitute a threat. There are too few capable of taking them seriously. Too few with a vision of the simple course of Nature, too few who recall the voice that speaks in great beginnings. These are still words in a little newspaper, a newspaper incomprehensible to too many, an *underground* newspaper.

But this newspaper is not much longer an underground newspaper, not for much longer will these pages and other pages across this country be underground, but they will awaken to the force of an awareness, a consciousness and a direction expanding within and behind them—to the ever widening walls and the chaos lashing before them, and their purpose will be too strongly defined and their own commitment made too deeply to evade. And then there will be no talk among them of being underground. But the voice will have been made, a voice that will not be stilled. For the words once out cannot be caught back, once spoken they cannot be unspoken. Spoken strongly they will not be forgotten.

Now we will begin to gather together our force and come together with ourselves. We will work as slowly, as deliberately as we can, building within ourselves, within the union of those who recognize our voice, returning to that voice behind all our voices that is speaking in the world today more strongly than ever before.

Now this voice is going out from place to place. It has no fears of not being heard. It will be heard because it will be pursued. It will be pursued because of the life that is in it. A new voice and new things are snatched for exploitation. But this voice has no fear of exploitation. Having nothing but its commitment and its dedication it has nothing to lose and everything to gain. For it knows that each situation that arises, does arise only for its amplification. Each moment will be seized as a *new* moment. And it will be a new voice only because of its authority. Because it will not be diverted or separated or categorized, but it will stand quietly pointing out the lie by contrast and by example. Even as it is ridiculed and derogated it will grow more strongly in the minds of its detractors.

We will speak as we *feel* and act as we *feel* and we shall be courted by the established media of communications. Because our actions are driven by conviction and commitment we will simply shine in their papers and upon their programs because of the life we represent.

And we will tell the truth of who we are and where we live. What we are building and have built. We will tell that we are the secret government coming into power. And there will be one that hears and one will come to us. And always one has in these first ventures even in these days.

If hippies exist, or have ever existed, they were made possible in large measure by the insistent refusal of adults to understand what is intolerable about American values. "Mutants Commune" is a total response to that refusal—a closely argued diatribe against the present socio-political configuration, combined with a comprehensive history of a new life style.

Mutants Commune

```
INMATES   fellow mutants

     break out of the mental institutions
     break out of the mental institutions

     break out of the mental institutions........political systems

     p o l     c!!!?                    coercion    p         p
     o      ic    o  **            ula              a      o      o
     w         e  n  **       pu     t              r   w------- l
     e         n          an i death i              e      e      i
     r*dea th*    trol    m         o n             r      r      c
                                                                  e

     break out of the mental institutions........economic systems

     mo n      p$$$$                    efficiency  m         m
     o    op   r                                    m      o      o
     n      o  o___      u  l so r y                o   ndeath $ n
     e    y l  p       p    m*consumpt   $          n      e      e
     y$$$$$$    erty$  co            i on           e      y      y
                                                    y

     break out of the mental institutions........education systems

     condi        r******                  ½diploma-   c       ½
     fi      ti   i                i gen c     con      o
     s        o   g 1111         l l      e½            ½    ditioni
     o         n  t  2222       ll censor  in           ½          n
     r      n     e          in t        g              *    ½     g
     ingllg n     ousness       t ell    in             *    ½
            24                        42  g

     break out of the mental institutions........military systems

     f#vio l       t!!!!                    terrorism  f         d
     o        l    e                  a l*             #      o      e
     r      n      r***           i o n  gu            #   r####    a
     c        e c  r o        n a t #death#ar          #      c      t
     e# #  e       ism##     n          d##                   e      h
```

break out of the mental institutions........religious systems

```
g (sin),    sin ()                      (secretness)   d      ;
u        ,   a              e   n s                  ;        e
i       s   c(;;;)           t      s;                ;       a(sin  s
l      i    r                r(death);s              ;        t      i
        n   e               e                                 h      n
t ,,,       dness         s c         i
                                       n
```

break out of the mental institutions........language systems

```
m sy        mass.                          mass....    m    :
a    n t     .                ph           y          a    :
s     a x   p          or      o l          n          semant
s      .    h ...       m       o    g     t          s     i
         e  o          s s death.     y.   a          :     c
.  c d      n         m a                   x               s
.ab         ology
```

break out of the mental institutions........mafia systems

```
pros t       money                  t t i   betting    l    $
.     i t u   o            i u   o n         o          o   -shark
h      u     n###          t t i             p          a    i
e     o i    e          r o s gambling #      i          n    n
r    n       y$sex      p                $ $$ u          $    g
oin$                                          m
```

break out of the mental institutions........family systems

```
alim o       m.death                 o P l   $alimony$   a    @
$     n      a                       e     e     d       d    @
d    y $    r @@@@             p      e   r  a    e       ultery@@
i    @      i             t w  o*death- m      a    @    @
                                          i l   t       @    @
vorc e .     age()..      t            y      h
```

FREE YOU ARE OPEN PEOPLE NOT TO BE CLOSED INTO

THE MENTAL INSTITUTIONAL SYSTEMS.

mutants revolve your head and nervous system. do acid. do

the holy cities. spinspiril. do yourself and bod. create

free forms. novas. do free.

freeall

freal

f real l

1750 ECONOMIC institutional systems are horizontal and
vertical pyramid hierarchies
boxed and frozen for coordinating programmed
corpses. (workers)
G.M. A.T.&T. Dow giving you the wheeler-dealer
alternatives of

becoming a workable taxpaying efficiency gnome
or
going to jail for vagrancy (no money) for not obeying
established leader authorities—the pop executive
idol images.

1919 FAMILY institutional systems are horizontal and
vertical pyramid hierarchies
boxed and frozen for coordinating programmed
corpses. (households)
father mother grandparents giving you the "my how
you've grown"
alternatives of
following in the footsteps of dear old dad's and mom's
together head
or
being sent out into the world without any cookies
for not obeying
established leader authorities—the pop mom-dad
team idol images.

1854 POLITICAL institutional systems are horizontal and
vertical pyramid hierarchies
boxed and frozen for coordinating programmed
corpses. (citizens)

Rep. Dem. Blk. Panthers giving you the "a vote for me
is a vote for you"
alternatives of
voting for war, monopolies, police, and the national guard
or
being totally non-represented for not obeying
established leader authorities—the pop president
idol image.

prehistoric MILITARY institutional systems are horizontal
and vertical pyramid hierarchies
boxed and frozen for coordinating programmed
corpses. (soldiers)
army navy air force giving you the "go get 'em"
alternatives of

burning and killing people
or
going to jail for not obeying
established leader authorities—the pop general
idol images.

1860 EDUCATIONAL institutional systems are horizontal and
vertical pyramid hierarchies
boxed and frozen for coordinating programmed
corpses. (students)
Harvard Yale Vassar M.I.T. giving you the "rah rah"
alternatives of
successful mental programming and physical conditioning
or
jail until you're sixteen and guilt forever after for not
obeying
established leader authorities—the pop teacher
idol images.

1367 RELIGIOUS institutional systems are horizontal and
vertical pyramid hierarchies
boxed and frozen for coordinating programmed
corpses. (members of the multitude)
Catholic Jewish Protestant giving you the blessed
alternatives of
believing in their gods
or
being condemned to doo-doo land for not obeying
established leader authorities—the pop god-representative
idol images.

1936 GANGSTER institutional systems are horizontal and
vertical pyramid hierarchies
boxed and frozen for coordinating programmed
corpses. (big wheels)
Mafia Cosa Nostra small-time hood giving you
the bang-bang
alternatives of
paying 6 for 5, house rates and rakes
or
getting beat up or shot for not obeying
established leader authorities—the pop good bad guy
idol images.

GET OUT OF THE RECTILINEAR BOXED STRAIGHT LINE 1600's STATIC
CARTESIAN COORDINATE SYSTEMS. HELP EACH OTHER DYNAMICALLY
FLOW TOGETHER AND APART IN POST ATOMIC, POST RELATIVITY FREE
FORM ONE TO ONE NOVAS

presidents, kings, generals, mothers, teachers, executives,
gangsters, and other leader authority icons, idols, and
images are death. nova and novas are born free and
die free as doing is done. be. be. be free.
free-ly choose nova or novas. find
natural identity in nova, not
pre-fabricated identity in
plastic formulas and
mass planned
obsolete
images.

FUCK the poor boy image always getting bargains and always
working overtime. CLASS.
FUCK the middle boy image grey in cordovans going to college
to get a head. SUCCESS.
FUCK the rich boy image always saying that's the way it
always was and will be and one
can't flux it. ADORABLE.

combine in one to one relations-novas.

novas are constellations of people who voluntarily
free form—the alternative to groups
that are
hired to function in the mental institutional
systems. novas are
freely open to all all
the time in all ways forever.
move. flex. pulse. undulate. expand. inpand.
grow.

one to one is confronting each thing and situation as itself, as specific,
as unique, free, open, flowing, changing, dynamic, on the wing, mysterious, infinite-sided, beyond reference. being. beyond games of power,
property, force, guilt, money.

decentralize language—the Establishment controls
attitudes and opinion by using
mass language and
mass images censored through the mass media—
API newspapers UPI images
LUCE magazines U.S. News and World images
NBC t.v. CBS images
ABC radio WOR images
COLUMBIA movies M.G.M. images

decentralize language—consciously communicate on
non-verbal levels.
telempathy-mime, hand gestures, facial
expression, body movements, babble sounds, telepathy. twitch.

decentralize language—each community should have a
language that is continually and
rapidly fluxing.
language created from own environment and
situations.
any crowd-be-in
any cop-Guerrins
free form-nova
communications company-c.c.

There exists a lag between the psyche of the leader authorities, controlling the great-grandfather mental institutions, and the psyche of
the fuck-leader youth trying to be free in the cybernated-pill-acid-mis-
sile technological environment they have no free in.

The leader authorities are agents of the death penalty.
The fuck-leader youth want to open life.
The leader authorities command work and inductions
under penalty of jail.
The fuck-leader youth want voluntary novas.

THE FUCK-LEADER YOUTH SEARCHER AND MAKER
OF VOLUNTARY LIFE IS A MUTANT.

mutation-n. (ME.; mutacion; L. mutation/to change) change
under threat of extinction

> maybe. chromosome flux. a discreet
> change. abrupt. snap. drop off.

drop out.................open..................flow

a mutant is
a hippie is an automation 1916 1942 conputer acid 1943 t.s. 1938 the
  pill 1952
1942 missile 1945 atom-bomb youth explosion 67. always. infinite. forever. now.

> —and changing—

and where are you at mr jones doe smith?
  the anonymous mass institution death trip—

> 1854 donkey elephant political institution.
> 1750 industrial revolution factory institution.
> 1267 "who you know" union guild institution.
> 1860 steam heat school house institution.
> 1919 007 betty crocker miss clairol family institution.
> prehistoric john wayne military institution.
> 1367 bing crosby renaissance church institution.
> 1936 ed g. robinson gangster institution.

1620 uncle tom institution.

and your creation is niggers
  (you can't tell a book by its color)
  your creation is bookmakers
  (don't take candy from strangers)
  your creation is Spellmans
  (god helps those who help themselves)
  your creation is war
  (laugh and the world laughs with you)
  your creation is thalidomide babies
  (I'll be ready as soon as I put on my face)
  your creation is juvenile delinquency
  (children should be seen and not heard)

  YOUR CREATION IS MASSIVE STIFF DEATH MASKED WITH
  EFFICIENCY STATISTICS

and you are right. right in the 1854, 1750, 1267, 1860, 1919, prehistoric, 1367, 1936, 1620, niggers, bookmakers, spellman, war, thalidomide, delinquency, stiff death bag.

and you're afraid to change because you're afraid
to face the unfamiliar
the unknown   LSD

and you hide in your locked houses, cars, and offices, and
you create paranoid children.

and now you have unconsciously helped create the mutants, the freaks.
and they will tell what you are afraid to tell.

LIFE, TIME, MENTAL AND PHYSICAL INSTITUTIONAL
INSURANCE POLICIES ARE DEATH.

and they will do what you are afraid to do.

create free   give free
take free   be free
everyways

GET OUT OF THE 1860 EDUCATION FORM—

the 1860 steam heat schoolhouse institution is a death form. the
grammar school-high school-university mass education-death trip. little
classrooms, cramped with sitting, suffocating children.

"Don't talk, children, sit there and listen to me for the next six
hours, for the next five days, for the next forty weeks. If you successfully pass through the first eight years imprisonment, you can do
four more years in high school. Then, if you are intelligent, fortunate,
and have money enough, you can do four more years in a university.
Then you can graduate and proudly be imprisoned in offices, factories,
and institutions throughout the world until, at long last, you are sixty-
five. Then you are free to take off more than two weeks in a row."
("Don't ask stupid questions")
("I'm busy right now")
Amen, brother.

THIS MAY BE
In a free form, the child's natural curiosity could flow. Their growth
in certain subjects which interest them would not be stunted by the
compulsion to study the same subjects with the same teacher at the
same time in the same room with students of the same age.

(IMAGE FLASH ON A SCREEN WITH THE NAME OF THE IMAGE PRINTED

UNDER IT. PRESSING KEYS TO LIGHT UP LETTERS UNDER THE PRINTED
WORDS)

There are teaching machines that could start to teach two-year olds
to read, write, and type. Machines like this could be made available to
every child.

If a child wanted to know about the t.v., you could take or send him
to an automated t.v. factory, where there would be classes for various
levels of instruction. A five-year old could assemble his own t.v. by
inserting proper numbered parts in their matching holes. Just like blocks.
A ten-year old could solder some parts on the chassis of the t.v. or hand-
operate a machine that is now automated. A twelve-year old could alternate various parts to get different effects. A fourteen-year old could design different sets around the same principles. A sixteen-year old could
start feeling God.

When doctors came to their house, they could inform the children of
medical realities. When plumbers come to the house, the kids could go
on a plumbing trip.

Along with the decentralized teaching of various subjects in automated factories and from personal contact, there could be the University
where all the different elements of the community could be represented.
This would offer all subjects to all ages.

In the Haight-Ashbury community, none of these ideas were carried
out in the past year. The ideas are still a little too far out to exist under
the existing conditions. Most of the education of children came from
personal contact with people living in communes. The only developments
in the Haight-Ashbury besides personal contact were two free nursery
homes and the Huckleberry House for kids under eighteen who split
from their parents.

GET OUT OF THE 1919 FAMILY FORM—

The 1919 007 betty crocker miss clairol family institution is a death
form. Marriage, responsibility for children, alimony are death. Let's do
away with the meaningless, unnecessary bullshit of "I want my kids to
have more than I had," "My kids will starve," "I don't have time to listen
to your abstract ideas, I have to support my family."

THIS MAY BE

The basic unit of the culture could be the commune instead of a house with one man and one woman in it. The commune would not be owned by one person or one group but it would be open to all people at all times, to do whatever they wished to do in it.

There would be no marriage contracts, but people could still have huge ceremonies when they met someone they dug. And if someone dug a different person every day, he could have a different ceremony every day.

All children, from the moment they were born, would be the responsibility of everyone, not only of the blood mother and father.

In the Haight-Ashbury during the last year, there was none of the shut-in paranoid one-man-and-woman-and-children family structure. Most people lived in communes because they were open and fun. People taught other people what they knew, whether it was about guitars, printing presses, dope, confronting slumlords, cooking, confronting police, raising children, painting, sex, etc. People became aware of the hassles of living with people, and had their minds blown by being continuously and intimately involved with ten or fifteen people.

Children were confronted with multiple character images rather than just their mother's and father's. For most people, it was more stimulating, more open, more knowledge-giving, more self-expressive than any other family form they had lived in.

GET OUT OF THE 1750 ECONOMIC FORM

The 1750 industrial revolution factory institution we live in is a death form. Really straight people, let's put it down. Let's burn all the dollars under pots and pop popcorn together. Let's put the budget books in the archives for future history freaks who wish to groove on the past. Let money, credit, capital, debts, and banking flow away. For really straight people these ideas are anachronisms.

THIS MAY BE

Production of goods can be done almost totally by machines.
Free.

Distribution of goods can be done free.
        dig this scene:
fifteen people getting stoned and doing their thing in some room in a commune. someone decides to turn on the t.v. and by some weird coincidence he is staring at channel 137. some cat in a clown outfit is in the

middle of a riff about how ten people are needed to deliver bread to a few of the free stores. so one cat says, "Let's go down there and goof" and they split./cut

There would be an unlimited supply of some goods. These could be distributed to individuals. There would be a limited supply of others. For example, jet planes. These could be distributed equally to areas instead of to individuals. There would be, say, ten jet passenger planes per county. The only restriction on the use of the plane would be that it had to be broadcast on channel 168 at least a half hour before it was taken. If someone tries to take the plane who doesn't know how to fly it, we wish him lots of luck.

Services can be done free.

People performing these services wouldn't have to hurry, kill time, or be efficient. If you wanted your car fixed, you could notify channel 438 and then start getting the goodies necessary for the party in honor of the car mechanic when he comes over to fix the car.

Division of labor (doing)

So many people have to be farmers . . . so many people have to be scientists . . . so many people have to be mechanics . . . so many people have to be carpenters . . . etc. If all things were free and people were free to do what they chose, people would willingly and happily learn to do the things that necessarily had to be done, in order for those conditions to continue to exist.

Value—this is the hang-up, brother mutants.

People groove on making things, giving them away, and fixing them up. It gives people identity. You are what you do. The problem is that there is only a limited amount of things can be made. Who is going to decide what to do with the limited resources that exist? In the United States today, the Federal Government makes the decision of what will be done with the resources. They do this by appropriating 60% of the budget to the industrial-military complex. The rationale goes that if we don't have the strongest military force, we will be conquered by those who do, the commie bastards, whoever they are. Since 1945, no one could conquer the United States and its allies unless the whole fucking solar system was thrown out of balance.

In the Haight-Ashbury during the last year, most aspects of a free economic form were accomplished.

PRODUCTION—There are no production plants in the Haight-Ashbury, so there were few things produced from raw resources into finished objects. The few exceptions have been the food grown and brought into the city from free farms, fish brought in from fishing boats, and guitars, jewelry, etc., made out of rocks, shells, and wood.

DISTRIBUTION—Almost every kind of article has been distributed free in the Haight-Ashbury—cars, clothes, paper clips, children, television sets, record players, ice-cream pops, bananas, LSD, cardboard boxes, ecstasy, cameras, leather, eyebrow pencils, birth control pills, fish 'n chips, bubble gum, belly button lint, harmonicas, rosaries, cookie makers, parking tickets, i.d.s., flowers, beds, sunshine, dynamite.

SERVICES—Every service has been performed free. Free food, free clothes, free shelter, free stores, free dances, free lawyers, free doctors, free painters, free sculptors, free engineers, free garbage collectors, free cooks, free actors, free joint-rollers, free house-painters, free clothes-makers, free carpenters, free mechanics, free printers, free chemists, free buses, free firemakers, free sandalmakers, free glassblowers, free electronic bugs, free guitar makers. Few office jobs have been done free.
If all things were free, there would be little need of office jobs.

It is beyond doubt that people will produce, distribute, and service things free. The problem under the present conditions is getting the resources and getting the space to use the resources free.
The people who run the Avalon and Fillmore dance halls are willing to give free dances all of the time, but they're caught in the bag of paying rent for the space. Most of the musicians who play in the dance halls are willing to play for free, but they need money to pay for their equipment and to pay rent for living space.

(If we may digress for a minute—the idea of property is bullshit, someone gets money for a piece of space on the planet earth because he says he owns it. well, who owns the earth? if one of the flying saucer people landed and took out a piece of stone and said that it said right there that he owned the earth, and that everyone on it had to pay him rent, would you believe it? believe it! and the next time the landlord comes around to collect the rent, tell him not to worry, you already paid the rent to the saucer people.)

The same willingness to always do free applies to lawyers, carpenters, and all the other people mentioned above, but they are hung up in the same space and resources bag. In fact, we are all hung up in the space and resources bag. And now we are going through the phase of doing free and doing money.

There are those who believe free and who do free all the time, but who are still forced to be dependent on other people to freely give them space and resources. There are those who think and say they believe free and who do free once a week or once a month. And there are the liberals and shuck-people who think and say they believe free, but who never do free.

The free spirit will grow when people do more free stores, free dances, free papers, etc. In cities, towns, high-schools, and colleges throughout the United States and the Universe.

give free take free

GET OUT OF THE 1854 POLITICAL FORM—

The 1854 donkey elephant political institution is a death form. After 113 years of success, the people in this country are where they're at. Straight people, we don't like to have to break your stiff security, but let's dig the cliché "it's time to change" and let's blow our brains and do more than just change candidates—let's change from a political system to a free form. novas.

THIS MAY BE

There are only two functions of government: to protect property and to protect people. In a free form, all property would be freely owned by all. In a free form there would be only one limitation, one restriction, one action that would be forbidden, one action that would be against orders (one action that is stupid), one action that would be unlawful: that you cannot cause physical restraint or damage to another person's bod, regardless of age.

As an alternative to breaking up the area of the United States into fifty states, the area could be broken up into a thousand counties that are already demarcated. These boundaries would be used not only for equal distribution of goods, but also for the judging of violations against the one and only law stated above.

If it took you twenty years to build and furnish your house, and someone wanted to destroy it, the physical destruction of the house of which you were a resident would imply your physical destruction. In this case, you would go before the county judging t.v. channel 675 and you would state your case and let the people of the county judge your case to decide whether or not the house should be destroyed. Everyone would have the right to appeal the county judging and appear before the national judging channel 4567.

Any violators of the one and only law would be ostracized to the state of Kansas which would be isolated from the rest of the country. The state of Kansas might be broken up according to the seriousness of the violation. There would be the crime of irresponsibility creating a machine or structure that caused physical damage, i.e., an unqualified person who built a bridge or structure that collapsed or ran amuck. There would be the crime of distributing drugs that cause damage to another person's bod. The crime of psychopathic killing.

From around September of 1966 until around April of '67, before all the national publicity and the coming of the tourists, in the free community part of the Haight-Ashbury, there were very few power, control, manipulation, and coercion games. When people do free they do free.

It has been learned that when you do free, if someone tries to control, manipulate or have power over you, you just split. When you do free, you have nothing to lose and nothing to gain. When you do free, you have something to lose and something to gain. When you live on a power level, you lose your freedom. When you live on a free level, you lose your power.

The only people who try to have power over others are the stiff paranoids wanting self-insurance. The only people who will conform to these power plays are the mass sheep self-insurance people.

Millions of free events on individual and large novas scale have been enacted in the last year. These free actions have generated energies of free joy to tens of millions of people in the United States and the world. Tens of thousands of people have lived here during the last year, free from power games and almost totally free from violence.

Until April, we lived on the street for over a year, and we saw only one fight and heard of only five others (not counting incidents of police brutality). If you're wondering what this riff is about, the point is that it is totally believable that men can live in an almost totally free environment without power games or violent performances.

Free people have offered to do the city dog pound, the city's Farmers Market, and the city's Weights and Measures Department for free. The Board of Supervisors in the city of San Francisco has denied the free spirit of these people and also denied the taxpayers the hundred thousand dollars that would have been saved, if these doings had been done free.

And 3 free stores have been closed by the San Francisco Building

Department, dozens of free houses have been closed by the Health
Department.

And bands have been busted for playing free music in the parks, and
the tens of thousands of busts made by the cops, who protected America
the Beautiful from

the mutants.

The only alternatives open for these free people are either to ignore
the city's political institution or to violently attack it.

GET OUT OF THE PREHISTORIC MILITARY FORM—

The prehistoric john wayne military nationalism institution is a death
form. Being drafted into the army against one's choice is death.

THIS MAY BE

If all the institutions were made voluntary, we would become the most
revolutionary country in the world. We would become the model for
every revolution whose purpose was to free. We would need a military
novas, not only to protect free in this space, the United States, but also
to help other people to become free if we decided to do this.

There would be a rule that any military movement would have to be
agreed upon by the whole country.

In the Haight-Ashbury, it developed that the Hell's Angels was the
military force. And it was really, really strange, fellows, to find out that
they would just as well fuck as fight, and just as well get stoned and be
friendly as terrorize. Can you dig it?

GET OUT OF THE 1936 GANGSTER INSTITUTION—

The 1936 Mafia, Cosa Nostra gangster ed g. robinson institution is a
death form. Horse-betting, card-betting, ball game-betting, number-
betting, prostitution, heroin, opium, downer dealing, loan sharking
money, money-sex, money-dope is death.

THIS MAY BE

atrophied

Before April, the Haight-Ashbury was a sort of upper-lower class
district where nothing happened in the heroin, prostitution, loan-sharking
categories. A few hippies distributed their own grass, acid, and mescaline.

Now it is t.v. radio newspaper magazine merchant paradise neon quickly spreading along the walls for looking tourists who have ventured once again into buy-buy land, and in the love-shuck consumer carnival emerges prostitution of a street kind, gangland murders, underworld opium and heroin, and bits of loan-sharking.

GET OUT OF THE 1367 RELIGIOUS FORM—

The 1367 bing crosby spellman renaissance church institution is a death form. Segregated churches of every denomination.

And the congregation parades through the door,
                    nylon, girdled life virgins dressed in their sunday best

                    Sermons about love of your fellow man
                         Blessings   the collection of money

And the congregation shuffles out the door,
                    to become soldiers.

THIS MAY BE

In the Haight-Ashbury, the origins and endings of the universe are mysterious and unknown, which each individual has to seek out for himself. May each man see the unknown in everything. May each man find his own God.

AND

we all had the experience, when we were in grammar school, of the leader-authority teacher who became so oppressive and stiff that the idea spread around the class that everyone should get up and walk out.

There was the small artistic smart kid
who probably originated the idea.
                    He would do it.

There was the medium-sized athletic kid
who was friendly with everyone in class.
                    He would do it.

There was the powerful tough kid.
He would do it.

And the smart kid would confront the other smart kids and find out
that they were afraid to do it because they were afraid the teacher would
get angry at them and lower their grades. And besides, why should they
do it? They were at the head of the class and had everything to lose.
The kids at the bottom of the class goofed and were stupid and had
nothing to lose.
And the athletic kid would confront the middle-grade kids, and find
out that they would do it if everyone else in the class would do it.
And the athletic kid and the tough kid would confront the lower part
of the class and find out that they were afraid to do it because they were
afraid they would flunk.

?jones brown and carmichael?

The impulse for free had been created by the stiff oppressiveness of
the teacher, but it was killed by the stiffness and oppressiveness of their
own IDENTITY.

The smart kids didn't want to lose their identity of being
the smartest in the class, and they didn't want their
parents to know they were naughty in class.

The middle kids did not want to lose their identity of
almost being as smart as the smart kids and as tough
as the tough kids, and they didn't want their parents
to know they were naughty in class.

The tough kids were afraid of getting the identity of being
flunkees, and they didn't want their parents to
know they were naughty in class.
. . . . So they stayed in class
and they stayed not free, and they insisted on keeping their not free
identities. And the girls sat there, not knowing what to do, smiling
once in awhile.
And the kids got a little older and they saw the city black man hate
the middle class white man. The middle class white man threatened the
IDENTITY of the black man. The middle class white man was better than
the city black man because he had all those cadillacs and color t.v.'s.
And the city black man threatened the IDENTITY of the middle class

white man. The middle class white man said he believed in freedom and
equality, and all he had to do was to look at that black to know that he
was a liar.

And the middle class man hates the rich man. The rich man threatens
the identity of the middle class man. The rich man is better than the
middle class man because he goes on all those groovy vacations, and has
those groovy cars, and that groovy house, and he doesn't have to worry
about money after he retires.

And the rich man hates the middle class man because the middle
class man threatens his identity. The rich man dangles the jobs in front
of the nose of the middle class man and says that he can make it if he
works hard enough, but all the rich man has to do is to take one look
at those middle class men to know that he's a liar. There is only one job
like that for every 30,000 middle class men.

    but on

         and on

             and on

                 and on

                    the Niggers

                          threaten the identity of the spicks
the spicks

        threaten the identity of the limeys

            the mockies

                threaten the identity of the square-heads
the square-heads

    threaten the identity of the greaseballs   the greaseballs

           threaten the identity of the guineas
the micks

  threaten the identity of the dagos

                  AND

the dealers threaten the identity of the musicians . . . the musicians
threaten the identity of the cops . . . the cops threaten the identity of
the merchants . . . the merchants threaten the identity of the politicians . . . the college kids threaten the identity of the high school
kids . . . the two-year old threatens the identity of the father

everybody has something to lose—

THEIR FIXED MENTAL INSTITUTIONALIZED IDENTITY.

and all the time they choose to lose their freedom rather than their
identity

And all that horseshit about leaving your wife, as if there
    weren't at least one million other women you could groove with.
And all that fixed identity horseshit about leaving your
    blood children as if there weren't at least a billion other
    kids you could groove with.
And all that fixed identity horseshit about leaving
    your job, as if there weren't an infinite number of jobs
    you could groove with.
And all that fixed identity horseshit about cars, t.v.'s,
    cameras, equipment, houses, as if you couldn't use them
    without owning them.
THEY COULD BE YOURS FREE, IF YOU HAD A FREE IDENTITY
    INSTEAD OF THE STATIC FIXED IDENTITY WHICH YOU CLING TO.

A FREE PERSON HAS NO NEEDS, NO NECESSITIES. HE IS FREE TO CHOOSE
ANY ALTERNATIVE.

    get a few tabs of acid and go into the mountains with a friend. go
during the wintertime. stay in the mountains for a couple of days and
get the feel of the country around you. then, on a bright, sunshiny day
at 12 o'clock, drop some acid. there will be the warmth of the sun, and
the multiple smells, colors, sounds, and patterns of nature. and somewhere around 5 o'clock, you will see that the sun is about ready to go
over the horizon. and you will notice that as it approaches the horizon,
it gets colder and colder. and you will become aware that if you don't
collect wood and build a fire soon, you will probably freeze to death.
and your friend and you will build a fire and you will keep warm and
you will find that you have made it through the night.
and you will do this together for a time and you will find that you do
not need any help from your friend. and maybe you will venture out
into the mountains by yourself. and learn that the stars can give you
directions.
and one night you will look up for direction and you will see that the
stars are gone. and it will start raining. and you will find a place where
you can have shelter from the rain and keep warm, and you will survive
the night.
and as you go on you will become aware of the stars, and the clouds, and
the animals, and the trees, and the flowers, and the winds, and you will
continue to grow more secure in all your surroundings. you will learn
where to fish, where to trap, where to pick berries. your efficiency and
skill and security will become greater as they feed each other. then one

day you will twist and break your ankle on a rock, and in a flash, you will reflect that you had become too secure and self-confident.

and you'll lie there on the ground not knowing what to do

you'll lie there on the ground in pain

you will be about to die

and then by some magic, a little old man will probably appear and he will show you how to fix your ankle so you will be able to walk alone again. and after a few days, you will go off alone again. a little bit stronger.

and then you will notice that there are more men who travel in the mountains and after awhile you will become aware of where they will be about what time. and you will form a sometimes community with them. and then one day you will probably decide to go back to the city. And in the city you will see sheep running around saying that they need to do that and they need this and they need this and they need that, and you will find that they identify with things and ideas which they do not need to identify with, even though they think they do. and you will tell them that the only things they need are warmth, shelter, a little food, and some clothing. and that if they know they always can have these they can be free anywhere. that if they understand this, they can leave any situation that a free man can fulfill all his needs if he has to.

maybe he's just a country boy.

and maybe he can become a city boy, if the city people want to be free.

The revolutionaries talk about the unbearable conditions of poverty, ghettos, no jobs, collapsing family structures, brutal police forces, etc. They concentrate on all the unbearable conditions outside to each individual. And the politicians for millennia have been saying "Don't worry, folks, things will be better in the future. Heaven, Paradise, and Utopia are just around the program before your eyes. We are trying, trying, the world can't be free, you know." And descriptions, explanations, and promises are sometimes well intended and true, but they grossly miss the point.

You can stick a gun in his hands, and fulfill the
    IMAGE of a man.
You can stick a girl in his arms, and fulfill the
    IMAGE of a lover.
You can stick money in his pockets, and fulfill the
    IMAGE of success.
You can stick a suit on his back, and fulfill the
    IMAGE of dignity.

You can stick a t.v. before his eyes, and fulfill the
   IMAGE of being informed.
                                  And you can give him a house, a
job, radios, cars, refrigerators, telephones and fulfill the image of being
affluent
BUT
the only thing that will make him free in nitty-gritty marrow soul is
the knowing that he can take care of all his needs himself. Alone. Only
then will he have the alternatives of either being with someone or not.

Each individual has to have no needs, no necessities, in order to be
free. This is impossible, since he is a living organism. So he has to
travel second best. He has to know that he can fulfill his necessary needs
of food, clothing, shelter, and warmth. When he can fulfill all those
needs alone, he can leave any situation and the identity that goes with
the situation, knowing that he hasn't lost anything, that he will survive,
and that he is still free.

The world is filled with horrors because people identify with gripping
images which they think they need to become. They viciously struggle
for objects and situations that will make the image become reality. They
rationalize it and set up rules to make leaders who have power.

Power is the ability to execute or throw someone in jail for not obeying
established leader authorities. DEATH. It may be that people could
INFLUENCE people. INFLUENCE. In fluid. Flowing. A geographical area
where all objects, where all groups, were voluntary. nova. Where each
individual knew within himself that he could fulfill all his needs without being trapped by identity. BEING.
                    Amen, brother
                        FREE

"The Ideology of Failure" is as close as most readers will come to the Diggers; as the ultimate activists of hip, dispensing food and services for free, they generally distrust the literary form as a means of communication. The liberals, as one of their number argues, would attempt to teach by precept rather than by example —for the Diggers, and their impoverished constituency, the hour is getting late and talk is being devalued by the minute.

The Ideology of Failure

I knew it but I could not say it, and if I can begin to say it now, it is because I have left reality behind. Dead, the others have not been separated. They still hover around their corpses. I am not dead, but I am separated.

From the time we begin to call our childhood our past we seek to regain its simplicity. Its sense of presence. We tumble into drugs and cleave reality into so many levels of game. We turn our backs on the mess and walk into the woods, but only for a time. A game is a game is a game is a game and we return to the silent-crowded-uptight sidewalks with our pockets full of absurdity and compromise between cowardice and illusion.

Wearing hipsterism on our sleeves, we make music with mercenary groups who bleed money from any fools on the street, or we carve leather into sandals for twenty dollars a pair, or shape forms into art while a psychiatrist whispers formulae for a healthy life-lihood into our ear. And we smile all the time and stack a stereo with names we meet at parties and scoff at all the Sanpaku people cluttering up outside. We explode the myth of seriousness and wrap our bodies in a vinyl shield to coat our minds with microcosmic awareness of our own safety. We sophisticate our tastes in order to tap dance by hassles and shove the poignancy of "bring downs" into impersonal shadows. We focus everything towards the transcendence of daily consciousness: macrobiotic diets, hallucinogens, eastern and western aesthetics, philosophies, etc.

Our salaried hipness blankets us in the warmth of security until we masturbate ourselves into an erection of astral rapaciousness and grab whatever pleasures we might in the name of Love, always quick to contrast ourselves with middle-class man.

Berkeley Barb, November 18, 1966

If there is a contrast, it is slight. Hip and middle-class (as well as communist, fascist, socialist, and monarchist) values, goals, reactions and attitudes offer different styles, but amount to the same end: personal, national, or racial success. *Rien ne réussi comme le succès.*

The hipster, however, invites the indignation of his allies with a mockery of "straightness" and his alienation from the social norms of morality and dress. He is the perfection of success—liberated from the inhibitive life of bourgeois conformity and established in a packed class of happiness which combines the highest material pleasure with a total lack of commitment to middle-class humanism.

He is hated, feared, and envied. He is a man who can sing about the evils of the world, the beauty of touch, the delicacy of flowers, and scream systemicide from beneath a satin pillow while margining profits into war economies and maintaining his comfort on a consumer level of luxury. (Oh, excuse me. I see. He's educating the mass and his pay is only incidental compared to the millions of converts he has inspired with this orchestrated love. Ho, hum. . . .)

Well, when some of us get to that bracket, either through fame or fortune, we look at ourselves and remember the "Funk" that pushed us into the Lime, and we react. We may open peace centers with our money and contribute to the cause of freedom, or we may plow ourselves into the corner of "who cares" and paddy-cake fortunes, or we may drop out all over again and go back to the woods, and stare at the preposterousness of doing our thing within the frame of a reality that can incorporate and market anyone, anything, anytime. And then we may begin to understand that if some attempt is not made to manage the world with love, it will run mad and overwhelm everything, including the woods.

And so, we stay dropped-out. We won't, simply won't play the game any longer. We return to the prosperous consumer society and refuse to consume. And refuse to consume. And we do our thing for nothing. In truth, we live our protest. Everything we do is free because we are failures. We've got nothing, so we've got nothing to lose.

We're not foiled anymore by the romantic trappings of the marketeers of expanded consciousness. Love isn't a dance concert with a light show at $3 a head. It isn't an Artist Liberation Front "Free" Fair with concessions for food and pseudo psychedelia. It is the SF Mime Troupe performing Free Shows in the parks while it is being crushed by a furious $15,000 debt. It is Arthur Lisch standing under a blue flag in Hunters Point scraping rust off the tin-can memorial to Matthew Johnson from two to five everyday. It is free food in the Panhandle where anyone can do anything with the food they bring to each other. It is Love. And when love does its thing it does it for love and separates itself from the false-witness of the Copsuckers and the Gladly Dead.

To Show Love is to fail. To love to fail is the Ideology of Failure. Show Love. Do your thing. Do it for FREE. Do it for Love. We can't fail. And Mr. Jones will never know what's happening here, do you Mr. Jones.

—george metesky

Allen Ginsberg is the grand old man of the underground. As poet, philosopher, and guru, he energetically embraces the youth revolt, appearing at benefits for the victims of drug busts, speaking at love-ins, gracing the walls of hundreds of poster shops. As ever, he is visionary and controversial, in an attempt to prepare his constituency for the next new insight.

Renaissance or Die

ALLEN GINSBERG

Because our governors and polis have to perceive the obvious I wish to make some political suggestions to this community; make them as Poet and claim powers of Prophecy as did the good grey bards before me in this country because one who looks in his heart and speaks frankly can claim to prophecy.

The present condition of life for American Person is one of deathly public solitude. We've built a technological Tower of Babel around ourselves and are literally (as in Gemini) reaching into heaven to escape the planet. New giant over-population depends on a vast metallic superstructure to feed and transport all the bodies here together. The stupendous machinery surrounding us conditions our "thoughts, feelings and apparent sensory impressions," and reinforces our mental slavery to the material universe we've invested in.

How can we Americans make our minds change theme? For unless the theme changes—encrustation of the planet with machinery, inorganic metal smog, violent outrage and mass murder will take place. We witness these horrors already.

Abruptly then, I will make a first proposal—on one level symbolic, but to be taken as literally as possible, it may shock some and delight others—that everybody who hears my voice, directly or indirectly, try the chemical LSD at least once, every man woman and child American in good health over the age of 14—that, if necessary, we have a mass emotional nervous breakdown in these States once and for all, that we see bankers laughing in their revolving doors with strange staring eyes. May everybody in America turn on, whatever the transient law, because

The East Village Other, January 10, 1967

individual soul development (as once declared by a poet in jail in this city) is our law transcending the illusions of the political state. Soul also transcends LSD, may I add, to reassure those like myself who would fear a chemical dictatorship. I propose, then, that everybody including the President and his and our vast hordes of generals, executives, judges, and legislators of these States go to nature, find a kindly teacher or Indian peyote chief or guru guide, and assay their consciousness with LSD.

Then, I prophesy, we will all have seen some ray of glory or vastness beyond our conditioned social selves, beyond our government, beyond America even, that will unite us into a peaceable community.

The LSD I am proposing is literal. I hope it will be understood as not THE solution, but a typical and spiritually revolutionary catalyst, where many varieties of spiritual revolution are necessary to transcend specifically the political COLD WAR we are all involved in.

Anger and control of anger is our problem. Already we have enough insight into politics to be aware of one very simple thing: that we can judge all politics and all public speech and ideology by perceiving the measure of anger manifested therein. All present political parties propose violence to resolve our confusions, as in Vietnam. We might look for a third party, specifically named a Peace Party—referring to individual subjective peaceableness (such as we have not seen in our populace or our leaders) as well as consequent public peaceableness, a party founded on psychology not ideology. We obviously need to feed China and India, not ignore, manipulate or threaten to destroy them.

What can the young do with themselves faced with this American version of the planet? The most sensitive and among the "best minds" do drop out. They wander over the body of the nation looking into the faces of their elders, they wear long Adamic hair and form Keristan communities in the slums, they pilgrimage to Big Sur and live naked in forests seeking natural vision and meditation, they dwell in the Lower East Side as if it were an hermetic forest. And they assemble thousands together as they have done this year in Golden Gate Park in San Francisco or Tompkins Park in New York to manifest their peaceableness in demonstrations of Fantasy that transcend protest against—or for—the hostilities of Vietnam. Young men and women in speckled clothes, minstrels' garb, jesters' robes, carrying balloons, signs "President Johnson we are praying for you," gathered chanting Hindu and Buddhist mantras to calm their fellow citizens who are otherwise entrapped in a planetary barroom brawl.

But there has been no recognition of this insight on the part of the fathers and teachers (Father Zossima's famous cry!) of these young.

What's lacking in the great institutions of learning? The specific wisdom discipline that those young propose: search into inner space.

Children drop out of schools because there are no, or very few, Gurus. Those elders concerned with this practical problem might consider that there is an easy practical solution: the establishment within centers of learning of facilities for wisdom search which the ancients proposed as the true function of education in the first place; academies of self-awareness, classes in spiritual teaching, darshan with holymen of disciplined mind-consciousness. One might well, in fact, employ the drop-out beatniks as instructors in this department, and thereby officially recognize and proclaim the social validity of exploration of inner space. Tibetan monks, swamis, yogins, and yoginis, psychedelic guides, Amerindian peyote chiefs, even a few finished Zen Roshis and many profound poets are already present and available in our cities for such work though at present they battle immigration bureaucracies and scholarly heads of departments of Oriental Religion.

What I am proposing as policy, for us elders, for what community we have, is self-examination as Official Politics, an Official Politics of Control of Anger. With state propaganda reversed in that direction, church and university teaching and research in that direction, and requests to the government for vast sums of money equal to the outer-space program and consequent billboards on the highways "Control Your Anger—Be Aware of Yourself."

There is a change of consciousness among the younger generations, in a direction always latent to Elder America, toward the most complete public frankness possible. As the Gloucester poet Charles Olson formulated it, "Private is public, and public is how we behave." This means revision of standards of public behavior to include indications of private manners heretofore excluded from public consciousness.

Thus, new social standards, more equivalent to private desire—as there is increased sexual illumination, new social codes may be found acceptable to rid ourselves of fear of our own nakedness, rejection of our own bodies.

Likely an enlarged family unit will emerge for many citizens, possibly, as the Zen Buddhist anarchist anthropologist Gary Snyder observed, with matrilineal descent as courtesy to those dakinis whose saddhana or holy path is the sexual liberation and teaching of Dharma to many frightened males (including myself) at once. Children may be held in common, with the orgy an acceptable community sacrament, one that brings all people closer together. Certainly one might seduce the Birch Society to partake in naked orgy and the police with their wives together with Leroi Jones the brilliantly angry poet. America's political need is orgies in the parks, on Boston Common and in the Public Gardens with naked bacchantes in our national forests.

I am not proposing idealistic fancies, I am acknowledging what is already happening among the young in fact and fantasy and proposing official blessing for these breakthroughs of community spirit. Among the young we find a new breed of White Indians in California communing with illuminated desert redskins; we find our teenagers dancing Nigerian Yoruba dances and entering trance states to the electric vibration of the Beatles who have borrowed shamanism from Africa sources.

Ideas I have dwelled on are mixed. There is some prescription for public utopia through education in inner space. There is more prescription here for the individual, as always, the old command to free ourselves from social conditioning, laws and traditional mores.

And discover the Guru in our own hearts. And set forth within the New Wilderness of machine America to explore open spaces of consciousness in Self and fellow Selves. If there be the necessary revolution in America it will come that way. It's up to us older hairs who still have relation with some of the joy of youth to encourage this revolutionary individual search.

But how can peaceful psychological politics succeed when $50 billion a year is spent to busy participation in armed conflict? "Vietnam War Brings Prosperity"—headline Lincoln Nebraska *Star,* February 1966. Certainly the awareness itself of this condition will help some of us, as did Ike's warning against the military-industrial complex running the mind of the nation.

As a side note, there ARE specific methods for combatting the mental dictatorship over "thoughts feelings and apparent sensory impressions" imposed on us by military-industrial control of language and imagery in public media. W. S. Burroughs has provided a whole armamentarium of counter-brainwash techniques: cut-up of newspapers and ads, collage of political and entertainment news to reveal the secret intention of the Senders, observation of TV imagery with sound off and simultaneous apperception of noises on the radio or street. These methods are effective in jolting the soft machine of the brain out of its conditioned hypnosis.

Cutting out, or dropping out, of the culture will not lead to a chaos of individuality. What it will mean, for the young, is training in meditation and art (and perhaps neolithic lore), and responsibility of a new order, to the community of the heart, not to our heart-less society wherein we have read the headline in the Omaha *World Herald:* "Rusk Says Toughness Essential For Peace."

The "oversoul" to be discovered is a pragmatic reality. We can all tell signs of an illuminated man in business or the church—one who is open-hearted, non-judging, empathetic, compassionate to the rejected and condemned. The tolerant one, the Observer, the Aware. And we see that these should influence action.

Finally, detachment comes naturally: we all know the war is camp, hate is camp, murder is camp, even love is camp, the universe is a grand camp according to Chuang Tzu and the Prajnaparamita Sutra. This detachment is salvation. We have an international youth society of solitary children—stilyagi, provo, beat, mofada, nadaista, energumeno, mod and rocker—all aghast at the space age horror world they are born to and are now questioning the nature of the universe itself as is proper in the space age.

There are many contradictions here, especially between proposed communal sex orgy and contemplative choiceless awareness. Whitman noticed that too, "Do I contradict myself? Very well, I contradict myself." A dialogue between these contradictions is a good healthy way of life, one correcting the other. Indulgence in sexuality and sensational ecstasy may well lead to contemplative awareness of desire and cessation of desire.

> "I know although when looks meet
> I tremble to the bone,
> The more I leave the door unlatched
> The sooner love is gone."

What satisfaction is now possible for the young? Only the satisfaction of their Desire: love, the body, and orgy—the satisfaction of a peaceful natural community where they can circulate and explore persons, cities and the nature of the planet—the satisfaction of encouraged self-awareness, and the satiety and cessation of desire, anger, grasping and craving.

Respect for the old? Yea when the old are tranquil and not nervous, and respect the sport of the young. Holymen do inspire respect. One conservative Vaishnavite Swami Bhaktivedanta moved into the Lower East Side this year and immediately dozens of young LSD freakouts flocked to sing the Harekrishna Mahamantra with him—chant for the preservation of the planet.

But a nation of elders convinced that spiritual search is immaturity and that national war and metallic communication is maturity, cannot ask for respect from the young. For the present conduct of the elders in America is a reflection of lack of self-respect.

II. The Redefinition
of Culture:
Life as Art

When drug use becomes common in even the squarest college fraternities, when a major tobacco company patents the slang names of varieties of marijuana, and when television advertising is unashamedly psychedelic, it is no longer outrageous to speak of a "turned-on generation." Even without drugs, minds are expanding; as Teilhard de Chardin noted, the population increase means that we come more in contact with each other, and the mental temperature rises. Hard work is no longer the sole measure of success in our schools, and a *B* earned with persevering application takes second place to the inspired, imaginative performance of the less diligent genius.

Confronted with the paradox of an increasingly intelligent audience and an incessantly banal culture, we should not be surprised that people take drugs. For hallucinogens provide Instant Art; life becomes a movie, and you are the world's greatest director, screening reality through dilated eyes. But even the ritual of turning on becomes boring—"Now that you've found another key, what are you going to play?" as the Beatles phrase it.

Establishment myth has it that drugs make you politically passive and culturally indiscriminate, but judging from the cultural explosion of the popular arts in the last few years, the reverse is closer to the truth. The limitations of traditional forms have been found arbitrary, and experimentation, even at the risk of artistic anarchy, has revolutionized pop music, art, and, to a lesser extent, the theater. "We can't jettison the old stuff fast enough," claims one young poet. "The literature of the past few centuries is the product of minds limited by a single cultural orientation. With drugs, we can detach ourselves from our own consciousness."

So the world of drugs and the newer art forms enjoy a symbiotic relationship; even artists who don't use them have learned from the techniques of those who do. However repressive government controls on drugs may become, the process has been set in motion, and the healthy experimentation in both form and content should yield even more emphasis on psychedelic manifestations in the arts.

The revolution in popular music has raced along with virtually no standards of criticism adequate to its increased scope. Students await new records with the same controlled frenzy observed on the New York docks when a new chapter of a Dickens novel was arriving. Quality production is now justified by a quality product, and the most ambitious groups speak of attempting symphonies and operas. "Notes for the New Geology" represents a tentative and somewhat crude attempt to define the nature of this massive shift in aesthetics, as well as the articulation of a workable critical approach.

Notes for the New Geology

CHESTER ANDERSON

I

Rock's the first head music we've had since the end of the baroque. By itself, without the aid of strobe lights, day-glo paints and other sub-imaginative copouts, it engages the entire sensorium, appealing to the intelligence with no interference from the intellect. Extremely typographic people are unable to experience it, which—because TV didn't approach universality till 1950—is why the rock folk are so young, generally. (Most of the astounding exceptions are people, like the poet Walter Lowenfels, who have lived a long time but have not become old.)

II

SOME PRINCIPLES:
 —That rock is essentially head (or even psychedelic) music.
 —That rock is a legitimate avant garde art form, with deep roots in the music of the past (especially the baroque and before), great vitality, and vast potential for growth and development, adaptation, experiment, et cetera.
 —That rock shares most of its formal/structural principles with baroque music (wherein lie its most recent cultural roots), and that it

San Francisco *Oracle*, January, 1967

and baroque can be judged by the same broad standards (the governing principles being that of mosaic structure of tonal and textural contrast: tactility, collage).

—That is evolving Sturgeonesque *homo Gestalt* configurations:

* the groups themselves, far more intimately interrelated and integrated than any comparable ensemble in the past;

* super-families, like Kerista and the more informal communal pads;

* and pre-initiate tribal groups, like the teenyboppers; all in evident and nostalgic response to technological and population pressures.

—That rock is an intensely participational and non-typographic art form, forerunner of something much like McLuhan's covertly projected spherical society.

—That far from being degenerate or decadent, rock is a regenerative and revolutionary art, offering us our first real hope for the future (indeed, for the present) since August 6, 1945; and that its effects on the younger population, especially those effects most deplored by typeheads, have all been essentially good and healthy so far.

—That rock principles are not limited to music, and that much of the shape of the future can be seen in its aspirations today (these being mainly total freedom, total experience, total love, peace and mutual affection).

—That today's teenyboppers will be voting tomorrow and running for office the day after.

—That rock is an intensely synthesizing art, an art of amazing relationships (collage is rock and roll), able to absorb (maybe) all of society into itself as an organizing force, transmuting and reintegrating what it absorbs (as it has so far); and that its practitioners and audience are learning to perceive and manipulate reality in wholly new ways, quite alien to typeheads.

—That rock has reinstated the ancient truth that art is fun.

—That rock is a way of life, international and verging in this decade on universal; and can't be stopped, retarded, put down, muted, modified or successfully controlled by typeheads, whose arguments don't apply and whose machinations don't mesh because they can't perceive (dig) what rock really is and does.

—That rock is a tribal phenomenon, immune to definition and other typographical operations, and constitutes what might be called a 20th-century magic.

—That rock seems to have synthesized most of the intellectual and artistic movements of our time and culture, cross-fertilizing them and forcing them rapidly toward fruition and function.

—That rock is a vital agent in breaking down absolute and arbitrary distinctions.

—That any artistic activity not allied to rock is doomed to preciousness and sterility.

—That group participation, total experience and complete involvement are rock's minimal desiderata and those as well of a world that has too many people.

—That rock is creating the social rituals of the future.

—That the medium is indeed the message, and rock knows what that means.

—That no arbitrary limitations of rock are valid (i.e., that a rock symphony or opera, for example, is possible.)

—That rock is handmade, and only the fakes are standardized.

—That rock presents an aesthetic of discovery.

III

Marshall McLuhan makes no sense at all, not as I was taught to define *sense* in my inadequately cynical youth. He's plainly no Aquinas. And yet, somehow, he embarrassingly manages to explain to perfection an overwhelming array of things that used to make even less sense than he does and were somewhat threatening as well: things like pop, op and camp (which sounds like a breakfast food); the psychedelic revolution, the pot and acid explosion; the Haight-Ashbury community, and especially what we'll keep on calling Rock and Roll until we can find some name more appropriate for it. (I nominate Head Music, but I don't expect it to catch on.)

Not that McLuhan mentions any of these things. He simply gives the clues. Synthesis and synaesthesia; non-typographic, non-linear, basically mosaic and mythic modes of perception; involvement of the whole sensorium; roles instead of jobs; participation in depth; extended awareness; preoccupation with textures, with tactility, with multisensory experiences—put 'em all together and you have a weekend on Haight Street.

The electronic extension of the central nervous system, the evolutionary storm that's happening right now (which is having, slowly, exactly the same effect on the whole world as acid has had on us), makes everything else make sense, and McLuhan taught us how to see it. He doesn't *have* to make sense.

IV

We're still so hooked on mainly visual perceptions that the possibilities of our other senses are almost unimaginable. We still interpret highs in visual terms, for instance: though acid is mainly tactile, spatial, visceral and integrative; whilst pot affects mostly hearing and touch. It's all a matter of conditioning; we'll learn.

The things a really imaginative engineer could accomplish by working on our many senses, singly and in orchestrated combinations, are staggering. Imagine: sensory counterpoint—the senses registering contradictory stimuli and the brain having fun trying to integrate them. Imagine *tasting* G-minor! The incredible synaesthesiae!

Rock and roll is toying with this notion.

Though we've been brought up to think of music as a purely auditory art, we actually perceive it with the whole body in a complex pattern of sympathetic tensions and interacting stimuli.

Melodies, and especially vocal melodies or tunes in the vocal range, affect the larynx. It follows the tune, subvocalizing. As the line ascends, the larynx tightens, and as the line descends, it relaxes, responding sympathetically to the tension of the tones. (The larynx also tightens in response to strong emotion, just before the tears begin.) That's what makes an unexpected high note such an emotional event, because the part of the brain in charge of such things can't tell one kind of tension from the other. That's also much of what makes melodies work. Whether you want to or not, you participate.

Meanwhile, low notes—especially on the bass, and most acutely if it's plucked and amplified—are experienced in the abdomen as localized vibrations, an amazingly private sensation impossible to resist. The deeper the note, furthermore, the lower down on the trunk it seems to be felt. A properly organized R & R bass line is experienced as a pattern of incredibly intimate caresses: still more unavoidable participation.

(The same visceral perception yields a sense of musical space.)

A steady bass line in scales induces something like confidence and/or well-being. A jagged, syncopated bass can range you from nervous exhilaration to utter frenzy. (Old Bach knew all about this.) The possibilities are next to endless.

Rhythms, meanwhile, affect the heart, skeletal muscles and motor nerves, and can be used to play games with these pretty much at will. Repeated patterns (ostinati) and drones induce an almost instant light hypnosis (just like grass), locking the mind on the music at hand and intensifying all the other reactions. Long, open chords lower the blood pressure; crisp, repeated chords raise it.

And this is only the beginning, the barest outline of our physical response to music, but data enough for me to make my point. An arranger/composer who knew all this, especially if he had electronic instruments to work with, could play a listener's body like a soft guitar. He could score the listener's body as part of the arrangement, creating an intensity of participation many people don't even achieve in sex. (So far this seems to have happened mainly by accident.) And there's no defense but flight; not even the deaf are completely immune.

"Learning from the Beatles" . . . Well, of course. But from the chairman of the Rutgers English department, who serves additionally as an editor of the Partisan Review? *A monumental achievement, a tour de force. Poirier has absorbed in near-record time a huge, unwieldy body of work, analyzed it with the critical methods he initiated with Harvard's Reuben Brower, and produced the most lucid critique of the Beatles' total musical career. It confounds the imagination of those who were skeptical of the sensitivity of the last generation; Poirier's piece may inadvertently encourage talented but unenthusiastic students to study similar techniques. And if his own generation gets the message, so much the better.*

Learning from the Beatles

RICHARD POIRIER

Has anyone been able completely to ignore *Sgt. Pepper's Lonely Hearts Club Band?* Probably not. But the very fact of its immense popularity with people of every age and persuasion is almost a guarantee of its not receiving the demanding critical attention it calls for. It isn't enough to say that it is the latest * and most remarkable of the thirteen albums composed and performed by the Beatles since 1964; some such claim could have been made for each album when it appeared. *Sgt. Pepper* isn't in the line of continuous development; rather, it is an eruption. It's an astounding accomplishment for which no one could have been wholly prepared, and it therefore substantially enlarges and modifies all the work that preceded it. It sends us back to the earlier Beatles not for confirmation of the fact that they've always been the best group of their kind. Rather, we listen for those gestations of genius that have now come to fruition. And the evidence is there: in each album which, while being unmistakably theirs, is nonetheless full of exploratory peculiarities not heard on the others; in the way the release even of a single can

* The Beatles have since produced *Magical Mystery Tour*, but of its eleven songs four had appeared as singles when this article was written, and I discuss three of these at length: "Penny Lane," "Baby You're a Rich Man," and "All You Need Is Love."

Partisan Review, Fall, 1967

set off a new surge of energy in their many imitators; in a self-delight-
ing inventiveness that has gradually exceeded the sheer physical ca-
pacities even of four such brilliant musicians. The consequent necessity for expanded orchestral and electronic support reached the point
where the Sgt. Pepper album had to be wholly conceived in studio with
as many as forty-eight instruments. Meanwhile, still in their mid-
twenties they have made two movies, *A Hard Day's Night* and *Help!*,
which are in spots as good as the Marx Brothers, and their most versatile
member, John Lennon, has written two books of Joycean verbal play
that suggest why no one is ever in danger of reading too much into the
lyrics of their songs. The Beatles are now beyond patronization, and this
is especially satisfying to those like myself who have wondered how
much longer the literary academic adjudicators could claim to be taking
the arts seriously by promoting a couple of distinguished novels every
year, a few films, some poems, maybe a museum show and, if they're
really lucky, a play.

Of course to delay a revolution there are ways and ways of finally
paying considered attention to the lower orders. One way is to socialize in
the manner, McLuhan or pre-McLuhan, that forces the good and the
bad in the popular arts to lie down in the same categories. There'll surely
be a piece announcing, say, that the Beatles "represent"—a favorite
word in the shelving process—not just the young but an aristocracy of
the young. And of course they are aristocratic: in their carelessness,
their assumption that they can enact anyone else's life just for the fun
of it, their tolerance for the things they do make fun of, their delight
in wildness along with a disdain for middle-class rectitudes, their easy
expertness, their indifference to the wealth they are happy to have,
their pleasures in costume and in a casual eccentricity of ordinary dress,
their in-group language not meant, any more than is Bob Dylan's—another such aristocrat—to make ordinary sense. That kind of accommo-
dation is familiar by now, and so is another, which is to admit them
into the company of their "betters." You know, the way jazz is like Bach?
Well, sometimes they are like Monteverdi and sometimes their songs
are even better than Schumann's. But that won't work either. Liverpool
boys of their sort have been let into Eton before, and not on the assumption that it would be the style of Eton that would change.

It won't be easy to accommodate the Beatles, and that's nowadays
almost the precondition for exciting the pastoral concern of Responsible
Critics. Literary and academic grown-ups will discover that their favorite
captive audience, the young in school, really have listened to the Beatles'
kind of music and won't buy the yarn of significance that ensnares most
adult talk about the other arts. Any effort to account for what the

Beatles are doing will be difficult, as I've learned from this not very extensive and inexpert try, but only to the extent that talking about the experience of any work of art is more difficult than talking about the theory of it, or the issues in it or the history around it. The results of any such effort by a number of people would be of importance not just for popular music but for all the arts. People who listen to the Beatles love them—what about that? Why isn't there more talk about pleasure, about the excitement of witnessing a performance, about the excitement that goes into a performance of any kind? Such talk could set in motion a radical and acutely necessary amendment to the literary and academic club rules. Since the exalted arts (to which the novel, about a century ago, was the last genre to be admitted) have all but surrendered the provision of fun and entertainment to the popular arts, criticism must turn to film and song if it is to remind itself that the arts really do not need to be boring, no matter how much copy can be made from the elaboration of current theories of boredom.

Critical confrontations initiated in this spirit could give a new status to an increasingly unfashionable kind of criticism: to close-up, detailed concern for performance, for enactment and execution in a work of art. Film and song, the two activities in which young people are now especially interested, and about which they are learning to talk fairly well, may yield something to other kinds of scrutiny, but they yield much more to this kind. So does literature, on the very infrequent occasions when it is so treated. The need is for intense localization of interest and a consequent modesty of description, in the manner of Stark Young's dramatic criticism, or Bernard Haggin's writing about classical music and jazz or Edwin Denby and, more recently, Robert Garis on ballet. Imagining an audience for such criticism, the critic thinks not of a public with Issues and Topics at the ready, but rather of a small group of like-minded, quite private people who find pleasure in certain intensive acts of looking and listening. Looking and listening to something with such a group, imaginary or real, means checking out responses, pointing to particular features, asking detailed questions, sharing momentary excitements. People tend to listen to the Beatles the way families in the last century listened to readings of Dickens, and it might be remembered by literary snobs that the novel then, like the Beatles and even film now, was considered a popular form of entertainment generally beneath serious criticism, and most certainly beneath academic attention.

The Beatles' music is said to belong to the young, but if it does that's only because the young have the right motive for caring about it—they enjoy themselves. They also know what produces the fun they have, by phrase and instrument, and they're very quick, as I've discovered, to shoot down inflated interpretations. They should indeed exercise proprietary rights. This is the first time that people of school age have been tuned in to sounds invented not by composers approved by adults but in to sounds invented by their own near contemporaries, sounds associated with lyrics, manners and dress that they also identify as their own. David Amram, the New York Philharmonic's first resident composer, is understandably optimistic that this kind of identification will develop an avidity of attention to music that could be the salvation of American musical composition and performance. Perhaps in some such way the popular arts can help restore all the arts to their status as entertainment.

To help this process along it isn't necessary that literary and academic grown-ups go to school to their children. Rather, they must begin to ask some childlike and therefore some extremely difficult questions about particular works: Is this any fun? How and where is it any fun? And if it isn't why bother? While listening together to recordings of popular music, people of any age tend naturally to ask these questions, and I've heard them asked by young people with an eager precision which they almost never exhibit, for want of academic encouragement, when they talk about a poem or a story. Their writing about this music isn't as good as their talk, at least in the magazines I've been able to get hold of, like *Vibrations*, *The Broadside* and, perhaps the best, *Crawdaddy*. In written criticism they display some of the adult vices, including at times a nearly Germanic fondness for categorization: the Mersey beat, the raving style, trip songs, the San Francisco school, the love sound, folk-rock and the rock-folk-pop tradition are typical of the terms that get bandied about with desperate and charming hope. Reviews of popular music in the major newspapers and magazines are much worse, however, and before the Sgt. Pepper album practically no space even for an intelligent note was given the Beatles in any of them. Now that they've begun to appear, any adult easily victimized by a reputed generational gap need only read reviews of *Sgt. Pepper* in the *New York Times* and the *Village Voice* by Richard Goldstein to discover that youth is no guarantee of understanding. In his early twenties, he is already an ancient. Some of his questions—does the album have any real unity?— were not necessary even when originally asked some two thousand years ago, while others are a bad dream of Brooks and Warren: the "lyrical technique" of "She's Leaving Home" is "uninspired narrative, with a dearth of poetic irony." The song is in fact one of *Sgt. Pepper*'s satirically funniest cuts, though someone Goldstein's age mightn't as easily see this as someone older. Recognition of its special blend of period sentimentality and elegance of wit is conferred upon the listener not by his being chronologically young but by his having once lived with that especially English blend of tones from Beatrice Lillie or Noel Coward, and their wistful play about the genteel.

Nearly all the songs on the Sgt. Pepper album and the two singles released here since then—"All You Need Is Love" and "Baby You're a Rich Man"—are in fact quite broadly allusive: to the blues, to jazz hits of the thirties and forties, to classical music, early rock and roll, previous cuts by the Beatles themselves. Much of the comedy in these songs and much of their historical resonance, as in the stately Wagnerian episode in "A Day In the Life," is managed in this way. Mixing of styles and tones remind the listener that one kind of feeling about a subject isn't enough and that any single induced feeling must often exist within the context of seemingly contradictory alternatives. Most good groups offer something of this kind, like the Who, with the brilliant drummer Keith Moon. In songs like "Don't Look Away" and "So Sad About Us," Moon, working with the composer-guitarist Pete Townsend, calls forth a complicated response in a manner nicely described in *Crawdaddy* by Jon Landau, one of the best of the reviewers I've read: "Townsend scratches his chorus, muffles his strings, or lets the chord stand out full depending on what Moon is doing—the result being a perfectly unified guitar-drum sound that can't help but make you feel happy even while the lyrics tell you to feel sad." The Beatles have often in the past worked for similar mixtures, but they now offer an additional nuance: especially in later songs, one of the interwoven strands is likely to be an echo of some familiar, probably clichéd musical, verbal or dramatic formula. These echoes, like the soap-opera background music of "She's Leaving Home" or the jaunty music-hall tones of "When I'm Sixty-four," have the enriching effect that allusiveness can have in poetry: of expanding a situation toward the simultaneous condition of pathos, because the situation is seen as recurrent and therefore possibly insoluble, and comic, because the recurrence has finally passed into cliché.

Any close listening to musical groups soon establishes the fact that as composers and performers the Beatles repay attention altogether more than does any other group, American or English. They offer something for nearly everyone and respond to almost any kind of interest. The Rolling Stones, the Left Banke and the Bee Gees are especially good, but in none of these is there an inventive productivity equal to that of Lennon, McCartney or their producer George Martin, whose contributions of electronic and orchestral notation really make him one of the group, particularly now that their performances are to be exclusively in studio. Only Dylan shows something equivalent to the Beatles in his combination of talents as composer, lyricist and performer. In performance the Beatles exhibit a nearly total theatrical power. It is a power so unencumbered and so freely diverse both for the group and for each of its members that it creates an element of suspense in whatever they do, an expectation that this time there really will be a failure of good taste—that attribute shared by only the greatest theatrical performers. They never wholly lose themselves in anyone else's styling, however, or in their own exuberance; they never succumb to the excitements they generate, much less those of their audience. It's unthinkable that they would lend themselves for the rock and wreck sequence of the Yardbirds in Antonioni's *Blow-up*. That particular performance, quite aside from what it contributed to a brilliant film, is a symptom of the infiltration even into popular music of the decadence by which entertainment is being displaced by a self-abasing enactment of what is implicit in the *form* of entertainment—in this instance, of group playing that gives way to animosities and a destructive retaliation against recalcitrant instrumental support. When the Beatles sound as if they are heading orchestrally into self-obliterating noise, it is very often only that they may assert their presence vocally in quite the opposite direction: by contrasting choir-boy cooing, by filigrees of voice-play coming from each of them, as in the reprise of "Sgt. Pepper," for instance, or, as in "Lovely Rita," the little choral oo's and gaspings—all of these suggesting, in their relation to solo, crosscurrents of feeling within an agreed area of play. Manners so instinctively free and yet so harmonious could not be guided from outside, either by an audience or even by directorial guidance, however much the latter did help in rescuing them from the tawdry enslavement to Elvis Presley, an otherwise profitable influence, in their first, fortunately hard-to-find recording of 1961 made in Hamburg with Ringo's predecessor at the drums, Peter Best.

As is the taste of all great performers—in athletics, in politics, in any of the arts—the taste of the Beatles or of Dylan is an emanation of personality, of a self that is the generous master but never the creature of its audience. Taste in such instances is inseparable from a stubbornness of selfhood, and it doesn't matter that the self has been invented for the theater. Any self is invented as soon as any purpose is conceived. But the Beatles are a special case in not being *a* self at all. They are a group, and the unmistakable group identity exists almost in spite of sharp individuation, each of them, except the invisible Martin, known to be unique in some shaggy way. There are few other groups in which even one or two of the members are as publicly recognizable as any of the Beatles, and this can't be explained as a difference simply in public relations. It is precisely this unusual individuation which explains, I think, why the Beatles are so much stronger than any other group and why they don't need, like the Who, to play at animosities on stage. The pretense doesn't communicate the presence of individual Who but rather an anxiety at their not instinctively feeling like individuals when they are together. The Beatles, on the other hand, enhance the individuality of one another by the sheer elaborateness by which they arrive at a cohesive sound and by a musical awareness of one another that isn't distinguishable from the multiple directions allowed in the attainment of harmony. Like members of a great athletic team, like such partners in dance as Nureyev and Fonteyn or like some jazz combos, the Beatles in performance seem to draw their aspirations and their energy not from the audience but from one another. Their close, loyal and affectionate personal ties are of course not irrelevant.

The incentive for what they accomplish seems to be sequestered among them, a tensed responsiveness that encourages from Harrison, as in "And Your Bird Can Sing," what sounds like the best guitar playing in the world and which provokes the immense productivity of Lennon and McCartney. The amount they have composed might be explained by commercial venture but not the daring and originality of each new single or album. Of course the promise of "new sounds" is itself a commercial necessity in their business, as the anxieties of the second album of the Jefferson Airplane indicate, but the Beatles will soon release their fourteenth, and it's not merely "new sounds" that they produce, an easy enough matter with orchestral support, electronics and Asiatic importations. They produce different styles, different musical conceptions and revisions of sentiment that gives an unprecedented variety to an artistic career that had its proper beginning a mere four or five years ago. The freshness of each effort is often so radically different from the one before, as any comparison among *Rubber Soul, Revolver* and *Sgt. Pepper* will indicate, as to constitute risk rather than financial ambition—especially three such albums, along with a collection of earlier songs, *Yesterday and Today,* in a period just over eighteen months. They are the ones who get tired of the sounds they have made, and the testings and teasings that produce each new album are self-inflicted. If they are careerist it is in the manner not of Judy Garland, reminding us in each concert of "Somewhere Over the Rainbow" and the pains of show biz, but of John Coltrane who, when he died in July at forty, was also about to give up performance in public altogether, even though his reputation as one of the most influential musicians in jazz and its greatest saxophonist guaranteed him an increasingly profitable concert career. His interest in music was a continually exploratory one, an effort to broaden the possibilities, as the Beatles do now in studio, of his music and his instruments. Like Harrison with his guitar, he managed with the soprano sax to produce a nearly oriental sound, and this discovery led him to an interest in Indian music much as Harrison was led to the study of the sitar. And again like the Beatles, Coltrane's experimentation was the more intense because he and his sidemen, Elvin Jones and McCoy Tyner, achieved a remarkable degree of liberating, energizing empathy. Almost all such champions are extraordinary and private men who work with an audience, as the phrase goes, only when that audience is composed of the few who can perform with them. Otherwise, the audience is what it ought to be: not participants but witnesses or only listeners to a performance. The audience that in the theme song of *Sgt. Pepper* is so "lovely" that "we'd like to take you home with us" is a wholly imaginary one, especially on a record contrived as an escape from public performance.

Aloof from politics, their topicality is of music, the sentiments and the social predicaments traditional to folk songs and ballads. Maybe the most important service of the Beatles and similar groups is the restoration to good standing of the simplicities that have frightened us into irony and the search for irony; they locate the beauty and pathos of commonplace feelings even while they work havoc with fashionable or tiresome expressions of those feelings. A particularly brilliant example is the record, released some weeks after the Sgt. Pepper album, with "Baby You're a Rich Man" on one side and "All You Need Is Love" on the other. "Baby You're a Rich Man" opens with an inquiry addressed by McCartney and Harrison to Lennon, who can be said to represent here a starry-eyed fan's version of the Beatles themselves: "How does it feel to be/One of the beautiful people?" This and subsequent questions are asked of the "rich man" in a reverentially high but devastatingly lilting voice, to the accompaniment of bursts of sitar music and the clip-clopping of Indian song. The sitar, an instrument Harrison studied in India for six weeks with the renowned Ravi Shankar ("George," he reported, "was truly humble") here suggests not the India of "Within You, Without You" evoked on the Sgt. Pepper album, the India of the Bhagavad-Gita. It is rather another India, of fabulous riches, the India of the British and their Maharajahs, a place for exotic travel, but also for joss sticks and the otherworldliness of a "trip." All these possibilities are at work in the interplay of music and lyrics. Contributing to the merely social and satiric implications of the song, the Indian sounds operate in the manner of classical allusion in Pope: they expand to the ridiculous the cant of jet-set, international gossip columns—"one of the beautiful people" or "baby, you're a rich man now," or "how often have you been there?" But, as in Pope, the instrument of ridicule here, the sitar, is allowed in the very process to remain unsullied and eloquent. The social implications of the song carry more than a hint of self-parody since the comic mixtures of verbal and musical phrasing refer us to similar mixtures that are a result of the Beatles' fantastic fortune: Liverpool boys, still in their twenties, once relatively poor and now enormously rich, once socially nowhere and now internationally "there," once close to home both in fact and in their music but now implicated not only in the Mersey beat but in the Ganges sound, in travel to India and "trips" of a kind for which India set the precedent for centuries.

Most remarkably, the song doesn't sort out its social satire from its implicitly positive treatment of drugs. Bob Dylan often puns with roughly the same intention, as in "Rainy Day Woman #12 & 35," a simple but effective example:

> *Well, they'll stone you when you're trying to be so good,*
> *They'll stone you just like they said they would.*
> *They'll stone you when you try to go home,*
> *Then they'll stone you when you're there all alone.*
> *But I would not feel so all alone:*
> *Everybody must get stoned.*

In the Beatles' song, the very same phrases that belong to the platitudes of the "beautiful people" belong also with favorable connotations, to the drug scene. The question, "and have you travelled very far?" is answered by Lennon, the "beautiful" person, with what socially would be a comfortable cliché: "Far as the eye can see." But the phrase is really too outmoded for the jet age and thus sends us back to the original question and to the possibility that the "travel" can refer to a "trip" on LSD, the destination of which would indeed be "as far as the eye can see." Most of the lyrics operate in this double way, both as social satire and drug talk: "How often have you been there?/Often enough to know," or "What did you see when you were there?/Nothing that doesn't show" or "Some do it naturally" (presumably an acidhead by nature) to which the answer is "Happy to be that way." The song could pass simply as social satire, of not knowing what implications are carried even by the language you make fun of for its imprecisions. The point, and it's one that I'll come back to, is that the argot of LSD isn't much different from the banalities of question and answer between a "beautiful" person and his bedazzled interviewer. The punning genius of Lennon is evident here perhaps more effectively than in his two books, *In My Own Write* and *A Spaniard in the Works,* with their affinities to Edward Lear as well as to the Joyce of *Finnegans Wake.*

The Beatles won't be stuck even within their most intricate contrivances, however, and they escape often by reminding us and themselves that they are singers and not pushers, performers and not propagandists. The moment occurs in "Baby You're a Rich Man," as it does in other songs, near the end, in the question "Now that you've found another key/What are you going to play?" Necessarily the question refers us to their music while at the same time alluding to the promised results of drugs—a new "key" to personality, to a role as well as to the notes that one might "play." Similar uses of words that can allude both to the subject of the moment and to their constant subject, musical creation, occur in "All You Need Is Love" ("Nothing you can sing that can't be sung"), with implications we'll get to in a moment, and in the second song on the Sgt. Pepper album, "A Little Help From My Friends." Sung by Ringo the "help" refers most simply to affection when there is no one around to love and it also means pot supplied by a friend. However, at the beginning of the song it explicitly means the assistance the others will give Ringo with his singing, while the phrases "out of tune" and "out of key" suggest, in the broadest sense, that the number, like the whole occasion, is in the mode not of the Beatles but of Sgt. Pepper's Lonely Hearts Club Band: "What would you think if I sang out of tune,/Would you stand up and walk out on me./Lend me your ears and I'll sing you a song,/And I'll try not to sing out of key./Oh, I get by with a little help from my friends,/Mmmm, I get high with a little help from my friends,/Mmmm, going to try with a little help from my friends, . . ."

One of the Beatles' most appealing qualities is their tendency more to self-parody than to parody of others. The two are of course very close for performers who empathize with all the characters in their songs and whose most conspicuous moments of self-parody occur when they're emulating someone whose style they'd like to master. At such moments their boyishness really does shine forth as a musical virtue: giving themselves almost wholly to an imitation of some performer they admire, their necessary exaggeration of his style makes fun of no one so much as themselves. It's a matter of trying on a style and then—as if embarrassed by their own riches, by a self-confident knowledge that no style, not even one of their own invention, is more than a temporary exercise of strength—of laughing themselves out of imitation. Listen to the extravagant rendering on *Beatles '65* of Chuck Berry in "Rock and Roll Music" or their many early emulations of Presley, whose importance to their development is everywhere apparent, or the mimicry of Western music in "Act Naturally" on one of their very first albums, *Yesterday and Today,* or the McCartney imitation of Little Richard singing "Long Tall Sally" on the *Beatles Second Album.* It's all cowboys and Indians by people who have a lot of other games they want to play and who know very well where home is and when to go there. Parody and self-parody are frequent among the other groups in the form of persistent stylization, but its object is almost always some clichéd sentiment or situation. Parody from the Beatles tends usually, and increasingly, to be directed toward musical tradition and their own musical efforts. This is at least one reason why "All You Need Is Love," recorded on the reverse side of "Baby You're a Rich Man," is one of the most important they have ever done, an indication, along with the Sgt. Pepper album, of so sophisticated an awareness of their historical achievements in music as to make it seem unlikely that they can continue much longer without still further changes of direction even more radical than their decision not to perform henceforth for live audiences. "All You Need Is Love" is decisive evidence that when the Beatles think about anything they think musically and that musical thinking dictates their response to other things: to "love," in this instance, to drugs and social manners in "Baby You're a Rich Man Now" and throughout the Sgt. Pepper album.

I doubt that any of these subjects would in itself prove a sufficient sustenance for their musical invention until first called forth and then kindled by some musical idea. At this point in their career it is impossible, given their and George Martin's musical knowledge and sophistication, that the title "All You Need Is Love" should mean what it would mean coming from any other group, namely hippie or flower love. Expectations of complications are satisfied from the outset: the repetition, three times and in a languorous tone, of the phrase "love, love, love" might remind us of the song of the aging Chaplin in *Limelight,* a song in which he keeps repeating the word throughout with a pitiable and insistent rapidity. Musical subterfuge of lyric simplicity occurs again when the title line, "all you need is love," picks up a musical trailer out of the thirties ballroom. The historical frequency of the "need" for love is thus proposed by the music, and it is as if this proposition emboldens the lyrics: "Nothing you can do that can't be done," "nothing you can sing that can't be sung," "nothing you can know that can't be known," "nothing you can see that can't be shown—it's easy"—this is a sample of equally ambiguous assertions that constitute the verbal substance of the song, even while the word "love" is being stretched out in choral background. And like the ambiguous language of "Baby You're a Rich Man," the phrasing here sounds comfortably familiar—if you had love you could do anything. Except that isn't really what the lyrics imply. Rather, the suggestion is that doing, singing, knowing, seeing have in some sense already been done or at least that we needn't be in any particular sweat about them; they're accepted as already within the accustomed range of human possibility. What has not been demonstrated to anyone's satisfaction, what hasn't been tried, is "love." "Love" remains the great unfulfilled need, and the historical evidence for this is in endless musical compositions about it. Far from suggesting that "love" will solve everything, which would be the hippie reading of "all you need is love," the song allows most things to be solved without it. Such a nice bit of discrimination issues from the music and thence into the lyrics. Interestingly enough, the lyrics were meant to be simple in deference to the largely non-English-speaking audience for whom the song was especially written and performed on the BBC worldwide TV production of "Our World." "Normally," the Beatles' song publisher Richard James later observed, "the Beatles like to write sophisticated material, but they were glad to have the opportunity to write something with a very basic appeal." But so was Shakespeare at the Globe, and we know how unsophisticated *he* could be. The simplicity is entirely in the initial repetitions of title line and the word "love," a verbal simplicity first modified by the music and then turned into complications that have escaped even most English-speaking listeners.

Lennon and McCartney's recognition through music that the "need" for love is historical and recurrent is communicated to the listener by instrumental and vocal allusions to earlier material. The historical allusiveness is at the outset smart-alecky—the song opens with the French National Anthem—passes through the Chaplin echo, if that's what it is, to various echoes of the blues, and boogie-woogie, all of them in the mere shadings of background, until at the end the song itself seems to be swept up and dispersed within the musical history of which it is a part and of the electronics by which that history has been made available. The process begins by a recurrence of the "love, love, love" phrase, here repeated and doubled as on a stalled record. It then proceeds into a medley of sounds, fractured, mingled musical phrases drifting into a blur which my friend Paul Bertram pointed out to me is like the sounds of a radio at night fading and drifting among the signals of different stations. We can make out fragments of old love songs condemned to wander through the airways for all time: "Green Sleeves," a burst of trumpet sound I can't identify, a hit of the thirties called "In the Mood," a ghostly "love you, yeah, yeah, yeah" of "She Loves You" from the *Beatles Second Album* of 1964 and, in the context of "All You Need Is Love," a pathetic "all together now . . . everybody!" of the old community sing. Far from being in any way satiric, the song gathers into itself the musical expression of the "need" for love as it has accumulated through decades of popular music.

This historical feeling for music, including their own musical creations, explains, I think, the Beatles' fascination with the invented aspects of everything around them, the participatory tenderness and joy with which they respond to styles and artifact, the maturity with which they have come to see the coloring of the human and social landscape of contemporary England. It's as if they naturally see the world in the form of *son et lumière:* as they say in a beautiful neighborhood song about Liverpool, "Penny Lane is in my ears and in my eyes." Not everyone their age is capable of seeing the odd wonder of a meter maid—after all, a meter maid's a meter maid; fewer still would be moved to a song of praise like "Lovely Rita" ("When it gets dark I tow your heart away"); and only a Beatle could be expected, when seeing her with a bag across her shoulder, to have the historically enlivened vision that "made her look a little like a military man." Now of course English boys out of Liverpool can be expected, it says here, to be more intimate than American boys from San Francisco with the residual social and cultural evidences from World War II and even from the First World War. In response to these and other traces of the past, however, the Beatles display an absolutely unique kind of involvement. It isn't simply that they have an instinctive nostalgia for period styles, as in "She's Leaving Home" or "When I'm Sixty-four," or that they absorb the past through the media of the popular arts, through music, cinema, theatrical conventions, bands like Sgt. Pepper's or music-hall performers. Everyone to some extent apprehends the world in the shapes given it by the popular arts and its media; we all see even the things that are new to us through that gridiron of style that Harold Rosenberg imagines as a debilitating shield in front of the British Redcoats even as they first entered the American terrain. No, the Beatles have the distinction in their work both of *knowing* that this is how they see and feel things and of enjoying the knowledge. It could be said that they know what Beckett and Borges know but without any loss of simple enthusiasm or innocent expectation, and without any patronization of those who do not know. In the loving phrases of "Penny Lane," "A pretty nurse is selling poppies from a tray/ And tho' she feels as if she's in a play,/She is anyway."

It isn't surprising that drugs have become important to their music, that they are leading an effort in England for the legalization of marijuana, partly as a result of the conviction and sentencing on drug charges of two of the Rolling Stones, and that in response to questions, Lennon, McCartney and Harrison have let it be known that they've taken LSD. At least four of the songs on the Sgt. Pepper album are concerned with taking a "trip" or "turning on": "A Little Help from My Friends," "Lucy in the Sky with Diamonds," "Fixing a Hole," and "A Day in the Life," with a good chance of a fifth in "Getting Better." Throughout the album, the consciousness of the *dramatis personae* in the songs is directed more or less by inventions of media or of the popular arts, and drugs are proposed as one kind of personal escape into the freedom of some further invention all on one's own. Inventing the world out of the mind with drugs is more physically risky than doing it by writing songs, films or wearing costumes, but danger isn't what the songs offer for consideration, and it's in any case up to the Beatles alone to decide what they want for their minds and bodies. Instead, the songs propose, quite delightfully and reasonably, that the vision of the world on a "trip" or under the influence of a drug isn't necessarily wilder than a vision of the world through which we travel under the influence of the arts or the news media. Thus, the third song on the album, "Lucy in the Sky with Diamonds," proposes that the listener can "picture" a "trip" scene without taking such a "trip" himself. Here, as in "Baby You're a Rich Man," the experience of a "trip" is wittily superimposed on the experience of ordinary travel: "Picture yourself on a train in a station,/With plasticine porters with looking glass ties,/Suddenly someone is there on the turnstile,/The girl with kaleidoscope eyes." Of course the images could come as easily from Edward Lear as from the experience of drugs, and Lennon has claimed that the title of the song is not an anagram for LSD but was taken from a drawing his son did at school. Lennon, the author of two books of Joycean punning, knows to the point of hilarity that one meaning denies the presence of another, which it has hidden inside, only to all strangers and the police. Still his reticence is obviously a form of the truth. The Beatles won't be reduced to drugs when they mean, intend and enact so much more. "Acid," Harrison told the Los Angeles *Free Press* in August, "is not the answer, definitely not the answer. It's enabled people to see a little bit more, but when you really get hip, you don't need it." Later, to Hunter Davies of the London *Sunday Times*, McCartney announced that they'd given up drugs. "It was an experience we went through and now it's over we don't need it any more. We think we're finding other ways of getting there." In this effort they're apparently being helped by Maharishi Mahesh Yogi, the Indian founder of the International Meditation Society, though even on the way to their initiation in Bangor, North Wales, Lennon wondered if the experience wasn't simply going to be another version of what they already knew: "You know, like some are EMI and some Decca, but it's really still records."

The notion that we "picture" ourselves much of the time anyway without even willing it, that we see ourselves and the world in exotic images usually invented by someone else, is suggested throughout the Sgt. Pepper album, even on the cover, with its clustered photographs of world-shaping "stars" of all kinds. In "A Day in the Life," the last song and a work of great power and historical grasp, the hapless man whose

role is sung by McCartney wants to "turn on" himself and his lover—
maybe us too—as a relief from the multiple controls exerted over life
and the imagination by various and competing media. The sad little "oh
boy" interjected by McCartney's sweet, vulnerable voice into orchestral
movements of intimidating, sometimes portentous momentum, expresses
wonderfully how the victim is further confounded by the fact that these
controls often impose themselves under the guise of entertainment:

> *I read the news today oh boy*
> *About a lucky man who made the grade*
> *And though the news was rather sad*
> *Well I just had to laugh*
> *I saw the photograph.*
> *He blew his mind out in a car*
> *He didn't notice that the lights had changed*
> *A crowd of people stood and stared*
> *They'd seen his face before*
> *Nobody was really sure*
> *If he was from the House of Lords.*
> *I saw a film today oh boy*
> *The English Army had just won the war*
> *A crowd of people turned away*
> *But I just had to look*
> *Having read the book.*
> *I'd love to turn you on. . . .*

The news in the paper is "rather sad" but the photograph is funny, so
how does one respond to the suicide; suicide is a violent repudiation of
the self but it mightn't have happened if the man had followed the orders of the traffic lights; the victim isn't so much a man anyway as a
face people have seen someplace in the news, in photographs or possibly even on film; and while a film of the English army winning the
war is too dated for most people to look at, and maybe they don't believe
in victory anyway, the man in the song has to look at it (oh boy—a film)
because he has read a book about it and therefore it does have some
reality for him. "Turning on" is at least a way of escaping submission
to the media designed to turn on the mind from the outside—quite
appropriately the song was banned on the BBC—and loving to turn
"you" on, either a lover or you, the listener, is an effort to escape the
horror of loneliness projected by the final images of the song:

> *I read the news today oh boy*
> *Four thousand holes in Blackburn*
> *Lancashire*

And though the holes were rather small
They had to count them all
Now they know how many holes it takes
To fill the Albert Hall.
I'd love to turn you on.

The audience in Albert Hall—the same as the "lovely audience" in the first song that the Beatles would like to "take home" with them?—are only so many holes: unfilled and therefore unfertile holes, of the earth and therefore holes of decomposition, gathered together but separate and therefore countable, utterly and inarticulately alone. Is this merely a bit of visionary ghoulishness, something seen on a "trip"? No, good citizens can find it, like everything else in the song, in the daily news— of how Scotland Yard searched for buried bodies on a moor by making holes in the earth with poles and then waiting for the stench of de- composing flesh.

Lennon and McCartney in their songs seem as vulnerable as the man in "A Day in the Life" to the sights and sounds by which different media shape and then reshape reality, but their response isn't in any way as intimidated, and "turning on" isn't their only recourse. They can also tune in and play the game, sometimes to show, as in "A Day in the Life," how one shaped view of reality can be mocked out of exist- ence by crossing it with another. They mix their media the way they mix musical sounds or cross lyrics of one tone with music of quite an- other—with a vengeance. It's unwise ever to assume that they're doing only one thing or expressing themselves in only one style. "She's Leav- ing Home" does have a persistent cello background to evoke genteel melodrama of an earlier decade, and "When I'm Sixty-four" is inten- tionally clichéd throughout both in its ragtime rhythm and in its lyrics. The result is a satiric heightening of the love-nest sentimentality of old popular songs in the mode of "He'll build a little home/Just meant for two/From which I'll never roam/Who would, would you?" The home in "When I'm Sixty-four" is slightly larger to accommodate children, but that's the only important difference: "Every summer we can rent a cottage/In the Isle of Wight, if it's not too dear/We shall scrimp and save/Grandchildren on your knee/Vera Chuck & Dave." But the Beatles aren't satisfied merely with having written a brilliant spoof, with scor- ing, on their own authority, off death-dealing clichés. Instead, they quite suddenly at the end transform one cliché (of sentimental domesticity) into another (of a lonely-hearts newspaper advertisement) thereby proposing a vulgar contemporary medium suitable to the cheap and public sentiments that once passed for nice, private and decent: "Send me a postcard, drop me a line,/Stating point of view/Indicate precisely what you mean to say/Yours sincerely, wasting away/Give me your answer, fill in a form/Mine for evermore/Will you still need me, will you still feed me/When I'm sixty-four."

The Sgt. Pepper album and the singles released here just before and after it—"Penny Lane," "Strawberry Fields Forever," "All You Need is Love" and "Baby You're a Rich Man"—constitute the Beatles' most audacious musical effort so far, works of such achieved ambitiousness as to give an entirely new retrospective shape to their whole career. Nothing less is being claimed by these songs than that the Beatles now exist not merely as a phenomenon of entertainment but as a force of historical consequence. They have placed themselves within a musical, social and historical environment more monumental in its surroundings and more significantly populated than was the environment of any of their early songs. Listening to the Sgt. Pepper album one thinks not simply of the history of popular music but of the history of this century. It doesn't matter that some of the songs were composed before it occurred to the Beatles to use the motif of Sgt. Pepper, with its historical overtones; the songs emanated from some inwardly felt coherence that awaited a merely explicit design, and they would ask to be heard together even without the design.

Under the aegis of an old-time concert given by the type of music-hall band with which Lennon's father, Alfred, claims to have been associated, the songs, directly or by chance images, offer something like a review of contemporary English life, saved from folksong generality by having each song resemble a dramatic monologue. The review begins with the Sgt. Pepper theme song, followed immediately by "A Little Help From My Friends": Ringo, helped by the other Beatles, will, as I've already mentioned, try not to sing out of "key," try, that is, to fit into a style still heard in England but very much out of date. Between this and the reprise of Sgt. Pepper, which would be the natural end of the album, are ten songs, and while some are period pieces, about hangovers from the past, as is the band itself, no effort is made at any sort of historical chronology. Their arrangement is apparently haphazard, suggesting how the hippie and the historically pretentious, the genteel and the mod, the impoverished and the exotic, the Indian influence and the influence of technology are inextricably entangled into what is England. As I probably shouldn't say again, the Beatles never for long wholly submerge themselves in any form or style, so that at the end of the Indian, meditative sonorities of "Within You, Without You" the burst of laughter can be taken to mean—look, we have come through, an assurance from the Beatles (if it is their laughter and not the response of technicians left in as an example of how "straights" might react) that they are still

Beatles, Liverpool boys still there on the far side of a demanding foreign experience. This characteristic release of themselves from history and back to their own proper time and place occurs with respect to the design of the whole album in a most poignant way. Right after the reprise of the Sgt. Pepper song, with no interval and picking up the beat of the Sgt. Pepper theme, an "extra" song, perhaps the most brilliant ever written by Lennon and McCartney, breaks out of the theatrical frame and enters "a day in the life," into the way we live now. It projects a degree of loneliness not to be managed within the conventions of Sgt. Pepper's Lonely Hearts Club Band. Released from the controls of Sgt. Pepper, the song exposes the horrors of more contemporary and less benign controls, and it is from these that the song proposes the necessity of still further release. It does so in musical sounds meant to convey a "trip" out, sounds of ascending-airplane velocity and crescendo that occur right after the first "I'd love to turn you on," at midpoint in the song, and after the final, plaintive repetition of the line at the end, when the airplane sounds give way to a sustained orchestral chord that drifts softly and slowly toward infinity and silence. It is, as I've suggested, a song of wasteland, and the concluding "I'd love to turn you on" has as much propriety to the fragmented life that precedes it in the song and in the whole work as does the "Shantih, Shantih, Shantih" to the fragments of Eliot's poem. Eliot can be remembered here for still other reasons: not only because he pays conspicuous respect to the music hall but because his poems, like the Beatles' songs, work for a kaleidoscopic effect, for fragmented patterns of sound that can bring historic masses into juxtaposition only to let them be fractured by other emerging and equally evocative fragments.

Eliot is not among the sixty-two faces and figures, all unnamed and in some cases probably quite obscure, gathered round the Beatles on the cover, a pictorial extension of the collage effect which is so significant to the music. In making the selection, the Beatles were understandably drawn to figures who promote the idea of other possible worlds or who offer literary and cinematic trips to exotic places: Poe, Oscar Wilde, H. G. Wells, along with Marx, Jung, Lawrence of Arabia and Johnny Weissmuller. They are also partial to the kind of theatrical person whose full being is the theatrical self, like W. C. Fields, Tom Mix, Brando and Mae West, who has delightfully adapted such Beatle songs as "Day Tripper" to her own style. Above all, the cover is a celebration of the Beatles themselves who can now be placed (and Bob Dylan, too) within a group who have, aside from everything else, infused the imagination of the living with the possibilities of other ways of living, of extraordinary existences, of something beyond "a day in the life." So it is indeed like a funeral for the Beatles, except that they'd be no more "dead" than anyone else in attendance. There they are in the center, mustachioed and in the brassed and tasseled silk of the old-time bands, and, with brilliant, quite funny implications, they are also represented in the collage as wax figures by Madame Tussaud, clothed in business suits. Live Beatles in costumes from the past and effigies of the Beatles in the garb of the present, with the name of the Beatles in flowers planted before the whole group—this bit of slyness is a piece with not sorting out past and present and promised future in the order of the songs, or the mixed allusiveness to period styles, including earlier Beatles' styles or the mixing and confounding of media in songs like "When I'm Sixty-four" or "A Day in the Life." The cover suggests that the Beatles to some extent live the past in the present, live in the shadows of their own as well as of other people's past accomplishments, and that among the imaginative creations that fascinate them most, the figures closest at hand on the cover, are their own past selves. "And the time will come," it is promised in one of their songs, "when you will see we're all one, and life flows on within you and without you." As an apprehension of artistic, and perhaps of any other kind of placement within living endeavor, this idea is allowable only to the very great.

Idolized by more young girls than Jesus himself, honored by the Queen, and financially successful beyond the wildest hopes of any other rock group, the Beatles found themselves superficially fulfilled in their early twenties. But success bought time and, with it, contemplation; soon each Beatle had developed his own area of interest. George Harrison, the charmingly sinister lead guitarist, learned to play the sitar and studied Oriental philosophy. Paul McCartney, the cherub-faced songwriter, similarly went beyond material preoccupations to deal with the world of the soul. Their example has undoubtedly encouraged the present interest in the East, and their interviews not surprisingly concentrate on their philosophical interests.

The Buzz of All Buzzes:

George Harrison Interviewed

GEORGE HARRISON: If you could just say a word and it would tell people something straight to the point, then, you take all the words that are going to say everything, and you'd get it in about two lines. Just use those. Just keep saying those words.

MILES: * Like the "Hari Krishna" chants, except there the meaning of the words gradually fades away anyway.

G.H. That's right. They got hung up on the meaning of the word rather than the sound of the word. "In the beginning was the word" and that's the thing about Krishna, saying Krishna, Krishna, Krishna, Krishna, so it's not the word that you're saying, it's the sound: Krishna Krishna Krishna Krishna Krishna Krishna, Krishna and it's just sounds and it's great. Sounds are vibrations and the more you can put into that vibration, the more you can get out, action and reaction, that's the thing to tell people. You see it's all very obvious, the whole thing of life and all the answers to everything are in one divine law, Karma action and reaction. It's obvious: everybody knows that if they're happy then usually the people around them are happy, or that people around them happy

* Miles is a well-known British underground journalist and London reporter for *The East Village Other.*

International Times, May, 1967

make them a little happier; that's a proved thing, like "I give to you and you give to me"; they all know that but they haven't thought about it to the point of every action that they do. That's what it is with every action that you do, there's a reaction to it, and if you want a good reaction then you do a good action, and if you want a bad one, then you punch somebody. But that's where it is at. Just that one thing. That's why there is the whole scene of heaven and hell; heaven and hell is right now, right at this moment. You make it heaven or you make it hell by your actions . . . it's just obvious, isn't it?

M: People don't realize all of the possibilities, they don't realize how much they are in charge of the reality of their situation.

G.H.: Well that's because of ignorance; everybody is great really and has got to be great because they're going to be here until they get straight and that's it. . . . Everybody would like to be good, that's the silly thing, everybody always likes it when they're having a nice time or when they're happy or when it's sunny, they all dig it; but then they go and forget about it, they never really try to make it nice. They think that it just comes along and it's nice if you're lucky, or if you're un- lucky it's bad for you.

M: People act unconsciously at this level, they don't realize that they are purposely going out to stop things from getting any better.

G.H.: They're all ignorant, they fear new things, they fear knowledge somehow, I don't know why. Everything that I ever learned was always so good. I never thought so at the time, it was just that little bit more in your mind an expansion of consciousness or awareness. Even those of us who are very very aware are still so unaware. Everything's relative so that, the more you know, the more you know you don't know any- thing. . . .

Christ was the one washing the leper's feet so he was very, very hum- ble, but it's not the way they're putting it down now. They feel as though God is *that* up there and they are *that* down there and they don't realize that they *are* God and that Christ was exactly the same as us but he realizes that he was God. That's all it is, we're God too but we don't realize it. . . .

I'm a person who's trying to live within divine law, to the best, and it's very hard because it's self-discipline, because the more you realize, the more you've got to get yourself straight, so it's hard, you know. I'm trying and there are a lot of people who are trying, even people who are not conscious that they are doing it, but they are really . . . doing things for the good, or just to be happy or whatever. But then there's those other people, but you've got to have them to have this. . . . I'm not a part of anything in particular, because it's not really 1967 and it's not half-past eight, that's still what people have said it is. So it's just a little bit of time out of the cycle. There's this Indian fellow who worked out a cycle like the idea of stone-age, bronze-age, only he did it on an Indian one. The cycle goes from nothing until now and 20th century and then on and right round the cycle until the people are really grooving and then it just sinks back into ignorance until it gets back into the beginning again. So the 20th century is a fraction of that cycle, and how many of those cycles has it done yet? It's done as many as you think and all these times it's been through exactly the same things, and it'll be this again. Only be a few million million years and it'll be exactly the same thing going on, only with other people doing it. . . . I am part of the cycle, rebirth death, rebirth death, rebirth death. Some of the readers will know exactly what I mean, the ones who believe in reincarnation. It's pointless me trying to explain things like rebirth and death because I've just accepted that, you know, I can leave that.

M: The final death comes when the energy of consciousness reaches a point of complete unity with the universal energy flow and then ZAP, no more rebirth.

G.H.: But that's in that book [*Autobiography of a Yogi*]. That is the final release of that bit of you that is God so that it can merge into everything else. It's a far-out book, it's a gas. Through Yoga, anybody can attain; it's a God realization; you just practice Yoga and if you really mean it then you'll do it. You'll do it to a degree . . . there's Yogis that have done it to such a degree that they're God, they're like Christ and they can walk on the water and materialize bodies and they can do all those tricks. But that's not the point; the point is that we can do that and we've all *got* to do that and we'll keep on being reborn because for the law of action and reaction: "Whatsoever a man soweth, that shall he also reap"; you reap when you come back in your next birth, what you've sown in your previous incarnation. That's why I'm me and you're you and he's him and we are all whoever we are. From when I was born where I am now, all I did was to be *me* to get *this;* whatever you've done, you get it back, so you can either go on, or you can blow it.

The Buzz of All Buzzes

M: Are you concerned with communication?

G.H.: Oh, yes, of course, we are all one, I mean communication, just the realization of human love reciprocated, it's such a gas, it's a good vibration which makes you feel good. These vibrations that you get through Yoga, cosmic chants and things like that, I mean it's such a buzz, it buzzes you out of everywhere. It's nothing to do with pills or anything like that. It's just in your own head, the realization, it's such a buzz, it buzzes you right into the astral plane.

Nobody can become a drug addict if they're hip. Because it's obvious that if you're hip then you've got to make it. The buzz of all buzzes which is the thing that is God—you've got to be straight to get it. I'm sorry to tell you (turning to microphone) . . . you can get it better or more if you're straight because you can only get it to a degree. You know even if you get it, you only get it however long your pill lasts. So the thing is, if you really want to get it permanently, you have got to do it, you know . . . be healthy, don't eat meat, keep away from those night clubs and MEDITATE. . . .

The clan. The Klu Klux Klan or whatever they are. Do you know, it's stupid, isn't it, they're only little fellows who just put on their outfit, it's like we could be them, you just get your outfit and you go out with your little banner shouting at somebody like that. There was all that thing about the "Klan are coming to get us" at a concert somewhere in the States—and there were about four or five of them walking up and down, shouting, "Don't go in there . . ." something about that Christ thing, and there was all the kids shouting at them and laughing at them and that and then the police came around and told them to move away. It wasn't like you imagine . . . people with all fiery crosses and coming to burn us. Oh yes that was silly.

M: Did you find it easy to communicate with people in India?

G.H.: With most of the people you just communicate you don't have to talk. There are such great musicians; it was so nice and it was really just so . . . straight. They have a whole thing of trying to be humble, you've got to be humble really to be yourself or to get a chance to be yourself. If you're not humble, your ego and your big cabbage head are getting in the way. There were these musicians who are all advanced students of Ravi's and he'd been giving them a lesson. We were there just to watch a bit, and he sat in the middle and sang and they all followed him and went through about two and a half hours . . . improvised the whole lot. He was singing—which was pretty far out. All these people playing knocked me out so much, it was so great yet they were so humble and saying "It's such a pleasure to meet you," which was horrible because I was trying to be humble there. I was there for that, not for anything to do with being a Beatle. Ravi Shankar is so brilliant and these fellows, as far as I was concerned, were very far out . . . with people you communicate, there is no bullshit, because they don't create it. It's not so much a game as Western thought because they're a bit more spiritually inclined and they just sort of feel . . .

M: Did you just realize this yourself?

G.H.: I felt the vibrations all the time from the people I was with. They've all got their problems but they're just happy and vibrate.

M: You didn't search out a Guru?

G.H.: Ravi's my musical Guru, but the whole musical thing was too much just to be able to appreciate it whether I play or not. I've never been knocked out with anything for so long. But then later I realized that there wasn't the real thing, that was still only a little stepping stone for me to see. Through the music you reach the spiritual but the music's very involved with the spiritual as we know from Hari Krishna we just heard. It's so attuned to the spiritual scene, it depends how spiritual the musician is. Ravi is fantastic. He just sits there with a bit of wire and just does all that and says all that, things that you know and can't say because there's no words and he can say it like that.

M: Why does it come across best in music?

G.H.: Because music is sound, vibrations, whereas paintings are vibrations of whatever you pick up. It's not actually an energy vibration you get from a groovy painting, but music and sound seem to travel along vibrations, you know the whole thing with mantras is to repeat and repeat those sounds . . . it's vibrations in everything like prayers and hymns. They don't know about this over here. Prayer is to vibrate, do the devotion, whatever it is, to whoever you believe in, Christ or Buddha or Krishna or any of them. You get the response depending on how much you need it. Those people become that because they give it out, they want so much, they get back so much, they give out so much, they get back so much, it snowballs until you're Christ. You know we're back to that again. I'm not really hip to too much of the Zen or the Buddhist point of view, but you see I don't have to because I just know that they're all the same, it's all the same, it's just which ever one you want to take and it happens that I'm taking the Hindu one. . . . Be straight with yourself just to maybe save a few more people from being stupid and being ignorant. That's what we're doing here now, talking, because we've got to save them, because they're all potentially divine.

M: Does that concern you much?

G.H.: I couldn't cut off from everyone, because I'm still leaning on them, so if I'm leaning on them then there's someone leaning on me, only very subtly. I'm part of a structure that's going on and rather than cop out now, just at the moment, because I'm not ready, I'll wait. Maybe later on I'll get into where it's peaceful. We're already getting going, so that we'll have somewhere nice to be, because that's what it is you know, everybody should just stay at home and meditate and they'd be so much happier. That'll all come for us, because we are going to make it. "You make and preserve the image of your choice." But still we've got to communicate. We've got to be doing things because we're part of it and because it's nice. You've got to have an outlet. It's like having a big intake in the front of your head and there's so much going on, and it's going through all this, and there's a little exhaust-pipe on the back, that goes POW and lets a bit out. The aim is to get as much going out the back as is coming in. You've got to do that because for everything you get in you've got to give something out. So the Beatles, and whatever our own personal interests are, what we're doing from day to day, then that's like our little exhaust, coming out the back.

M: Which seems to be getting bigger and bigger?

G.H.: Well it's got to be but it's great, just the realization of it all, everything feasible because it's all only a dream anyway and that gives you infinite scope. You just go on and on and on until you go right out there. The thing is we could go; there's times, I'm sure, where we hold back a lot with things like "Strawberry Fields." I know there's a lot of people who like that who probably wouldn't have liked us a year ago. And then there's a lot of people who didn't like it who did like us a year ago. It's all the same really. Just some people pretend it's not happening. But they know, they simply must know. Because we're all together on this thing, we're just part of it and we'd like to get as many people who want to be a part of it with us. And if we really freaked out . . .

M: Do you think you're bringing most of them along with you?

G.H.: Well, we're losing a lot but we're gaining a lot too, I think. I dunno. But what I think, whatever it is, it's good. When somebody does something which everybody really wants to do, then it makes everyone else try a bit harder and strive for something better, and it's good. If ever we've done something like that then everybody's been there. We're as much influenced by everybody else as they are by us, if they are. It's just all a part of the big thing. I give to you and you give to me and it goes like that into the music you know.

Guru and Disciples

G.H.: The Guru and Disciple relationship is where the person has a one hundred per cent belief in the Guru and that way you put your trust in the Guru, that he's going to get you out of this mess. If you are a Christian, then Christ is your Guru, and they're all disciples of Christ. If they are. So to put your full belief in your Guru, because it's for your own good, because you've decided that. . . . It's just having a lot of respect for the person and it's like that with music as well. . . . You should love your instrument and respect it. Whenever Ravi does a concert he'll put his special thing on, and get nice and clean and washed up and get his joss sticks going. He's very straight, he doesn't drink or smoke or anything like that and by his real devotion he's mastered the thing. By his own discipline. He's playing for eighteen hours a day for about fifteen years, that's why he's that good. I've got no illusions about being a sitar player, I mean it's nothing like that. I really see it in perspective because he's got about ten million students who are all so groovy playing the sitar and yet he's only got hope for one of them to really make it, so that's me out for a kickoff. But that's not the important thing you see. The thing is, that however little you learn of it, it's too much, it's too much. Indian music is brilliant and for me, anyway (this is only personal), it's got everything in it. I still like electronics and all sorts of music if it's good but Indian music is just . . . an untouchable you can't say what it is, because it just is.

. . . Your religion, or whatever you're doing, so if you're putting out something to make people happy and something that's a bit devotional. It's got to be. If you spend all your life in a studio; you can't last out if it's not. Stockhausen and all the others, they're just trying to take you a bit further out or in, further in, to yourself. The way out is in. It's since the newspapers started the drug craze. That's it, you see, isn't that a bizarre scene, I mean you're the only paper that can say this because you're the only honest paper, really, when you get down to it. What I mean is, that thing about the sales, that's all they're concerned with, how many . . . all this bullshit, on the front page how many papers we've sold today, and we're selling more than the *Daily Express*, hup yer. All their silly little games, all that crap. And another thing they're always saying, "The *Daily Mirror* carried thirteen thousand inches of advertising"—and fuck-all to read, just a lot of shit. Actually bragging about how, it's stupid isn't it, it's a newspaper, anyway, we forgive them, as always. But this is the great thing. When you've got yourself to a point where you've realized certain things about life and the world and everything like that, then you know that none of that can affect you at all because you know it's the same thing now with those newspaper people they were always writing all that, just making it up. The thing is we know what the scene is, and we know them, they're all those little fellows. They'd all really like to be happy and they try to be happy but they're in a nasty little organization and it's great really. The whole thing of hate, anybody who hates, I feel sorry for them you know, that they are in that position and the newspapers are like that. I feel we got away from the point, whatever it was. The point was, you can print your paper, you know that they can't touch you because you know more than them and it's obvious because they'd be the ones to puzzle about it. On our side of the fence there's no puzzling to it. We know what it is.

The police are people as well. All those nasty people aren't really nasty if they'd realize it. All those policemen can't be themselves and they've got to do that game and pretend to be a policeman and go all through that shit about what's in the book, they've got to make themselves into a little part of themselves which is a lie and an untruth. The moment they put a uniform on they're bullshitting themselves, just thinking that they're policemen, because they are not policemen. They think that they created a thing called policemen and so then they try and enforce their creation on others and say "Now we've made a thing and it's called The Police and we want you all to believe in it and it's all for your own good and if you don't look up to it you'll get your ass kicked and you'll go in the craphouse."

You just keep changing the subject onto what you think we should be talking about and I'll just talk it back out of it again onto this . . . to people who look at the scene negatively, then it is, and they stay in their drab world. We've got to get it back again, after the war, and get it back to how it should be—everybody's happy and smiling and leaping about and doing what they all know is there that they should be doing. There's something happening. If everybody could just get into it, great, they'd all smile and all dress up. Yes—that'd be good. "The world is a stage." Well he was right, because we're Beatles, and it's a little scene and we're playing and we're pretending to be Beatles, like Harold Wilson's pretending to be Prime Minister and you're pretending to be the Interview on *IT*. They're all playing. The Queen's the Queen. The idea that you wake up and it happens that you're Queen, it's amazing but you could all be Queens if you imagined it . . . they'll have a war quickly if it gets too good they'll just pick on the nearest person to save us from our doom. That's it, soon as you freak out and have a good time, it's dangerous, but they don't think of the danger of going into some other country in a tank with a machine gun and shooting someone. That's all legal and above board, but you can't freak out—that's stupid.

Everything Is Beautiful: An Interview with Paul McCartney

M: In the last few thousand years only the materialistic side of man has developed and built up.

P.M.: The drag about this is that everybody has realized there aren't such things as ghosts, there isn't such a thing as God, and there is no such thing as a soul, and when you die you die. Which is great, it's fine, it's a brave thought really. The only trouble is, that you don't have the bit that you did when you were a kid of innocently accepting things. For instance, if a film comes on that's superimposed and doesn't seem to mean anything, immediately it's weird or it's strange or it's a bit funny, to most people, and they tend to laugh at it. The immediate reaction would be a laugh. And that's wrong. That's the first mistake, and that's the big mistake that everyone makes, to immediately discount anything that they don't understand, they're not sure of, and to say, "Well, of course, we'll never know about that." There are all these fantastic theories people put forward about . . . "It doesn't matter anyway," and it does, it does matter, in fact that matters more than anything . . . that side of it. We've been in the lucky position of having our childhood ambitions fulfilled. We've got all the big house and big car and everything. So then, you stand on the plank, having reached the end of space, and you look across the wall and there's more space, and that's it. You get your car and house and your fame and your world-wide ego satisfaction, then you just look over the wall and there's a complete different scene there, that it really is and which is really the scene. And looking back, obviously you can still see everybody in the world trying to do what you've just done and that is what they believe life's about. And they're right, because that is what life's about for them. But I could tell a few people who are further down on the rung, trying to do exactly what I've just done, "That's completely the wrong way to do it, because you're not taking into account this scene on the other side of the wall. This is the bit you've also got to take into account. And then that bit will be easier, it'll all be easier then."

M: It's hard to take into account though, because to gain material things there is a well-established method, but how do you investigate the other scene?

P.M.: Well, did I tell you that George Martin was talking to us in the recording studio and he came down and said: "Somebody wants to see you, somebody wants to talk to you," and we said: "Who is it, then?" and he said: "Oh, it's some crank talking about peace." . . . and he was right, it was a crank talking about peace, because when you talk about peace, you are a crank, you're pigeonholed, you've associated yourself with Vietnam and sitting down in Trafalgar Square and everybody thinks they know what you are then, because they've seen these people in Trafalgar Square. And if you were to burn yourself they'd know why you'd burned yourself so it wouldn't matter.

The thing that's grown up out of this materialist scene that everyone's got into, is that for everything to exist on a material level you've got to be able to discount any things that happen which don't fit in with it. And they're all very neatly disposed of these days. It's great, it's really very neat, I mean the way for instance IT would just be immediately labeled as "just one of those papers, that's all." And pot is just that, pot is "just drugs" and LSD is "just drugs" and every form of drugs is "just the pit of iniquity, the black pit that terrible, decadent, disgusting people always fall into." There is no thought on anyone's part why anyone takes drugs. But there's thought on their part why they take a drink, why they need a drink. Though they're not maybe willing to admit that they take a drink to get drunk. Most people think, "Oh no, no, no, I don't drink to get drunk! No, No, No, I take a drink occasionally. I do take a drink at parties, but I must say I don't drink to get drunk!" There's something to get a bit drunk, it's all right. But nobody will ever admit that they're all standing there pissed because they wanted to get pissed which is the truth of it, it must be the truth. Otherwise they would stick to orangeade.

M: If you are able to see everything in its own terms, do you find that this has eliminated the Western concept of finding some things beautiful and others repulsive?

P.M.: No, you see the pity about operating like this is that my act is not adapted to it. All that I have learned and the way I talk and the way I act, doesn't really fit in. . . . There is still a lot of me which has learned a lot of wrong things, that has based a lot of things on fallacies. I can't just accept everything, I can't just suddenly say, "Right, everything is as I know it is, and I know I ought to accept it all." It's difficult when you've learned for twenty-two years of your life that it isn't like that at all and that everything is just the act and everything is beautiful or ugly, or you like it or you don't, things are backward or they're forward. And dogs are less intelligent than humans and suddenly you realize that with all of that is right, it's all wrong as well. Dogs aren't less intelligent . . . to dogs, and the ash tray's happy to be an ash tray. But of course we think it's just an ash tray and that kind of hang-up still occurs. I still keep thinking of people just like that as well. It's pretty difficult to see anything in them. It's still difficult to see the good in bad because I've been trained that bad is bad . . . there's no good in bad, and I know I'm wrong. And all this on a wider level.

M: How does this approach affect your dealings with people? I mean it's a very isolated position, very objective, existentialist. Does it make contact easier or . . . ?

P.M.: It can do. The trouble is at the moment that I haven't got it going yet. It's really a question of trying to put those things into practice because when I think something which says the kind of thing that I've learned in days gone by, it tends to still stick, obviously just because of sheer weight, twenty-two years as opposed to two, trying to learn it like this. I'm really at the beginning of this stage. So when people say: "I see all your ambitions as Beatles have been fulfilled, you've done just about everything, you've played in every country in the world, what does it feel like?" it feels exactly the same as it did when I was trying to get five quid for a guitar. It's a beginning again, there's no end. I know I'm going to need a new set of rules and the new set of rules have got to include the rule that there aren't any rules. So I mean . . . they're pretty difficult.

It can make it difficult because if you say a thing according to the new book of the prophet, they say things in reply according to the old testament, and you find yourself saying, "Well, yes, but I don't quite mean that. I know it sounds like that but is not. What I mean is working on a new assumption of everything being fluid," you find yourself getting into cock-ups with words. It's a big battle at the moment. Trying not to say too many words and if there's a pregnant pause in the conversation, not feeling that I've got to fill it. But let someone else, who fears the silence, fill it. I don't fear it anymore. Of course it will need a bit of training. But the good thing about it is that if you are prepared to accept that things aren't just broad and wide, they're infinitely broad and wide, then there's a great amount to be learned. And the changeover . . . it can be done. It just takes a bit of time, but it will be done, I think.

M: Are you trying to take anyone with you on it?

P.M.: Yes I'd like to. I'm trying to take people with me of course, I don't want to be shouting to people "Listen, listen, I've found it! Listen, this is where it's at!" and everyone going "Oh fuck off, you fucking crank," because I see the potentiality in them as well, not just in myself. I'm not just the great wizard who's going to sort it all out, I'm just one of them. And if I can see how I ought to have compassion then it would be nice if they were going to see that too. Rather than me just standing there getting slapped on the other cheek all the time. This is the gap in electronics. There are quite a few people that are prepared for the next sound, they are ready to be led to the next move. The next move seems to be things like electronics because it's a completely new field and there's a lot of good new sounds to be listened to in it, but if the music itself is just going to jump about five miles ahead, then everyone's going to be left standing with this gap of five miles that they've got to all cross before they can even see what scene these people are on . . . I can see that it is in a way a progression to accept random things as being planned. Random is planned, as well, but most people won't accept random things as being planned. Random is planned, as well, but most people won't accept that and they'd need a lead into it. You can't just say to somebody, "That machine plays random notes, but it's planned and I can control the amount of random in it." They'll say "What for? Why don't you write a nice tune, or why don't you just write some interesting sounds?" That's what I'd like to do. I'd like to look into that gap a bit.

M: Do people like Cage help you, just by their existence? Because they have done so much work with random sound, it enables you to be a bit more free without worrying too much about it.

P.M. These become the new idols. Like then it wasn't a question of listening to Elvis for him to become your idol, he was your idol. Elvis was the idol, there wasn't any question of ever having to seek him out. But the idols now, the people that I can appreciate now are all more hidden away in the little back corners, through performing for themselves. They seem to be but they're probably not, they've been pigeonholed into that because they're cranks talking about peace. But you've got to sort out these people, you've got to look much more, because Stockhausen isn't played on Radio London every day, so there's not much of a chance of him becoming an idol overnight.

M: Do you think that someone like Albert Ayler can help? His music reaches quite a lot of people.

P.M.: Yes, if you're talking about the communication thing, of helping in that kind of way, then it's all helping, but only in a small way at the moment, that is the trouble. I don't think it would be very easy to say to people: "Don't you think it's possible that the scene that someone like Albert Ayler or Stockhausen is getting into isn't necessarily a bad scene? It's not necessarily what you think it is, isn't necessarily weird. Why is it weird? It's weird because you don't know about it, because it's a bit strange to you. It's new. And gravity was very weird, gravity was very strange when he talked about it and microscopes, they're all strange until you know about them." The most important thing to say to people is, It isn't necessarily so, what you believe. You must see that whatever you believe in isn't necessarily the truth. No matter how truthful it gets, it's not necessarily ever the truth, because the fact that it could be right or wrong is also infinite, that's the point of it. The whole being fluid and changing all the time and evolving. For it to be as cut-and-dried as we've got it now, it's got to be cut-and-dried in an unreal way. It's a fantastically abstract way of living that people have got into without realizing it. None of it's real.

I was trying to think of the people that I meet in a day that aren't acting in some way. And of course I'm acting, all the time. But at least I'm making a serious effort not to act now, realizing that most of my acting is to no avail anyway. There's no point in anyone doing a Hollywood grin, because everyone knows it's a Hollywood grin. But everyone goes on in this fantastic surreal way, of accepting it as a genuine grin but knowing secretly that it isn't really. They take it and they do another grin back and they get on famously. They really get on well with each other doing these grins, and then one of them breaks a leg and the other one walks away and it falls apart a bit and something happens, and the one who's broken a leg wonders why the grin didn't work when he had a broken leg. And it all gets very strange and very very far out. But everyone thinks that's the normal thing, that that's life. Everyone's got these great surrealist expressions . . . "Oh well that's life," and "You can't have your cake and eat it," . . . "You can't burn your candle at both ends, you know." These great, very scientific truths like "You can't burn your candle at both ends," and who the fuck said that. [Laughter] All the time they're working . . . I say they, but I'm in with they, I too am working on false assumptions. . . .

M: It stems from people being afraid of each other . . . afraid to just open up the armor a little bit.

P.M.: I really wish that I could. At the back of my brain somewhere, there is something telling me now that . . . It tells me in a cliché too, it tells me that everything is beautiful and everything is great and fine and that instead of imposing things like, "Oh I don't like that television show" or "No I don't like the theater," "No, no, I don't like so and so," that I know really that it's all great, and that everything's great and that there's no bad ever, if I can think of it all as great. But this gets back to the other twenty-two years of me, it's only ever been in the last two years, at the most, that I've ever tried to think of anything as being beautiful, having realized that I could think of everything as being incredible, with a bit of effort, on my mind's part, on my part. So I'm only just starting to try and think of things like that, so it still is difficult, and it still is difficult to communicate with people. But the aim is to be able to, one day, sit there and not feel any of the hang-ups that people feel towards each other, not feel any of the hang-ups of say, food not being up to standard or anything. It would be too much of a hang-up to . . . fight this other twenty-two years and really try and kill it off in a year. To really try and sort it out in a year is too big a project. So at the moment I'm just trying to operate within the new frame of reference but not pushing it. Because to push it really would be to alienate myself completely from everything. It really would make me into a very sort of strange being, as far as other people were concerned.

M: You have a more difficult situation anyway being a Beatle, because people's responses to you are always conditioned quite a lot by this.

P.M.: Yes, sure, that's very difficult, but there is also the added advantage, of people being conditioned to listen to me in one kind of way. When you're listening to someone who's famous, you're prepared to listen. You're not going to shout them down quite as much. If I knew how to say this all in three words to get it over to everyone, I would be in a great position. At the moment it's not so good, because anyone I do talk to talks to me in a conditioned way, and I can break that down. That's not too hard to break down because it's pretty obvious anyway that it doesn't exist within me, it only exists for them. Having broken down that, it sometimes is easier to get through to people because they've got a vague respect for you, for what you've done in the one field. For instance in the money field, that happens to impress a lot of people, you know. Which is in fact the least impressive bit of it, but that's the bit that impresses most people and so you find that a lot of forty-year-old men who would have never listened to anything I had to say are now a bit more willing because they're trying to make the money like I've made. So they think, "Well Christ, he must have something to have made that."

By now, every television comic in search of a routine has satirized modern dancing, and most situation comedies have parodied the discotheque crowd. At its most opulent, with the "beautiful people" patronizing the scene, the ritual of dance becomes a desperate attempt to regain youth. But for those who understand the new ethic of total freedom of expression, dancing becomes elevated to the level of art. Although it is nothing if not impermanent, there are moments when the audience and the band fuse in a continuum of light, sound, and motion that seems far more agreeable than the stylized dancing of other eras.

To Dance

TOM ROBBINS

We, all of us, have a need to identify our bodily rhythms with those of the cosmos.

The wind in a forest of fir. The spilling of grain in the fields. The migration of bird and seed. The trek of atom and star.

That is why we dance.

Dance began as a co-ordination of motor impulses with universal energies which man only instinctively perceived. It developed into a playful Dionysian rite designed to help man get outside of himself, or rather, to get outside of the ego so that he might discover the self.

Dance is a fundamental human need. To deny that need is to become hostile, neurotic and menopausal. Everyone should dance every day. Dance at a discotheque. Dance in your living room. Dance in bed. Stick flowers in your typewriter and dance at the office. Dance at the supermarket with a smoking banana in your teeth. Dance in the streets. Dance in church. "Dance beneath a diamond sky with one hand waving free."

Shiva danced to release the countless souls of men from the snare of illusion. The Hopi danced in the desert and made rain. Muhammad Ali danced at the Houston induction center in his shorts and socks. To arrest

Helix, May 4, 1967

a human being for dancing is in itself an immoral act. A law which prohibits dancing is a crime against man and a sin against God.

Dance. Next time you are at a light show be especially sure to dance. So dance. Dance and if you should ever be arrested for dancing, dance in the paddy wagon. Dance in your jail cell and dance in court. Maybe the judge will dance with you.

The place of the dance is within the heart.
To dance is to love again.

All life is theater, the new sages claim, but the play's absurd. In that case, there's no reason to take life seriously, and the "script" of "Trip Without a Ticket" has amused the participants on several occasions, while totally infuriating the "straight" population of San Francisco. The burning of money in front of the New York Stock Exchange did not amuse the brokers of that city, and when it was discovered that one of the torchmen had been collecting welfare, the city terminated his income.

Trip Without a Ticket

Our authorized sanities are so many nembutals. "Normal" citizens with store-dummy smiles stand apart from each other like cotton-packed capsules in a bottle. Perpetual mental out-patients. Maddeningly sterile jobs for strait-jackets, love scrubbed into an insipid "functional personal relationship" and Art as a fantasy pacifier. Everyone is kept inside while the outside is shown through windows: advertising and manicured news. And we all know this. How many TV specials would it take to establish one Guatemalan revolution? How many weeks would an ad agency require to face-lift the image of the Viet Cong? Slowly, very slowly we are led nowhere. Consumer circuses are held in the ward daily. Critics are tolerated like exploding novelties. We will be told which burning Asians to take seriously. Slowly. Later.

But there is a real danger in suddenly waking a somnambulistic patient. And we all know this.

WHAT IF HE IS STARTLED RIGHT OUT THE WINDOW?

No one can control the single circuit-breaking moment that charges games with critical reality. If the glass is cut, if the cushioned distance of media is removed, the patients may never respond as normals again. They will become life-actors.

THEATER IS TERRITORY. A space for existing outside padded walls. Setting

Communication Company, Spring, 1967

down a stage declares a universal pardon for imagination. But what happens next must mean more than sanctuary or preserve. How would real wardens react to life-actors on liberated ground? How can the intrinsic freedom of theater illuminate walls and show the weak spots where a breakout could occur?

GUERILLA THEATER INTENDS TO BRING AUDIENCES TO LIBERATED TER-RITORY TO CREATE LIFE-ACTORS. It remains light and exploitative of forms for the same reasons that it intends to remain free. It seeks audiences that are created by issues. It creates a cast of freed beings. It will become an issue itself.

This is theater of an underground that wants out. Its aim is to liberate ground held by consumer wardens and establish territory without walls. Its plays are glass-cutters for empire windows.

The diggers are hip to property. *Everything is free, do your own thing. Human beings are the means of exchange.* Food, machines, clothing, materials, shelter and props are simply there. Stuff. A perfect dispenser would be an open automat on the street. *Locks are time-consuming.* Combinations are locks.

So a store of goods or clinic or restaurant that is free becomes *a social art form.* Ticketless theater. Out of money and control.

> "First you gotta pin down what's wrong with the
> West. Distrust of human nature, which means
> distrust of Nature. Distrust of wildness in oneself
> literally means distrust of Wilderness."
> —Gary Snyder

Diggers assume free stores to liberate human nature. First free the space, goods and services. *Let the theories of economics follow social facts.* Once a free store is assumed, human wanting and giving, needing and taking become wide open to improvisation.

A sign: IF SOMEONE ASKS TO SEE THE MANAGER TELL HIM HE'S THE MANAGER

Someone asked how much a book was. How much did he think it was worth? 75 cents. The money was taken and held out for anyone, "Eh, who wants 75 cents?" A girl who had just walked in came over and took it.

A basket labeled FREE MONEY.

No owner, no manager, no employees and no cash register. A salesman in a free store is a life-actor. Anyone who will assume an answer to a question or accept a problem as a turn-on.

QUESTION (whispered): Who pays the rent?
ANSWER (loudly): May I help you?

Who's ready for the implications of a free store? Welfare mothers pile bags full of clothes for a few days and come back to hang up dresses. Kids case the joint wondering how to boost.

Fire helmets, riding pants, shower curtains, surgical gowns and WW I Army boots are parts for costumes. Nightsticks, sample cases, water pipes, toy guns and weather balloons are taken for props. When materials are free, imagination becomes currency for spirit.

Where does the stuff come from? People, persons, beings. Isn't it obvious that objects are only transitory subjects of human value? An object released from one person's value may be destroyed, abandoned or made available to other people. The choice is anyone's.

The question of a free store is simply what would you have.

STREET EVENT: BIRTH OF HAIGHT—FUNERAL FOR MONEY NOW?

Pop Art mirrored the social skin, happenings X-rayed the bones. Street events are social acid heightening consciousness of what is real on the streets. To expand eyeball implications until the facts are established through action.

The Mexican Day of the Dead is celebrated in cemeteries. Yellow flowers are falling petal by petal on graves. In moonlight. Favorite songs of the deceased and everybody gets loaded. Children suck death's-head candy engraved with their names in icing.

A digger event. Flowers, mirrors, penny-whistles, girls in costumes of themselves, Hell's Angels, street people, Mime Troupe.

Angels ride up Haight with girls holding NOW signs. Flowers and penny-whistles passed out to everyone.

A chorus on both sides of the street chanting UHH!—AHH!—SHH BE COOL! Mirrors held up to reflect faces of passers-by.

Penny-whistle music, clapping, flowers thrown in the air. A bus-driver held up by the action gets out to dance a quick free minute. No more passers-by, everybody's together.

The burial procession. Three black-shrouded messengers holding staffs topped with reflective dollar signs. A runner swinging a red lantern. Four pallbearers wearing animal heads carry a black casket filled with blow-ups of silver dollars. A chorus singing *Get Out of My Life Why Don't You Babe* to Chopin's *Death March*. Members of the procession give out silver dollars and candles.

Now more reality. Someone jumps on a car with the news that two Angels were busted. Crowd, funeral cortege and friends of the Angels fill the street to march on Park Police Station. Cops confront 400 free beings: a growling poet with a lute, animal spirits in black, candle-lit girls singing *Silent Night*. A collection for bail fills an Angel's helmet. March back to Haight and street dancing.

Street events are rituals of release. Re-claiming of territory (sundown, traffic, public joy) through spirit. Possession. Public New-Sense.

Not street-theater, *the street is theater*. Parades, bank robberies, fires and sonic explosions focus street attention. A crowd is an audience for an event. Release of crowd spirit can accomplish social facts. Riots are a reaction to police theater. Thrown bottles and overturned cars are responses to a dull, heavy-fisted, mechanical and deathly show. People fill the street to express special public feelings and hold human communion. To ask "What's happening?" The alternative to death is a joyous funeral in company with the living.

WHO PAID FOR YOUR TRIP?

Industrialization was a battle with 19th-century ecology to win breakfast at the cost of smog and insanity. Wars against ecology are suicidal. *The*

U.S. standard of living is a bourgeois baby blanket for executives who scream in their sleep. No Pleistocene swamp could match the pestilential horror of modern urban sewage. No children of White Western Progress will escape the dues of peoples forced to haul their raw materials.

But the tools (that's all factories are) remain innocent and the ethics of greed aren't necessary. Computers render the principles of wage-labor obsolete by incorporating them. We are being freed from mechanistic consciousness. We could evaluate the factories, turn them over to androids, clean up our pollution. *North Americans could give up self-righteousness to expand their being.*

Our conflict is with job-wardens and consumer-keepers of a permissive looney-bin. *Property, credit, interest, insurance, installments, profit are stupid concepts. Millions of have-nots and drop-outs in the U.S. are living on an overflow of technologically produced fat. They aren't fighting ecology, they're responding to it.* Middle-class living rooms are funeral parlors and only undertakers will stay in them. Our fight is with those who would kill us through dumb work, insane wars, dull money morality.

GIVE UP JOBS SO COMPUTERS CAN DO THEM! Any important human occupation can be done free. Can it be given away?

Revolutions in Asia, Africa, South America are for humanistic industrialization. The technological resources of North America can be used throughout the world. Gratis. Not a patronizing gift, shared.

Our conflict begins with salaries and prices. The trip has been paid for at an incredible price in death, slavery, psychosis.

An event for the main business district of any U.S. city. Infiltrate the largest corporation office building with life-actors as nymphomaniacal secretaries, clumsy repairmen, berserk executives, sloppy security guards, clerks with animals in their clothes. Low key until the first coffee break and then pour it on. Secretaries unbutton their blouses and press shy clerks against the wall. Repairmen drop typewriters and knock over water-coolers. Executives charge into private offices claiming their seniority. Guards produce booze bottles and playfully jam elevator doors. Clerks pull out goldfish, rabbits, pigeons, cats on leashes, loose dogs. At noon 1000 freed beings singing and dancing appear outside to persuade employees to take off for the day. Banners roll down from office windows announcing liberation. Shills in business suits run out of the building, strip and dive in the fountain. Elevators are loaded with incense and a pie-fight breaks out in the cafeteria.

Theater is Fact/Action.

Give up jobs. Be with people. Defend against property.

THEATER IS FACT/ACTION

Weekly, it seems, some poor drudge of a drama critic asks why the theater seems so lifeless, so preoccupied with trivia. Concurrent Theater is one of several experimental forms intended by their creators to enlarge the scope of the theater by superimposing additional layers of reality—or fantasy. Although it is staggeringly vague, could it conceivably be the salvation of a declining theater?

Manifesto for a

Concurrent Theater

JAMES BROUGHTON

Theater as practiced for five centuries in the West is in its final death throes.

As an expressive medium in the present age it is quaint and irrelevant.

Its fixed perspective, emphasis on linear narrative logic, and artificial projection of voice and gesture are anachronistic in the world of film, TV, and multi-media participational events.

It is likely to become a costly museum of antiques like opera and the symphony orchestra.

Gertrude Stein gave up going to the theater because she got either way ahead of the play or way behind it.

The problem nowadays is how to get with it at all.

Following a single story line, logically worked out throughout a protracted evening, invites only ennui.

Life is no longer experienced by any of us as a single tale told by an idiot. Or a genius either.

The painful little individual misery does not illuminate our more inclusive world.

Our lives and those of everyone else on the globe now occur concurrently. This has been forced upon us by electronic media.

Berkeley Barb, October 27, 1967

Our tribal connections, our involvement in the whole world, our instantaneous information about the rise and fall of practically anybody (or everybody) require a new vision of reality.

We are all in the collective conscious and unconscious together, like some huge indecent Roman bath wired with speakers, screens and lights.

The theater of our times is no longer the playhouse; it is the entire world.

Expo 67, a Be-In, a State Fair, the funeral of President Kennedy, any large event or happening, political or religious rite, is far more involving than a clever psychodrama shouted at us in our fixed, uncomfortable and costly seats.

Multiple screens have entered film, TV has its many channels and crazy mosaic, radio and stereo are absorbed on double levels.

But the theater is trying to survive with only one channel.

Unless the theater recognizes that life is going on all at once and tries to capture a total environment, it will wind up on the bookshelves among the medieval manuscripts.

The only way that theater can remain a dynamic medium is for it to become the arena of paradoxes that is our actual life today.

Since we live on multiple levels, and perceive them simultaneously in all their compounded ambiguity, the theater of our time cannot be a meaningful force by continuing to put dreams into little boxes following one another single file.

Present day art thinks in multi-media, fusions and hybridizations, overlappings and interactions.

The child of the electronic world can keep track concurrently of several TV channels, records on the stereo, transistor programs, comic books, telephone conversations, and various personal activities.

Experts, like critics and professors, pride themselves on having developed a perception of only one thing at a time.

Concurrent Theater aims at a total experience, not at the serviceable illustration of a literary text.

Concurrent Theater attempts a form of communication programming:

an enlarged vision of the human dilemma, a more embracing involvement in the ecology of our lives.

Concurrent Theater can reveal the impotency and the idiocy of talk for telling us anything we really want to know.

Concurrent Theater can demolish the tyranny of the written script as the definitive basis for drama.

Concurrent Theater does not seek a more cultivated art form, since art is no longer separate from life.

It does seek a new means of grasping a more total picture of modern existence.

Concurrent Theater is a fugal form, a montage, a collage in time and space.

Thereby it seeks to bring the theater into some closer correlation to modern mental life.

Concurrent Theater is not a happening. It is not improvisational. It returns the desiccated literary drama to precise nourishing sources; back to J. S. Bach, to Barnum & Bailey, to the country fair, to *Finnegans Wake,* to the rites of Dionysus.

But it has nothing to do with tradition. It is free to use, instead, the inheritance of the whole of history.

All degrees of possibility and variation are open to it. The only limits are, as always, those of vision.

Ex-junkie of the century is one label pinned on William Bur-
roughs; his novels are, for the most part, highly influenced by
his drug experience. His prose is characterized by that dis-
connected sensibility which drugs often encourage in creative
people—enormous insights clash with unimaginable transitions,
profundity battles constantly against syntax.

Academy 23 is thus an antidrug testimony of the most im-
pressive order. Burroughs has indeed been there, he's seen all
there was to see, and it just wasn't enough. A word to the wise
should be sufficient, but it never has been, and there's every
assurance that even the newly enacted federal restrictions will
fail to curb drug ingestion. The underground press in general is
less sanguine about drugs than its image suggests; at least, it
has enough responsibility to seek out the testimony of ex-users,
leaving sensationalism to the mass circulation, "responsible"
journals.

Academy 23: A Deconditioning

WILLIAM BURROUGHS

The drug problem is camouflage like all problems wouldn't be there if things had been handled right in the beginning considering a model drug problem in the United States where the addict is a criminal by legal definition and the proliferation of state laws making it a felony illegally to sell possess or be addicted to opiates, marijuana, barbiturates, benzedrine, LSD, and new drugs are constantly added to the list. A continual outcry in the press creates interest and curiosity people wanting to try these drugs so more users more outcry more laws more young people in jail. Until even senators ask themselves plaintively "Do we really want to put a good percentage of our young people in jail?" "Is this our only answer to the narcotics problem?"

The American Narcotics Department says frankly yes the drug user is a criminal and should be treated as such jail best Rx for addicts expert says the laws must reflect society's disapproval of the addict possessing a reefer cigarette in the state of Texas you will see fifteen years of society's disapproval reflected from decent church going eyes.

The Village Voice, July 6, 1967

Any serious attempt to actually enforce this welter of state and federal laws would entail a computerized invasion of privacy a total police terror a police machine that would pull the entire population into its orbit of violators, police, custody, courts, defense, probation, and parole. Just tell the machine to enforce all laws by whatever means and the machine will sweep us to the disaster of a computerized police state.

You see how this drug virus spreads in America and from there to England? LSD means pounds to the sensational press and I may say in passing there is a type of writing that does cause people to commit crimes and that is writing done in the world press . . . boy in Arizona reads all about it maniac sex killer slays eight women in Chicago nurses' home . . . that boy got five women before the fuzz nailed him and told police he got the idea from reading about that maniac killer in Chicago and he wanted people to notice him wanted his picture in the papers. Dig into your morgues and see how many times the prisoner got the idea from reading about it in the papers. Why do not children attack the passerby with cutlasses or force Uncle Rab to walk the plank from his Ozark house boat? Because they know "Treasure Island" is make believe. But something in the papers that really happened "Jeez he had nerve that guy musta took nerve to walk in cool like that making sure each one was dead I got nerve too plenty of it . . ."

Now the press gives LSD the build-up it's new it's exciting anybody who is anybody in literature and the arts has logged a trip and jolly dull reading too the pop stars are using it it's dangerous it's glamorous it's the thing to do so all the young people hear about it and want to try it that's what youth wants is adventure remember the needle beer in Sid's speakeasy over on Olive Street drunk before you put the glass down well a few illegal beers in Sid's speak was an adventure for Eddie and Bill back in the 1920s only the cops didn't put us in jail just told us to go home those dear dead days now we have a drug problem after shoving a sugar cube in every open mouth the press is now screaming to stamp out this evil jumped from a six floor window hacked his mother-in-law to death more laws more criminals more young people in jail more pot dogs sniffing through flats and country houses nuzzling young people in coffee bars now we have a "drug problem" that is to say the problem of a number of drugs now in common use varying considerably in destructive action. Pep pills and all variation of the benzedrine formulae present no valid excuse for continued existence. After an overdose of these drugs the user undergoes excruciating depressions, when high "meth heads" may become compulsive talkers who stalk the streets in search of victims when experienced friends have bolted their doors. His mouth is dry his hair is mussed his eyes are wild he's gotta talk to somebody. The whole spectrum of benzedrine intoxication is deplorable. Since these drugs have slight medical indication that could not be covered by a safer stimulant like caffeine why not close the whole ugly scene once and for all by stopping the manufacture of benzedrine or any variation of the formula?

Cannabis is certainly the safest of the hallucinogenic drugs in common use large numbers of people in African and Near Eastern countries smoking it all their lives without apparent ill effects. As to its legalization in Western countries I do not have an opinion. If English doctors are empowered to prescribe heroin and cocaine it seems reasonable that they should also be empowered to prescribe cannabis.

The strong hallucinogenic drugs: LSD, mescaline, psylocybin, dim-N, bannisteria caapi do present more serious dangers than their evangelical partisans would care to admit. States of panic are not infrequent and death has resulted from a safe dose of LSD. Recollect when I was traveling in the Putumayo town of Macoa laid up there a week with fever stumbled on the story man down from Cali if my memory serves serious young student believed in telepathy read Lorca wanted to experience the "soul vine" bannisteria caapi the Indians thereabouts call it "yage" so the brujo brewed up his brujo dose he took himself man and boy forty years and passed it to the unfortunate traveler: one scream of hideous pain he rushed out into the jungle. They found him in a little clearing he was clearing with his convulsions. No charges were brought against the brujo city feller got what he asked for. This sugary evil old man lived on to poison me some years later. However, mindful of the fate of my predecessor, I had provided myself with six nembutal capsules and twenty codeine tablets a piece of foresight to which I may well owe my life. Even so I lay on the ground outside the brujo's hut for hours paralyzed in a hermetic vice of pain and fear. A high tolerance is acquired with use and the brujo's daily dose to get his power up could readily be lethal to a novice. Setting aside the factor of tolerance there is considerable variation in reaction to these drugs from one individual to another a safe dose for one tripper could be dangerous for another. The prolonged use of LSD may give rise in some cases to a crazed unwholesome benevolence the old tripster smiling into your face sees all your thoughts loving and accepting you inside out. Admittedly these drugs can be dangerous and they can give rise to deplorable states of mind. To bring the use of these drugs in perspective I would suggest that academies be established where young people will learn to get really high . . . high as the Zen master is high when his arrow hits a target in the dark . . . high as the Karate master is high when he smashes a brick with his fist . . . high . . . weightless . . . in space. This is the space age. Time to look beyond this run down radioactive cop rotten planet. Time to look beyond this animal body. Remember anything that can be done chemically can be done in other ways. You don't need drugs to get high but drugs do serve as a useful short cut at certain stages of the training. The students would receive a basic course of training in the non-chemical disciplines of Yoga, Karate, prolonged sense with-drawal, stroboscopic lights, the constant use of tape recorders to break down verbal association lines. Techniques now being used for control of thought could be used instead for liberation. With computerized tape recorders and sensitive throat microphones we could attain insight into the nature of human speech and turn the word into a useful tool instead of an instrument of control in hands of a misinformed and misinforming press. Verbal techniques are now being used to achieve more reliable computer processed techniques in the direction of opinion control and manipulation the "propaganda war" it's called. The CIA does not give away money for nothing. It gives away money for opinion control in certain directions. Opinion control is a technical operation extending over a period of years. First a population segment—segment "prepara-tion" is conditioned to react to words rather than word referents. Count Korzybski who formulated General Semantics used to begin a lecture by pointing to a chair and saying, "Whatever that is it is not a 'chair.'"

That is the object chair is not the verbal or written label "chair." He considered the confusion between label and object the "is of identity" he called it, to be a basic flaw in Western thought this flaw is cultivated by the practitioners of opinion control. You will notice in the subsidized periodicals a curious prose without image. If I say the word "chair" you see a chair. If I say "the concomitance of societal somnolence with the ambivalent smugness of unavowed totalitarianism" you see nothing. This is pure word conditioning the reader to react to word. "Prepara-tions" so conditioned will then react predictably to words. The condi-tioned preparation is quite impervious to facts.

The aim of academy training is precisely decontrol of opinion the student being conditioned to look at the facts before formulating any verbal patterns. The initial training in non-chemical methods of ex-panding awareness would last at least two years. During this period the student would be requested to refrain from all drugs including alcohol since bodily health is essential to minimize mental disturbance. After basic training the student would be prepared for drug trips to reach areas difficult to explore by other means in the present state of our knowledge. The program proposed is essentially a disintoxication from inner fear and inner control a liberation of thought and energy to prepare a new generation for the adventure of space. With such possibilities open to them I doubt if many young people would want the destructive drugs. Remember junk keeps you right here in junky flesh on this earth where Boot's is open all night. You can't make space in an aqualung of junk. The problem of those already addicted remains. Addicts need medical treatment not jail and not prayers. I have spoken frequently of the apo-morphine treatment as the quickest and most efficacious method of treating addicts. Variations and synthesis of the apo-morphine formula might well yield a miracle drug for disintoxication. The drug lomotil which greatly reduces the need for opiates but is not in itself addicting might prove useful. With experimentation a painless cure would certainly emerge. What makes a cure stick is when the cured addict finds something better to do and realizes he could not do it on junk. Academies of the type described would give young people something better to do incidentally reducing the drug problem to unimportance.

The falling-domino theory of the drug-abuse agents argues that heroin is the logical outgrowth of marijuana and LSD use, but those who have talked to users know that those trips are quite different. For most people, marijuana gives a boost to the life-force, whereas heroin is strictly for those who want out. As yet there has been no mass conversion to needles and their deadly side effects, though if the Mafia succeeds in gaining control of the marijuana market, articles like this may appear more frequently.

Metaman and the Mirror Minds

PAUL DORPAT

THIS WEEK YOU HAVE ALREADY HEARD A WHOLE LOT ABOUT
    HEROIN.
Do you remember hearing about it before? . . . .
MIRRORMIND?
You must remember, for you go on repeating yourself . . . .
your prejudices, your duplicity, your repetitious follies.

We have received a phone call from an upset mother
Demanding in a shaken yet sweetly struggling voice that something be
    done.
THE CHILD IS RUNNING AWAY!
The mother wants us to save her from separation . . . from herself
    alone.
The child is only fifteen and "very impressionable . . ."
They never talked with one another . . . .
                    THE CHILD IS RUNNING AWAY.

MOTHERS . . . LISTEN! We live in an ignorant and confused world
    and in an ignorant and confused city.
You simply must understand that.   You must relax in the chaos.
                    You must be contradicted.
                    You must understand you don't
                    understand.

Helix, October 10, 1967

115

THE CHILD WHO IS RUNNING AWAY IS RUNNING OUT OF AND
INTO THE MIDST OF CHAOS. BUT SUPPLE AND CURIOUS
HE WILL MORE EASILY NAVIGATE THE ECSTATIC AND GRO-
TESQUE FLOW OF OUR CORPORATE INSANITY.
(GOVERNORS BACK JOHNSON'S POLICY IN VIETNAM)
(PRINCESS ALEXANDER VISITS LYNDA-BIRD. WHICH ONE'S THE
PRINCESS?)
(THE 1968 BUICK IS BIGGER AND BETTER THAN EVER!)
(WE'D BETTER WIND THINGS UP OVER THERE OR THEY'LL
THINK WE'RE COWARDS.)
(AN IDLE MIND IS THE DEVIL'S WORKSHOP.)

it is you who are afraid of losing your way. it is you who should run away.
"PROTECT THE CHILDREN" means "MY GOD! MY GOD! PRO-
TECT ME."
You speak it in the mirror . . .
For a people that goes on repeating itself—
FETISHED GLASS FONDLERS—

you have a lot to say about *PROGRESS* . . . that is,
(THE BARS NOW STAY OPEN SATURDAY NIGHT UNTIL TWO.
. . . IT TOOK ½ century TO ACCOMPLISH THAT.)
You are the *FACE-SAVERS* . . . You supply all the media with infor-
mation of yourselves. You mistake the heaping up of faces for *PROG-
RESS* . . . You sent out press-releases about how you can be found
most anywhere . . . .
ALL THE NEWS IS OLD NEWS REPEATED . . . YOU WON'T BREAK
THE VERBOSITY OF HISTORY: ITS REDUNDANCY.
NOW THE CHILD WHO IS RUNNING AWAY WILL COME TO
THE DISTRICT. HE COMES OUT OF A SILENT HOME WHERE
THE PARENTS NEVER TALKED MUCH. HE MOVES IN A
WORLD OF IGNORANCE AND CONFUSION. IN THE DISTRICT
THE CHILD WILL BE SOLD SMACK . . . HEROIN. THIS WEEK
YOU HAVE ALREADY HEARD A WHOLE LOT ABOUT HEROIN.
DO YOU REMEMBER HEARING ABOUT IT BEFORE? MIRROR-
MIND? YOU MUST REMEMBER, FOR YOU GO ON REPEATING
YOURSELVES . . . YOUR PREJUDICES, YOUR DUPLICITY,
YOUR REPETITIOUS FOLLIES.

THERE ARE MANY KINDS OF DEATH . . . .
Like the HARD-HIGH . . . the trip you get from taking smack.
THAT KIND OF DEATH IS NOT TOO UNLIKE YOUR OWN. Do not

be surprised, then, if the child who is running away buys the smack, takes it and keeps on taking it.

It's a soft buzz like a dream that keeps on repeating itself.

Like being feathered in the ease of an infinite Cadillac.

Like being carried through a hall of mirrors.

The Cadillac is the expensive hearse that leads the softly smiling procession of faces on the unending journey to the interment.

YOU NEVER TALK WITH ONE ANOTHER.

YOUR CHILD HAS BEEN SLEEP-WALKING AT HOME.

Don't be surprised if he takes smack and "likes" it.

"BETCHA CAN'T EAT JUST ONE."

THERE ARE MANY KINDS OF DEATH ....

And yours is the most deadly, for you carnivorously insist on sicking death on your already eaten life.

PROGRESS: You have a mind-body perfectly and variously suited to do many things. But when you learned that that involved risks you forgot it.

For an *EROTIC SENSE OF REALITY* . . . for the risk of being *AWARE* . . . you substituted the risk of NOT MAKING $10,000 BY THE TIME YOU'RE THIRTY.

A POCKET FULL OF FACES . . . OR . . . RUN NEXT DOOR AND TRADE DOLLARS WITH YOUR NEIGHBOR.

THERE ARE MANY KINDS OF DEATH . . . (some of these are creative.) the ego needs to be slaughtered the wisdom of masochism the wisdom of blowing your mind the psychedelic tool the religious technology: the happy alchemist who will as a gift to you ruin your pretensions for the flowering of the kingdom of god that is within you. the deathliness of lsd and marijuana.

THERE ARE MANY KINDS OF DEATH ....

Like the "death of the 'hippy.'" Another of your PRESS-RELEASES. BUT ADMITTEDLY IT IS APPROPRIATE THAT YOU ANNOUNCE HIS DEATH, FOR IT WAS OUT OF YOUR NEED TO FIRST HALF-CONSCIOUSLY FABRICATE THE "HIPPY" AND THEN DISCOVER AND DEFINE HIM AND NOW DESTROY HIM. IT IS LIKE AN OLD RITUAL OF RAISING THE FATTED-CALF FOR VIOLENT SLAUGHTER.

And in the game of hide-and-seek you need your criminals

And in the game of one-up you need the Joneses

And in the game of scapegoating you need the Negro

With a need so great why do you wonder that the Negro is rebelling, that the Joneses are escalating, that the criminals are proliferating and that the "hippy" is killing himself?

KILLING HIMSELF (1)

He is leaving the streets and going off by himself . . . or in small numbers.

He asks to be left alone and forgotten.

He had something to say, but that message has been swallowed up by the media-men . . . the sensational mirrorminds.

He is not so likely to act up front except to throw soot or dollars to the wind.

Perhaps you will run into him unexpectedly in the suburbs or out on the farm.

He is going back to where most of his "kind" have been all along . . . underground . . . or above in disguise.

He'll be about the business of hourly revolution in his own head. BEFORE WHEN HE WAS TALKING WITH YOU HE WAS YOUR MAIN CHANCE TO ESCAPE THE HALL OF MIRRORS . . . HE WAS YOUR

metaman

WITH YOUR OWN *ORDINARY LANGUAGE* . . . WHEN HE SAID "LOVE" HE MEANT *LOVE*. WHEN HE SAID "FLOWERS" HE MEANT *FLOWERS*.

With only so much METAPHOR as was necessary to break the mirrored reproduction of MASKS the METAMAN'S metaphor—his odd language —was not any difficult or esoteric conceit. It was the living understanding of the vital potential that existed in your own language . . . in "LOVE," "FLOWERS," "FREEDOM" in *"THE KINGDOM OF GOD IS WITHIN YOU"*

KILLING HIMSELF (2)

or he is sitting in the streets, doing-up smack doing your death trip super. Even here he's much better at it than you.

III. The Nature of the Revolt

Wanting out is one thing, and finding a viable alternative to the present system is quite another. The middle class in America is large, almost all-embracing, and defectors are usually welcomed back to the fold. Indeed, the self-imposéd exile has been accepted in some areas to a degree that makes it seem transitional, just another stage in the process of growing up. Erik Erikson calls this a "psycho-social moratorium," and for those who drop out of familial and societal structures, Bohemianism may serve roughly the same function as college. There are, one would assume, some parents who worry when their child fails to have an "identity crisis" at age nineteen.

How can anyone permanently escape middle-class values? It sounds like a deceptively easy question, but as George Orwell learned before us, one does not shake off a culture simply by going down and out. Converts are not won by prospects of hunger, illness, and free love-*cum*-venereal disease; to win, a new system must prove itself both more stable and more exciting than the America one leaves behind. The economics of such a structure defy imagination, and those who attempt to construct new models for a new order have generally succeeded in multiplying confusion and frustration. "There must be some way out of here," as Bob Dylan says, but the self-acknowledged wise men of the underground have failed to find it. The prophet of a better society is much awaited, but he has yet to appear.

To assemble Ginsberg, Leary, Snyder, and Watts in one room is to convene a summit conference of hip, a colloquium of those who have somehow assumed leadership roles in the underground subculture. The participants share roughly the same visions of the American reality they have repudiated; they differ primarily in their answers to the philosophical and economic needs of those who follow them in withdrawing from society. Although the discussion exposes the poverty of available solutions for those who join a deviant subculture in America—Leary, for example, reveals himself virtually incapable of intelligible thinking even about the implementation of his own doctrine—it does tell us a great deal about the ways these people relate to one another. Even as self-congratulatory dropouts, they are somewhat isolated from Social Darwinism by virtue of their celebrity, but there is some compensation for their otherworldliness in their ability to accept differences. It is this love of diversity within the subculture as it struggles for life that is most seductive to those who seek the renewal of spiritual affinities, but it is the difficulty of surviving the hardships of the initial break with society that has, no doubt, persuaded more than one potential vagabond to stay at home.

Changes

ALLEN GINSBERG, TIMOTHY LEARY, GARY SNYDER, ALAN WATTS

ALAN WATTS: Look then, we're going to discuss where it's going . . . the whole problem of whether to drop out or take over.
TIMOTHY LEARY: Or anything in between?
WATTS: Or anything in between, sure.
LEARY: Cop out . . . drop in . . .
GARY SNYDER: I see it as the problem about whether or not to throw all your energies to the subculture or try to maintain some communication network within the main culture.
WATTS: Yes. All right. Now look . . . I would like to make a preliminary announcement so that it has a certain coherence.
  This is Alan Watts speaking, and I'm this evening, on my ferry boat,

San Francisco *Oracle*, February, 1967

the host to a fascinating party sponsored by the San Francisco *Oracle*, which is our new underground paper, far-outer than any far-out that has yet been seen. And we have here, members of the staff of the *Oracle*. We have Allen Ginsberg, poet and rabbinic saddhu. We have Timothy Leary, about whom nothing needs to be said. (laughs) And Gary Snyder, also poet, Zen monk, and old friend of many years.

ALLEN GINSBERG: This swami wants you to introduce him in Berkeley. He's going to have a Kirtan to sanctify the peace movement. So what I said is, he ought to invite Jerry Rubin and Mario Savio, and his cohorts. And he said: "Great, great, great!"

So I said, "Why don't you invite the Hell's Angels, too?" He said: "Great, great, great! When are we gonna get hold of them?"

So I think that's one next feature . . .

WATTS: You know, what is being said here, isn't it: To sanctify the peace movement is to take the violence out of it.

GINSBERG: Well, to point attention to its root nature, which is desire for peace, which is equivalent to the goals of all the wisdom schools and all the Saddhanas.

A Pacifist on the Rampage

WATTS: Yes, but it isn't so until sanctified. That is to say, I have found in practice that nothing is more violent than peace movements. You know, when you get a pacifist on the rampage, nobody can be more emotionally bound and intolerant and full of hatred.

And I think this is the thing that many of us understand in common, that we are trying to take moral violence out of all those efforts that are being made to bring human beings into a harmonious relationship.

GINSBERG: Now, how much of that did the peace movement people in Berkeley realize?

WATTS: I don't think they realize it at all. I think they're still working on the basis of moral violence, just as Gandhi was.

GINSBERG: Yeah . . . I went last night and turned on with Mario Savio. Two nights ago . . . after I finished and I was talking with him, and he doesn't turn on very much. . . . This was maybe about the third or fourth time.

He was describing his efforts in terms of the motive power for large mass movements. He felt one of the things that move large crowds was righteousness, moral outrage, and *anger* . . . righteous anger.

Menopausal Minds

LEARY: Well, let's stop right here. The implication of that statement is: we want a mass movement. Mass movements make no sense to me, and I want no part of mass movements. I think this is the error that the leftist activists are making. I see them as young men with menopausal minds.

They are repeating the same dreary quarrels and conflicts for power of the thirties and the forties, of the trade union movement, of Trotsky-ism and so forth. I think they should be sanctified, drop out, find their own center, turn on, and above all avoid mass movements, mass leader-ship, mass followers. I see that there is a great difference—I say com-pletely incompatible difference—between the leftist activist movement and the psychedelic religious movement.

In the first place, the psychedelic movement, I think, is much more numerous. But it doesn't express itself as noisily. I think there are dif-ferent goals. I think that the activists want power. They talk about student power. This shocks me, and alienates my spiritual sensitivities.

Of course, there is a great deal of difference in method. The psyche-delic movement, the spiritual seeker movement, or whatever you want to call it, expresses itself . . . as the Haight-Ashbury group had done . . . with flowers and chants and pictures and beads and acts of beauty and harmony . . . sweeping the streets. That sort of thing.

WATTS: And giving away free food.

LEARY: Yes . . . I think this point must be made straight away, but because we are both looked upon with disfavor by the Establishment, this tendency to group the two together . . . I think that such con-fusion can only lead to disillusion and hard feelings on someone's part. So, I'd like to lay this down as a premise right at the beginning.

GINSBERG: Well, of course, that's the same premise they lay down, that there is an irreconcilable split. Only, their stereotype of the psychedelic movement is that it's just sort of like the opposite . . . I think you're presenting a stereotype of them.

SNYDER: I think that you have to look at this historically, and there's no doubt that the historical roots of the revolutionary movements and the historical roots of this spiritual movement are identical. This is something that has been going on since the Neolithic as a strain in human history, and one which has been consistently, on one level or another, opposed to the collectivism of civilization toward the rigidities of the city states and city temples. Christian Utopianism is behind Marx-ism.

LEARY: They're outs and they want in.

Utopian Religious Drive

SNYDER: . . . but historically it arrives from a Utopian and essentially religious drive. The early revolutionary political movements in Europe have this Utopian strain in them.

Then Marxism finally becomes a separate, nonreligious movement, but only very late. That Utopian strain runs right through it all along. So that we do share this . . .

GINSBERG: What are the early Utopian texts? What are the early mystical Utopian political texts?

SNYDER: Political?

GINSBERG: Yeah. Are you running your mind back through Bakunin or something?

SNYDER: I'm running it back to earlier people. To Fourier, and stuff . . .

WATTS: Well, it goes back to the seventeenth century and the movements in Flemish and German mysticism, which started up the whole idea of democracy in England in the seventeenth century. You have the Anabaptists, the Levellers, the Brothers of the Free Spirit . . .

SNYDER: The Diggers!

Secular Mysticism

WATTS: The Diggers, and all those people, and then eventually the Quakers. This was the source. It was, in a way, a secularization of mysticism.

In other words, the mystical doctrine that all men are equal in the sight of God, for the simple reason that they *are God*. They're all God's incarnations.

When that doctrine is secularized, it becomes a parody . . . that all men are equally inferior. And therefore may be evil-treated by the bureaucrats and the police, with no manners.

The whole tendency of this equalization of man in the nineteenth century is a result, in a way, of the work of Freud. But the absolute recipe for writing a best-seller biography was to take some person who was renowned for his virtue and probity, and to show, after all, that everything was scurrilous and low down.

You see? This became the parody. Because the point that I was making—this may seem to be a little bit of a diversion but the actual point is this: Whenever the insights one derives from mystical vision become politically active, they always create their own opposite. They create a parody.

Wouldn't you agree with that, Tim? I mean, this is the point I think you're saying: that when we try to force a vision upon the world, and say that everybody ought to have this, and it's *good* for you, then a parody of it is set up. As it was historically when this vision was forced upon the West, that all men are equal in the sight of God and so on and so forth . . . it became bureaucratic democracy, which is that all people are equally inferior.

SNYDER: Well, my answer to what Tim was saying there is that, it seems to me at least, in left-wing politics there are certain elements, and there are always going to be certain people who are motivated by the same thing that I'm motivated by.

And I don't want to reject the history, or the sacrifices of the people in that movement . . . if they can be brought around to what I would consider a more profound vision of themselves and society. . . .

LEARY: I think we should get them to drop out, turn on, and tune in.

GINSBERG: Yeah, but they don't know what that means even.

LEARY: I know it. No politician, left or right, young or old, knows what we mean by that.

GINSBERG: Don't be so angry!

LEARY: I'm not angry . . .

GINSBERG: Yes, you are. Now, wait a minute. . . . Everybody in Berkeley, all week long, has been bugging me . . . and Alpert . . . about what you mean by drop out, tune in, and turn on. Finally, one young kid said, "Drop out, turn on, and tune in." Meaning: get with an activity—a manifest worldly activity—that's harmonious with whatever vision he has.

Everybody in Berkeley is all bugged because they think, one: drop-out thing really doesn't mean anything, that what you're gonna cultivate is a lot of freak-out hippies goofing around and throwing bottles through windows when they flip out on LSD. That's their stereotype vision. Obviously stereotyped.

LEARY: Sounds like bullshitting . . .

The Newspaper Vision

GINSBERG: No, like it's no different from the newspaper vision, anyway. I mean, they've got the newspaper vision.

Then, secondly, they're afraid that there'll be some sort of fascist *Putsch*. Like, it's rumored lately that everyone's gonna be arrested. So that the lack of communicating community among the hippies will lead to some concentration camp situation, or lead . . . as it has been in

Los Angeles recently . . . to a dispersal of what the beginning of the community began.

LEARY: These are the old, menopausal minds. There was a psychiatrist named Adler in San Francisco whose interpretation of the group Be-In was that this is the basis for a new fascism . . . when a leader comes along. And I sense in the activist movement the cry for a leader . . . the cry for organization. . . .

GINSBERG: But they're just as intelligent as you are on this fact. They know about what happened in Russia. That's the reason they haven't got a big, active organization.

It's because they, too, are stumped by: How do you have a community, and a community movement, and cooperation within the community to make life more pleasing for everybody—including the end of the Vietnam war? How do you have such a situation organized, or disorganized, just so long as it's effective—without a fascist leadership? Because they don't want to be that either.

See, they are conscious of the fact that they don't want to be messiahs—political messiahs. At least, Savio in particular. Yesterday, he was weeping. Saying he wanted to go out and live in nature.

LEARY: Beautiful.

GINSBERG: So, I mean he's like basically where we are: stoned.

Genius of Nonleadership

WATTS: Well, I think that thus far, the genius of this kind of underground that we're talking about is that it has no leadership.

LEARY: Exactly!

WATTS: That everybody recognizes everybody else.

GINSBERG: Right, except that that's not really entirely so.

WATTS: Isn't it so? But it is so to a great extent now . . .

GINSBERG: There's an organized leadership, say, at such a thing as a Be-In. There is organization; there is community. There are community groups which cooperate, and those community groups are sparked by active people who don't necessarily parade their names in public, but who are capable people . . . who are capable of ordering sound trucks and distributing thousands of cubes of LSD and getting signs posted . . .

WATTS: Oh yes, that's perfectly true. There are people who can organize things. But they don't assume the figurehead role.

LEARY: I would prefer to call them *foci* of energy. There's no question. You start the poetry, chanting things . . .

WATTS: Yes.

LEARY: And I come along with a celebration. Like Allen and Gary at the Be-In.

Nature and Bossism

WATTS: And there is nobody in charge as a rule, and this is the absolutely vital thing. That the Western world has labored for many, many centuries under a monarchical conception of the universe where God is the boss, and political systems and all kinds of law have been based on this model of the universe . . . that nature is run by a boss.

Whereas, if you take the Chinese view of the world which is organic . . . they would say, for example, that the human body is an organization in which there is no boss. It is a situation of order resulting from mutual interrelationship of all the parts.

And what we need to realize is that there can be, shall we say, a movement . . . a stirring among people . . . which can be *organically* designed instead of *politically* designed. It has no boss. Yet all parts recognize each other in the same way as the cells of the body all cooperate together.

SNYDER: Yes, it's a new social structure. It's a new social structure which follows certain kinds of historically known tribal models.

LEARY: Exactly, yeah! My historical reading of that situation is that these great, monolithic empires that developed in history: Rome, Turkey and so forth . . . always break down when enough people (and it's always the young, the creative, and the minority groups) drop out and go back to a tribal form.

I agree with what I've heard you say in the past, Gary, that the basic unit is tribal. What I envision is thousands of small groups throughout the United States and Western Europe, and eventually the world, as dropping out. What happened when Rome fell? What happened when Jerusalem fell? Little groups went off together . . .

GINSBERG: Precisely what do you mean by drop out, then . . . again, for the millionth time?

SNYDER: Drop out throws me a little bit, Tim. Because it's assumed that we're dropping out. The next step is, now what are we doing where we're in something else? We're in a new society. We're in the seeds of a new society.

GINSBERG: For instance, you haven't dropped out, Tim. You dropped out of your job as a psychology teacher in Harvard. Now, what you've dropped into is, one: a highly complicated series of arrangements for lecturing and for putting on the festival . . .

LEARY: Well, I'm dropped out of that.

GINSBERG: But you're not dropped out of the very highly complicated legal constitutional appeal, which you feel a sentimental regard for, as I do. You haven't dropped out of being the financial provider for Millbrook, and you haven't dropped out of planning and conducting community organization and participating in it.

And that community organization is related to the national community, too. Either through the Supreme Court, or through the very existence of the dollar that is exchanged for you to pay your lawyers, or to take money to pay your lawyers in the theater. So you can't drop out, like *drop out,* 'cause you haven't.

LEARY: Well, let me explain . . .

GINSBERG: So they think you mean like, drop out, like go live on Haight-Ashbury Street and do nothing at all. Even if you can do something like build furniture and sell it, or give it away in barter with somebody else.

LEARY: You have to drop out in a group. You drop out in a small tribal group.

SNYDER: Well, you drop out one by one, but . . . you know, you can join the subculture.

GINSBERG: Maybe it's: "Drop out of what?"

WATTS: Gary, I think that you have something to say here. Because you, to me, are one of the most fantastically capable drop-out people I have ever met. I think, at this point, you should say a word or two about your own experience of how to live on nothing. How to get by in life economically.

This is the nitty-gritty. This is where it really comes down to in many people's minds. Where's the bread going to come from if everybody drops out? Now, you know expertly where it's gonna come from—living a life of integrity and not being involved in a commute-necktie-strangle scene.

SNYDER: Well, this isn't news to anybody, but ten or fifteen years ago when we dropped out, there wasn't a community. There wasn't anybody who was going to take care of you at all. You were really completely on your own.

What it meant was, cutting down on your desires and cutting down on your needs to an absolute minimum; and it also meant, don't be a bit fussy about how you work or what you do for a living.

That meant doing any kind of work. Strawberry picking, carpenter, laborer, longshore . . . Well, longshore is hard to get into. It paid very well. Shipping out . . . that also pays very well.

The Virtue of Patience

But at least in my time, it meant being willing to do any goddam kind of labor that came your way, and not being fussy about it.

And it meant cultivating the virtue of patience—the patience of sticking with a shitty job long enough to win the bread that you needed to have some more leisure, which meant more freedom to do more things that you wanted to do. And mastering all kinds of techniques of living really cheap . . .

Like getting free rice off the docks, because the loading trucks sometimes fork the rice sacks, and spill little piles of rice on the docks which are usually thrown away.

But I had it worked out with some of the guards down on the docks that they would gather fifteen or twenty-five pounds of rice for me, and also tea . . . I'd pick it up once a week off the docks, and then I'd take it around and give it to friends. This was rice that was going to be thrown away, otherwise. Techniques like that.

WATTS: Second day vegetables from the supermarket . . .

SNYDER: Yeah, we used to go around at one or two in the morning around the Safeways and Piggly Wigglies in Berkeley, with a shopping bag, and hit the garbage cans out in back. We'd get Chinese cabbage, lots of broccoli and artichokes that were thrown out because they didn't look sellable anymore.

So, I never bought any vegetables for the three years I was a graduate student at Berkeley. When I ate meat, it was usually horsemeat from the pet store because they don't have a law that permits them to sell horsemeat for human consumption in California like they do in Oregon.

GINSBERG: You make a delicious horsemeat sukiyaki. (laughter)

A Sweet, Clean Pad

WATTS: Well, I want to add to this, Gary, that during the time you were living this way, I visited you on occasion, and you had a little hut way up on the hillside of Homestead Valley in Mill Valley and I want to say, for the record, that this was one of the most beautiful pads I ever saw. It was sweet and clean, and it had a very, very good smell to the whole thing. You were living what I consider to be a very noble life.

Now, then, the question that next arises, if this is the way of being a successful drop-out, which I think is true . . . Can you have a wife and child under such circumstances?

SNYDER: Yes, I think you can, sure.

WATTS: What about when the state forces you to send the child to school?

SNYDER: You send it to school.

LEARY: Oh no, c'mon, I don't see this as drop-out at all.

SNYDER: I want to finish what I was going to say. That's the way it was ten years ago.

Today, there is a huge community. When any kid drops out today, he's got a subculture to go fall into. He's got a place to go where there'll be friends, and people that will put him up and people that will feed him—at least for a while—and keep feeding him indefinitely if he moves around from pad to pad.

LEARY: That's just stage one. The value of the Lower East Side, or of the district in Seattle or the Haight-Ashbury, is that it provides a first launching pad.

Everyone that's caught inside a television set of props, and made of actors . . . The first thing that you have to do is completely detach yourself from anything inside the plastic, robot Establishment.

A Way Station: A Launching Pad

The next step—for many people—could well be a place like Haight-Ashbury. There they will find spiritual teachers, there they will find friends, lovers, wives . . .

But that must be seen clearly as a way station. I don't think the Haight-Ashbury district—any city, for that matter—is a place where the new tribal . . .

SNYDER: I agree with you. Not in the city.

LEARY: . . . is going to live. So, I mean *drop out!* I don't want to be misinterpreted. I'm dropping out . . . step by step.

Millbrook, by the way, is a tribal community. We're getting closer and closer to the landing . . . We're working our way of import and export with the planet. We consider ourselves a tribe of mutants. Just like all the little tribes of Indians were. We happen to have our little area there, and we have to come to terms with the white men around us.

What Are You Building?

SNYDER: Now look . . . Your drop-out line is fine for all those other people out there, you know, that's what you've got to say to them. But,

I want to hear what you're building. What are you making?

LEARY: What are we building?

SNYDER: Yeah, what are you building? I want to hear your views on that. Now, it's agreed we're dropping out, and there are techniques to do it. Now, what next! Where are we going now? What kind of society are we going to be in?

LEARY: I'm making the prediction that thousands of groups will just look around the fake-prop-television-set American society, and just open one of those doors. When you open the door, they don't lead you in, they lead you *out* into the garden of Eden . . . which is the planet.

Then you find yourself a little tribe wandering around. As soon as enough people do this—young people do this—it'll bring about an incredible change in the consciousness of this country, and of the Western world.

GINSBERG: Well, that is happening actually . . .

LEARY: Yeah, but . . .

SNYDER: But that garden of Eden is full of old rubber truck tires and tin cans, right now, you know.

LEARY: Parts of it are . . . Each group that drops out has got to use its two billion years of cellular equipment to answer those questions. "Hey, how we gonna eat? Oh, there's no more paycheck, there's no more fellowship from the university! How we gonna eat? How we gonna keep warm? How we gonna defend ourselves? How we gonna eat? How we gonna keep warm?"

Those are exactly the questions that cellular animals and tribal groups have been asking for thousands of years. Each group is going to have to depend upon its turned on, psychedelic creativity and each group of . . .

I can envision ten M.I.T. scientists, with their families, they've taken LSD . . . They've wondered about the insane-robot-television show of M.I.T. They drop out.

They may get a little farm out in Lexington, near Boston. They may use their creativity to make some new kinds of machines that will turn people on instead of bomb them. Every little group has to do what every little group has done through history.

New Structures; New Techniques

SNYDER: No, they can't do what they've done through history. What is very important here is, besides taking acid, is that people learn the techniques which have been forgotten. That they learn new structures, and new techniques. Like, you just can't go out and grow vegetables, man. You've gotta learn *how* to do it. Like we've gotta learn to do a lot of things we've forgotten to do.

LEARY: I agree.

WATTS: That is very true, Gary. Our educational system, in its entirety, does nothing to give us any kind of material competence. In other words, we don't learn how to cook, how to make clothes, how to build houses, how to make love, or to do any of the absolutely fundamental things of life.

Cerebral "Freak Outs"

The whole education that we get for our children in school is entirely in terms of abstractions. It trains you to be an insurance salesman or a bureaucrat, or some kind of cerebral character.

LEARY: Yes . . . it's exactly there that, I think, a clear-cut statement is needed. The American educational system is a narcotic, addictive process . . .

WATTS: Right!

LEARY: . . . and we must have *nothing* to do with it. Drop out of school, drop out of college, don't be an activist . . .

WATTS: But we've got to do something else.

LEARY: Drop *out* of school . . .

GINSBERG: Where are you gonna learn engineering, or astronomy, or anything like that?

LEARY: The way men have always learned the important things in life. Face to face with a teacher, with a guru. Because very little . . .

GINSBERG: What about astronomy . . . like calculation of star ratios . . . things like that?

LEARY: If any drop-out wants to do that, he can do it . . . I can tell him how to do it.

SNYDER: I would suspect that within the next ten years—within the next five years probably—a modest beginning will be made in subculture institutions of higher learning that will informally begin to exist around the country, and will provide this kind of education without being left to the Establishment, to Big Industry, to Government.

WATTS: Well, it's already happening . . .

SNYDER: I think that there will be a big extension of that, employing a lot of potentially beautiful teachers who are unemployed at the moment . . . like there are gurus who are just waiting to be put to use; and also drawing people, who are working in the universities with a bad con-science, off to join that . . .

LEARY: Exactly . . .

SNYDER: There's a whole new order of technology that is required for this. A whole new science, actually. A whole new physical science is going to emerge from this. Because the boundaries of the old physical science are within the boundaries of the Judaeo-Christian and Western imperialist boss sense of the universe that Alan was talking about.

In other words, our scientific condition is caught within the limits of that father figure, Jehovah, or Roman-emperor model . . . which limits our scientific objectivity and actually holds us back from exploring areas of science which can be explored.

LEARY: Exactly, Gary. Exactly . . .

WATTS: It's like the guy in Los Angeles who had a bad trip on LSD and turned himself in to the police, and wrote: "Please help me. Signed, Jehovah." (laughter)

LEARY: Beautiful! (more laughter) It's about time he caught on, huh? (more laughter)

WATTS: Yes-ss (laughing) But, here though, is this thing, you see. We are talking about all this, which is really a rather small movement of people, involved in the midst of a *fantastic multitude* of people who can only continue to survive if automated industry feeds them, clothes them, houses them and transports them. By means of the creation of *immense* quantities of ersatz material: fake bread, fake homes, fake clothes and fake autos.

In other words, this thing is going on . . . you know, *huge, fantastic* numbers of people . . . *increasing, increasing, increasing* . . . people think the population problem is something that's going to happen five years from *now.* They don't realize it's right on us now! People are coming out of the *walls!*

SNYDER: And they're gobbling up everything on the planet to feed it.

WATTS: Right.

SNYDER: Well, the ecological conscience is something that has to emerge there, and that's part of what we hope for . . . hopefully in the sub-culture.

vfA. (Voice from the Audience): Gary, doesn't Japan clearly indicate that we can go up in an order of magnitude in population and still . . .

SNYDER: Well, who wants to? It can be very well argued by some people who have not been thinking very clearly about it, that we could support a larger number of people on this planet infinitely. But that's irresponsible and sacrilegious. It's sacrilegious for the simple reason it wipes out too many other animal species which we have no right to wipe out.

LEARY: Absolutely.

SNYDER: We have no moral right to upset the ecological balance.

WATTS: No, that's true. We've got to admit that we belong to the mutual eating society.

SNYDER: Furthermore, it simply isn't pleasant to be crowded that way. Human beings lose respect for human beings when they're crowded.

LEARY: Out of my LSD experiences I have evolved a vision which makes sense to my cells . . . that we are already putting to work at Millbrook. And that is, that life on this planet depends upon about twelve inches of topsoil and the incredible balance of species that Gary was just talking about.

On the other hand, man and his technological, Aristotelian zeal has developed these methods of laying down miles of concrete on topsoil, polluting the waters and doing the damage that Gary was just talking about. Now, we cannot say to this society: "Go back to a simple, tribal, pastoral existence." That's romantic.

Forward

SNYDER: You can say *"go forward to a simple, pastoral existence."*

LEARY: Yeah. I have come to a very simple solution. All the technology has to go underground. Because metal belongs underground. You take a hatchet out in the forest and let it go. It goes exactly where God and the Divine Process wants it to be: underground.

Now the city of New York—the megalopolis is going to exist from Seattle to San Diego in a few years—could just as well be underground. If it goes underground it's there, where it belongs, with fire and metal and steel.

I foresee that these tribal groups that drop out—and I mean absolutely drop out—will be helping to get back in harmony with the land, and we've got to start immediately putting a technology underground.

I can think of different ways we can do this symbolically. The Solstice, last April 21st [March 21st—*Oracle*], a group of us went out in front of the house in Millbrook and we took a sledge hammer and we spent about an hour breaking through the road. And we had this incredible piece of asphalt and rock—about four inches—and then we said: "Hey! Underneath this planet somewhere there's dirt!" It was really magical. And once you get a little piece taken out—it took about an hour to get one little piece—then you just go underneath it and it begins to crumble.

So I think we should start a movement to—one hour a day or one hour a week—take a little chisel and a little hammer and put a little hole in some of this plastic, and just see some earth come up, and put a seed there. And then put a little ring—mandalic ring—of something around it.

I can see the highways and I can see the subways and I can see the patios and so forth. Suddenly the highway department comes along, and: "There's a rose growing in the middle of Highway 101!" And then . . . then . . . the robot power group will have to send a group of the highway department to kill the rose and put the asphalt down on the gentle, naked skin of the soil.

Now when they do that, we're getting to them. There'll be pictures in the paper. And consciousness is going to change. Because we've got to get to people's consciousness. We've got to let people realize what they're doing to the earth.

GINSBERG: That's the area of poetry you're dealing with there.

LEARY: Here we go. I'm the poet and you're the politician. I've told you that for ten years!

GINSBERG: "There are no ideas but in things," said William Carlos Williams. How does this work out now?

SNYDER: Technologically?

vfa: I wouldn't want to work underground.

LEARY: Of course not. The only people that would want to work underground are people that would want to work with metal and steel. But if they're hung up that way, and they want to play with those kinds of symbols, fine. We'll have the greatest, air-conditioned, smooth, airport, tile gardens for them with all sorts of metal toys to play with.

vfa: Can I ask you for a clarification on one thing about drop out? You said that in another ten years the young men in the colleges are going to have degrees and the doctors, psychologists and so on, will all be turned-on people. But if they drop out from college now they won't have degrees and these people won't gain control of the apparatus—I mean, I know someone now at State who studies psychology and who doesn't know whether to drop out or not, and who's pulled in two directions. I think there are many people like this.

Drop Out: Yes or No?

LEARY: Yes, I think he should drop out. And I want to be absolutely clear on that. *Nobody* wants to listen to that simple, two-syllable phrase. It gets jargled and jumbled, and I mean it. . . . Now, everyone has to decide how he drops out and when, and he has to time it gracefully, but that's the goal.

SNYDER: We understand that . . .

LEARY: Well, Allen didn't. And Allen, I want you to tell the people in Berkeley that ask you what I mean, I mean *absolutely* have nothing to do with the university, and start planning step by step how you can detect . . .

GINSBERG: Of course, that's where the big argument is, over the *non-students*. The guys that dropped out are not involved, and their problem is what kind of communities they organize.

LEARY: Now, I can foresee that you might work for Sears and Roebuck for six months to get enough money to go to India. But that's part of your drop out. And what I'm doing today, Allen, is part of my drop out. I've got responsibilities, contracts . . . and I don't think that anyone should violate contracts with people that they love. . . . Contract with the university—ha! Fine—quit tomorrow. Therefore, I have to detach myself slowly. When I was in India two years ago . . .

GINSBERG: India . . . but look . . . you know the university is personal relationships also. They're in contact with persons. They can't reject those persons, necessarily . . . There might be a Bodhisattva among those persons.

SNYDER: . . . as Tim says, you can gracefully drop out . . .

LEARY: Aesthetically . . .

SNYDER: . . . at one time or another, which I take to mean . . .

GINSBERG: I was teaching at Berkeley last week—what do you mean "drop out"? (laughs)

LEARY: You've got to do your yoga as a college professor . . . it's part of the thing you're gonna have to go through, and after you do that then (laughs) you shudder and run to the door.

Sages in the Mountains

WATTS: Surely the fact of the matter is that you can do this on a small scale, as an individual, where just a few people are doing this . . . as they always have done. There have always been a kind of elite minority who dropped out—who were the sages in the mountains.

But now we are in a position where the conversations that you and I have go to millions, and people are asking this sort of question.

Let's suppose that everybody in San Francisco decided to take the six o'clock train from the Third Street Station to Palo Alto. . . . See?

We know there's no chance of their doing so. And therefore this catastrophe doesn't happen.

LEARY: That's exactly what I say to people who say: "Well, suppose everyone dropped out?" Ridiculous!

WATTS: Yeah, supposing everyone dropped out. . . . Of course they're not going to.

LEARY: Suppose everyone took LSD tonight—great! (laughs)

The Leisure Society: Puzzles and Paradoxes

WATTS: The thing is this: what we are facing, what's going to happen in this . . . if we do not encounter the final political catastrophe of atomic war, biological warfare and wipe the whole thing out, we're going to have a huge leisure society—where they're going to reverse taxation and *pay* people for the work that the machines do for them. Because there's no other solution to it.

In other words, if the manufacturer is going to be able to sell his products, the people gotta have money to pay for the products. All those people have been put out of work by the machines the manufacturer is using. Therefore, the people have got to be paid by the government—*credit* of some kind, so they can buy what the machines produce—then the thing will go on.

So this means that thousands and thousands of people are going to be loafing around, with nothing at all to do. A few people who are maniacs for work will go on . . .

LEARY: I think what you're defining, Alan, is . . .

WATTS: But that's the kind of situation we're moving into, *if* we survive at all.

LEARY: Well, there's another possibility. And, I think you're defining two possible new species. Let's face it, the evolution of mankind is not over.

WATTS: No!

LEARY: Just as there are many kinds of primates: baboons and chimpanzees and so forth. In a few thousand years we'll look back and see that from—what we call man—there may be two or more new species developing.

There's no question that one species, which could and probably will develop, is this anthill. It's run like a beehive with queens—or kings—[laughs] and it'll all be television and now, of course, in that, sexuality will become very promiscuous and almost impersonal. Because, in an anthill, it always turns out that way.

But you're gonna have another species who inevitably will survive, and that will be the tribal people, who won't have to worry about leisure because when you drop out then the real playwork begins. Because then you have to, as Gary says, learn how to take care of yourself and your loved ones on this . . .

SNYDER: I don't think that you're right about that anthill thing at all though. That's a very negative view of human nature. I don't think it's accurate.

LEARY: It's no longer even human nature. We won't call them human anymore.

Human Beings Want Reality

SNYDER: C'mon, Tim, they're humans and they're gonna be here. You're talking a drama now. You're not talking about—you know—anthropological realities. The anthropological reality is that human beings, in their nature, want to be in touch with what is real in themselves and in the universe.

For example, the longshoremen with their automation contract in San Francisco . . . a certain number of them have been laid off for the rest of their lives with full pay, and some of them have been laid off already for five years—with full pay—by their contract.

Now, my brother-in-law is a longshoreman, and he's been telling me about what's happening to these guys. Most of them are pretty illiterate, a large portion of them are Negroes. The first thing they all did was get boats and drive around San Francisco Bay . . . because they have all this leisure.

Then a lot of them got tired driving around boats that were just like cars, and they started sailing. They move into and respond to the possibility of challenge.

Things become simpler and more complex and more challenging for them. The same is true of hunting. Some guy says "I want to go hunting and fishing all the time, when I have my leisure . . . by God!" So he goes hunting all the time. Then he says, "I want to do this in a more interesting way." So he takes up bow hunting . . . Then the next step is—and this has happened—he says, "I want to try making my own arrowheads." And he learns how to flake his own arrowheads out.

Now, human beings want reality. That's, I think, part of human nature. And television and drinking beer and watching television is what the working man laid off does for the first two weeks.

But then in the third week he begins to get bored, and in the fourth week he wants to do something with his body and his mind and his senses.

LEARY: But if he's still being paid by the Establishment, then you have someone who's going back to childhood. Like, he's making arrows that he doesn't really need . . .

SNYDER: May I speak my vision about this?

LEARY: I object to that very much. I want him out there really fighting—not fighting, but working—for his family, not chipping . . .

SNYDER: Well, this is a transitional thing, too . . . . It's too transitional.

GINSBERG: This leads to violence because it divides everybody up into two separate . . .

SNYDER: Oh, he was talking poetry.

LEARY: No, I'm not! I want to be clear about this. We are doing this already . . .

SNYDER: No, but the difference is, the children of the ants are all going to be tribal people. That's way it's going to work. We're going to get the kids, and it's going to take about three generations.

The Change

And in the meantime, the family system will change, and when the family system changes the economy will change . . . and in the meantime, a number of spiritual insights are going to change the minds of the technologists and the scientists themselves, and technology will change.

There will be a diffused and decentralized technology . . . as I see it . . .

WATTS: Well, go on . . . Are you saying now what you said was your vision?

SNYDER: Now, what I was going to say was very simply this.

I think that automation in the affluent society, plus psychedelics, plus—for the same curious reason—a whole catalytic, spiritual change or bend of mind that seems to be taking place in the west, today especially is going to result—can result ultimately—in a vast leisure society in which people will voluntarily reduce their number, and because human beings want to do that which is real . . . simplify their lives.

The whole problem of consumption and marketing is radically altered if a large number of people voluntarily choose to consume less.

And people will voluntarily choose to consume less if their interests are turned in any other direction.

If what is exciting to them is no longer things but states of mind.

LEARY: That's true.

States of Mind

SNYDER: Now what is something else . . .

People are becoming interested in states of mind, and things are not going to substitute for states of mind. So what I visualize is a very complex and sophisticated cybernetic technology surrounded by thick hedges of trees . . .

Somewhere, say around Chicago. And the rest of the nation a buffalo pasture . . .

LEARY: That's very close to what I think.

SNYDER: . . . with a large number of people going around making their own arrowheads because it's fun, but they know better . . . (laughter) They know they don't have to make them. (more laughter)

LEARY: Now, this seems like our Utopian visions are coming closer together. I say that the industry should be underground, and you say it should be in Chicago. This interests me.

WATTS: Well, it's the same idea.

SNYDER: Well, those who want to be technological engineers will be respected . . . And the other thing is that you can go and live close to nature, or you can go back and . . .

LEARY: But you won't be allowed to drive a car outside this technological . . .

SNYDER: But you won't want to!

That's the difference, baby. It's not that you won't be allowed to, it's that you won't want to . . . That's where it's got to be at.

Civilized "Pap"

WATTS: Because, it's the same thing when we get down to, say, the fundamental question of food. More and more one realizes that the mass-produced food is not worth eating, and therefore, in order to delight in things to eat, you go back to the most primitive processes of raising and preparing food. Because that has taste.

And I see that it will be a sort of flip, that as all the possibilities of technology and automation make it possible for everybody to be assured of having the basic necessities of life . . . they will then say: "Oh, yes, we have all that. Now we can always rely on that, but now in the meantime while we don't have to work, let's go back to make arrowheads and to raising the most *amazing plants*."

SNYDER: Yeah . . . It would be so funny; the thing is that they would all get so good at it that the technology center of Chicago would rust away. (laughter)

WATTS: Right! Right! (laughter)

LEARY: That's exactly what's going to happen. The psychedelic dropouts are going to be having so much fun. They're going to be so much obviously healthier.

WATTS: But Tim, do you see any indication among people who at present are really turned on, that they are cultivating this kind of material competence? Now, I haven't seen too much of it yet . . .

SNYDER: Some of those kids at Big Sur have got it.

WATTS: Yeah, maybe you're right.

SNYDER: They're learning. A few years ago they used to go down to Big Sur and they didn't know how to camp or dig latrines.

Technological Handbook

But like what Martine has been telling me lately, is that they're getting very sharp about what to gather that's edible, how to get sea salt, what are the edible plants and the edible seeds, and the revolutionary technological book for this state is A. L. Kroeber's *Handbook of the California Indians,* which tells you what's good to eat and how to prepare it. And also what to use for tampax: milkweed fluff . . . (laughter) Diapers made of shredded bark . . . The whole thing is all there.

LEARY: Beautiful . . .

WATTS: But the thing is this. I've found so many people who are the turned-on type, and the circumstances and surroundings under which they live are just plain cruddy. You would think that people who have seen what you can see with the visions of psychedelics would reflect themselves in forms of life and art that would be like Persian miniatures. Because obviously Persian miniatures and Moorish arabesques are all reflecting the state of mind of people who were turned on. And they are rich and glorious beyond belief.

GINSBERG: Majestic.

WATTS: Majestic! Yeah! Well now, why doesn't it occur . . . It is slowly beginning to happen . . . 'Cause I've noticed that, recently, all turned-on people are becoming more colorful. They're wearing beads and gorgeous clothes and so on and so forth . . . and it's gradually coming out. Because you remember the old beatnik days when everybody was in blue jeans and ponytails and no lipstick and *drab*—and *crummy!*

SNYDER: What! (laughter)

WATTS: Now, something's beginning to happen!

SNYDER: Well, it wasn't quite that bad, but we were mostly concerned with not being consumers then . . . and so we were showing our non-consumerness.

WATTS: Yes, I know! The thing is I am using this as a symbol because the poor cons in San Quentin wear blue jeans.

SNYDER: The thing is that there are better things in the Goodwill now than there used to be.

WATTS: Yes, exactly. (laughter) But the thing is that now I see it beginning to happen. Timothy here, instead of wearing his old—whatever it was he used to wear—has now got a white tunic on with gold and colorful gimp on it.

GINSBERG: Gimp?

WATTS: Yes, and it's very beautiful, and he's wearing a necklace and all that kind of thing, and color is at last coming into the scene.

SNYDER: That's going back before the Roundheads, and before Cromwell . . .

WATTS: Yes, it is.

LEARY: Let's get practical here. I think we're all concerned with the increasing number of people who are dropping out and wondering where to go from there. Now let's come up with some practical suggestions which we might hope we could unfold in the next few months.

Bush, Farm, City

SNYDER: There's three categories: wilderness, rural, and urban. Like there's going to be bush people, farm people, and city people. Bush tribes, farm tribes, and city tribes.

LEARY: Beautiful. That makes immediate sense to me. How about beach people?

VFA: Let me throw in a word . . . the word is evil and technology. Somehow they come together, and when there is an increase in technology, and technological facility, there is an increase in what we usually call human evil.

SNYDER: I wouldn't agree with that . . . no, there's all kind of non-evil technologies. Like, Neolithic obsidian flaking is technology.

VFA: But in its advanced state it produces evil . . .

WATTS: Yes, but what you mean, I think, is this. When you go back to the great myths about the origin of evil, actually the Hebrew words which say good and evil as the knowledge of good and evil being the result of eating the fruit of the tree of knowledge . . .

Analytical Lag

These words mean advantageous and disadvantageous, and they're words connected with technical skills. And the whole idea is this, which you find reflected in the Taoist philosophy, that the moment you start interfering in the course of nature with a mind that is centered and one-pointed, and analyzes everything, and breaks it down into bits . . . The moment you do that you lose contact with your original know-how . . . by means of which you now color your eyes, breathe, and beat your heart.

For thousands of years mankind has lost touch with his original intelligence, and he has been absolutely fascinated by this kind of political, godlike, controlling intelligence . . . where you can go ptt-ptt-ptt-ptt . . . and analyze things all over the place, and he has forgotten to trust his own organism.

Now the whole thing is that everything is coming to be realized today. Not only through people who take psychedelics, but also through many scientists. They're realizing that this linear kind of intelligence cannot keep up with the course of nature. It can only solve trivial problems when the big problems happen too fast to be thought about in that way.

So, those of us who are in some way or other—through psychedelics, through meditation, through what have you—are getting back to being able to trust our original intelligence . . . are suggesting an entirely new course for the development of civilization.

SNYDER: Well, it happens that civilization develops with the emergence of a class structure. A class structure can't survive, or can't put across its principle, and expect people to accept it . . . if they believe in themselves. If they believe, individually, one by one, that they are in some way godlike, or Buddhalike, or potentially illuminati.

So it's almost ingrained in civilization, and Freud said this, you know "Civilization as a Neurosis," that part of the nature of civilization is that it must *put down* the potential of every individual development.

Private Visions

This is the difference between that kind of society which we call civilized and that much more ancient kind of society, which is still viable and still survives, and which we call primitive. In which everybody is potentially a chief and which everybody . . . like the Comanche or the Sioux . . . *everybody* in the whole culture . . . was expected to go out and have a vision one time in his life.

In other words, to leave the society to have some transcendental experience, to have a song and a totem come to him which he need tell no one, ever—and then come back and live with this double knowledge in society.

WATTS: In other words, through his having had his own isolation, his own loneliness, and his own vision, he knows that the game rules of society are fundamentally an illusion.

SNYDER: The society not only permits that, the society is built on that . . . And everybody has one side of his nature that has been out of it.

WATTS: That society is strong and viable which recognizes its own provisionality.

SNYDER: And no one who ever came into contact with the Plains Indians didn't think they were men! Every record of American Indians, from the cavalry, the pioneers, the missionaries, the Spaniards . . . say that every one of these people was men.

In fact, I learned something just the other day. Talking about the Uroc Indians, an early explorer up there commented on their fantastic self-confidence. He said, ". . . Every Indian has this fantastic self-confidence. And they laugh at me," he said, "they laugh at me and they say: 'Aren't you sorry you're not an Indian.' Poor wretched Indians!" (laughs) this fellow said.

Alone and at One

Well, that is because every one of them has gone out and had this vision experience . . . has been completely alone with himself, and face to face with himself . . . and has contacted powers outside of what anything the society could give him, and society expects him to contact powers outside of society . . . in those cultures.

WATTS: Yes, every healthy culture does. Every healthy culture provides for there being nonjoiners. Sanyassi, hermits, drop-outs too . . . every healthy society has to tolerate this . . .

SNYDER: A society like the Comanche or the Sioux demands that everybody go out there and have this vision, and incorporates and ritualizes it within the culture. Then a society like India, a step more civilized, permits some individuals to have these visions, but doesn't demand it of everyone. And then later it becomes purely eccentric.

LEARY: We often wonder why some people are more ready to drop out than others. It may be explained by the theory of reincarnation. The people that don't want to drop out can't conceive of living on this planet outside of the prop television studio, are just unlucky enough to have been born into this sort of thing . . . maybe the first or second time. They're still entranced by all the manmade props. But there's no question that we should consider how more and more people, who are ready to drop out, can drop out.

WATTS: If there is value in being a drop-out . . . that is to say, being an outsider . . . You can only appreciate and realize this value if there are in contrast with you insiders and squares. The two are mutually supportive.

LEARY: If someone says to me, "I just can't conceive of dropping out . . ." I can say, "Well, you're having fun with this go round . . . fine! We've all done it many times in the past."

GINSBERG: The whole thing is too big, because it doesn't say drop out of *what* precisely. What everybody is dealing with is people, it's not dealing with institutions. It's dealing with them but it's also dealing with people. Working with and including the police.

SNYDER: If you're going to talk this way you have to be able to specifically say something to somebody in Wichita, Kansas, who says, "I'm going to drop out. How do you advise me to stay living around here in this area which I like?"

LEARY: Let's be less historical now for a while, and let's be very practical about ways in which people who want to find the tribal way . . . How can they do it . . . what do you tell them?

SNYDER: Well, this is what I've been telling kids all over Michigan and Kansas. For example, I tell them first of all, Do you want to live here, or do you want to go some place else? All right, they say they want to stay where they are. I say, okay, get in touch with the Indian culture here. Find out what was here before. Find out what the mythologies were. Find out what the local deities were. You can get all of this out of books.

Go and look at your local archeological sites. Pay a reverent visit to the local American Indian tombs, and also the tombs of the early American settlers. Find out what your original ecology was. Is it short grass prairies, or long grass prairie here?

Go out and live on the land for a time. Set up a tent and camp out and watch the clouds and watch the water and watch the land and get a sense of what the climate here is. Because since you've been living in a house all your life, you probably don't know what the climate is.

LEARY: Beautiful.

SNYDER: Then decide how you want to make your living here. Do you want to be a farmer, or do you want to be a hunter and food gatherer?

You know, you start from the ground up, and you can do it in any

part of this country today . . . cities . . . and all . . . For this continent I took it back to the Indians. Find out what the Indians were up to in your own area. Whether it's Utah, or Kansas, or New Jersey . . .
LEARY: That is a stroke of cellular revelation and genius, Gary. That's one of the wisest things I've heard anyone say in years. Exactly how it should be done.

I do see the need for transitions though, and you say that there will be city people as well as country people and mountain people . . . I would suggest that for the next year or two or three, which are going to be nervous, transitional, mutational years—where things are going to happen very fast, by the way—the transition could be facilitated if every city set up little meditation rooms, little shrine rooms, where the people in transition, dropping out, could meet and meditate together.

It's already happening at the Psychedelic Shop, it's happening in New York. I see no reason why there shouldn't be ten or twenty such places in San Francisco.
SNYDER: There already are.

The Energy to Create

LEARY: I know, but let's encourage that. I was just in Seattle and I was urging the people there. Hundreds of them crowd into coffee shops, and there is this beautiful energy.

They are liberated people, these kids, but they don't know where to go. They don't need leadership, but they need, I think, a variety of suggestions from people who have thought about this, giving them the options to move in any direction. The different meditation rooms can have different styles. One can be Zen, one can be macrobiotic, one can be bhahte chanting, one can be rock and roll psychedelic, one can be lights.

If we learn anything from our cells, we learn that God delights in variety. The more of these we can encourage, people would meet in these places, and *automatically* tribal groups would develop and new matings would occur, and the city should be seen for many as transitional . . . and they get started. They may save up a little money, and then they head out and find the Indian totem wherever they go.

A Magic Geography

SNYDER: Well, the Indian totem is right under your ground in the city, is right under your feet. Just like when you become initiated into the

Haineph pueblo, which is near Albuquerque, you learn the magic geography of your region; and part of that means going to the center of Albuquerque and being told: There is a spring here at a certain street, and its name is such and such. And that's in a street corner in downtown Albuquerque.

But they have that geography intact, you know. They haven't forgotten it. Long after Albuquerque is gone, somebody'll be coming there, saying there's a spring here and it'll be there, probably.

LEARY: Tremont Street in Boston means "three hills."

GINSBERG: There's a stream under Greenwich Village.

vfA: Gary, what do you think of rejecting the week as a measure of time; as a sort of absurd, civilized measure of time, and replacing it with a month, which is a natural time cycle?

LEARY: What is the time cycle?

SNYDER: The week, the seven day week. Well, the seven day week is simply based on the Old Testament theory that the world was created in seven days, you know. So you don't need it, particularly.

vfA: Right. It seems to me a formal rejection of it and a cycling of social events around the idea of monthly cycle . . .

Holy Day!

WATTS: I don't agree with that, because . . . everywhere that this week thing has spread, people have adopted it, where they didn't have this time rhythm before. But people have not understood the real meaning of the week, which is that every seventh day is a day to goof off. It's to turn out of the whole thing. The rules are abrogated. "The six days thou shalt labor, and do all that thou has to do. The seventh day thou shalt keep holy." *Holy day!* and this means holiday. It means instead of a day for laying on rationality and preaching and making everybody feel guilty because they didn't operate properly the other six days.

LEARY: You turn on.

WATTS: The seventh day is the day . . . Yes, absolutely, to go crazy. . . . Because if you can't afford a little corner of craziness in your life, you're like a steel bridge that has no give. You're so rigid you're going to collapse in the first wind.

LEARY: There is also some neuro-pharmacological evidence in support of the weekly cycle. That is, you can only have a full-scale LSD session about once a week. And when they said in Genesis—actually it's the first page of Genesis—"On the seventh day He rested," it makes very modern sense.

GINSBERG: You can interpret it psychedelically, but that's like new criticism . . . (laughter) You can actually *like* new criticism . . .

LEARY: I want you to be very loving to me for the rest of . . . and the tape will be witness . . . whether Allen is loving or not to me, for the rest of the evening.

GINSBERG: That's all right, I can always use a Big Brother . . .

WATTS: May I point out, this has directly to do with what we've been talking about.

GINSBERG: But I was just getting paranoid of you interpreting the Old Testament as a prophecy of LSD. That's what I was *thinking*.

LEARY: My foot has often led to other people's paranoias at the time.

WATTS: One day in seven, one seventh, is the day of the drop out.

SNYDER: That's not enough. (laughter)

WATTS: Now wait a minute. You're going too fast, Gary.

vfa: Gary, the first six days of the week you drop out, and the seventh day you work.

SNYDER: Baby, we've gotta get away from this distinction between work and play. That's the whole thing, really. Like this one day in seven thing, the reason I don't agree with it is that it implies that making the world was a job.

WATTS: Oh, that's perfectly true. I entirely agree with you on that.

A Bad Scene

SNYDER: And any universe that is worth creating isn't any job to create. You dig it. I don't sympathize with his fatigue at all . . . He must have made a bad scene. (chuckles)

WATTS: You are talking on a different level than we're discussing at the moment. You are talking from the point of view where from the very deepest vision everything that happens is okay, and everything is play.

SNYDER: Well, I wasn't really talking from that vision.

WATTS: Well, that's where you really are. Now, I'm going one level below this, and saying . . .

SNYDER: What I'm saying is if you do enjoy what you're doing, it's not work.

WATTS: That's true. That's my own philosophy: that I get paid for playing.

Now, the thing is, though, that just as talking on a little bit lower level . . . now—one day in seven is for goofing off . . . and that's a certain less percentage. So in a culture, if the culture is to be healthy, there has to be a substantial but, nevertheless, minority percentage of people who are not involved in the rat race.

And this is the thing that it seems to me is coming out of this. We cannot possibly expect that everybody in the United States of America will drop out. But it is entirely important for the welfare of the United States that a certain number of people, a certain percentage, should drop out. Just as one day in seven should be a holiday.

vfA: That's the baby that's being born. That's the baby that's being born *now*. The problem that we have to deal with is how to get that baby out easily.

LEARY: I think we must be more practical than we have been, because there are hundreds and thousands of people who are very interested in what we are talking about in the most A-B-C practical sense like: What do I do tomorrow?

WATTS: Right!

Right Occupation

SNYDER: The subject is money, and point two is: right occupation, which is the sixth or the seventh stage in the eightfold path of the Buddha.

WATTS: Now, I want to put what I've said and what you've said together to make it one.

LEARY: Everyone has to become a Buddha.

WATTS: Those people who drop out are the ones who make work and play the same.

LEARY: That's a great slogan!

vfA: You said earlier that when automation comes people will be paid not to work.

WATTS: Yes.

vfA: Automation is already come in this country . . .

WATTS: It's coming, yes.

vfA: . . . but the country hasn't learned how to solve the problem of distribution. So it has a war in Vietnam to get rid of its surplus products . . .

WATTS: Exactly, because we are still under the superstition that money is real.

vfA: If now, people started dropping out—the most turned-on people started dropping out—instead of guiding our already automated society into a time when we can have leisure so that we can go into ourselves and become real people . . . if all these people drop out, isn't there a danger that it will leave the non-turned-on people in control of the machine, and it would just be Vietnam after Vietnam?

LEARY: No.

vfA: Because they react!

LEARY: Exactly, you see the only way to stop the war in Vietnam is for a hundred high school kids to quit school tomorrow. Don't picket, don't get involved in it at all . . . because they're watching . . .

WATTS: And there'll be too many to be picked off one by one.

Caesar's Garden

LEARY: Caesar watches! He's watching, and every time we dig a little hole in the pavement and plant a rose, a hundred thousand consciousnesses are changed.

Don't worry about it. We can have nothing to do with the steel. We can't fight with Caesar over who's going to run the television-prop-fake-show. The only way to end the war in Vietnam is to let's *all* drop out and change the American consciousness as quickly as possible.

WATTS: Well, fundamentally it's always been said and I think . . .

GINSBERG: Now, what can I drop out of?

LEARY: Don't take your teaching post at Cal.

GINSBERG: Don't take my teaching post at Cal . . . That's one way, but that involves money. I need the money.

vfA: You should just give it away.

GINSBERG: But I've been giving it away . . . that's why I need the money. (laughter) The Diggers say abandon money . . .

vfA: You don't necessarily have to abandon it.

LEARY: Get rid of it. Pass it on faster and faster . . .

vfA: Money is stored energy—it may be real or it may not be real and should be given away within the community.

GINSBERG: What about Pound's idea of money? Pound said that where money came from was that somebody got a million dollars in gold, and then the government gave him sixteen million dollars' credit.

In other words, he could issue sixteen million dollars' worth of dollars—for a million in gold. So just the people who had that gold, presumably, had credit. So Pound's idea was that all credit should come from the government.

SNYDER: Well, within the subculture it moves more and more towards exchange, toward giving and exchanging of what you've created, and getting food for pawns, literally . . . and keeping it within the community.

GINSBERG: What if you want a piano?

LEARY: Different ones of us, at different times, have more energy that can interact with the culture.

In the last four months, I have been making about eight thousand dollars a week and I didn't have enough money in Seattle yesterday to buy a package of cigarettes. Let's go on, and be more practical.

SNYDER: Well, I think there are two problems with practicality. The one is right now, and the second is when technological advances have made mass unemployment. I mean this society at least, is moving towards the point when everybody will just be given money.

As a matter of fact, the American economy could afford right now to put everybody on a minimum income dole. And it would cost them less, probably, than the one-tenth that goes into social work.

Money, Money, Money

WATTS: And incidentally, Gary, it would cost us less to bribe the whole of Asia than to fight any wars there.

SNYDER: Just dump money on China.

WATTS: To dump money on China, to give everybody enough clothes, enough food, enough housing, it would cost us less than fighting the Vietnam war!

SNYDER: So the problem of bread is merely an interim problem, and I see it as being a question of flexibility, and willingness, and a Bodhisattva spirit of service . . . like being willing to work for the post office. It's a temporary problem.

GINSBERG: If we were to bribe Asia . . . bribe China, and feed China and everything like that . . . how could we do that and simultaneously drop out into purely separated pueblos, or family units, or tribes?

LEARY: Well, that's a fantasy of the times. A delightful fantasy to show the ridiculousness of the robot-fake-prop-television show.

Now Practical Step Number One, I suggest, is that we encourage, in every way we can, including with our energies, the setting up of meditation centers of tribal landing pads in all the cities of the United States.

I would say Step Number Two would be to . . .

GINSBERG: That requires a corporation, doesn't it?

SNYDER: No, it doesn't.

LEARY: Not at all! Nothing like that. It requires Ron and Jay, who've already done that.

SNYDER: But it requires that you be able to serve food next . . . Any good ashram serves food.

LEARY: So the Diggers have been starting on that.

SNYDER: So now where are we gonna get the food?

GINSBERG: The International Society for Krishna Consciousness is incorporated.

vfA: You get the food by acquiring land. That's the basic thing, to acquire land for people to go to.

LEARY: That's Step Number Three. As the people move from the city they've got to meet each other and form these tribal . . . I would say, reincarnation groups because the people who are ready to drop out and turn on will come to these centers and they'll wander around and they'll form natural cellular groups and they will leave the city.

A Model Be-In

I would suggest, as Practical Step Number Two, that the Human Be-In in San Francisco be a model. We've all tried different models of summer schools, of institutes and research projects and individual dropouts . . . psychedelic celebrations and so forth . . . and the Avalon and Fillmore and so forth . . .

I would say that the Human Be-In was a tremendously important thing in the consciousness of San Francisco. Now if that thing could happen in every large city in the country . . . And again, the beautiful thing about the Be-In was it had no leadership, it had no big financing, it will just grow automatically.

GINSBERG: Yeah, but we're accused of being the leaders. We're not, though, you know. What were *we* doing up on that platform?

LEARY: That's a charge that doesn't bother me at all.

vfA: There were fifty people up on that platform and every one of them was a leader. So were the people in the audience. The reason was that nobody came out and said, "We *are* the leaders," because that's bullshit!

GINSBERG: Nobody claims to be the leader, but I remember sitting up there showing my body off.

vfA: Every time they say "you're a leader" you point to Snyder, you see?

GINSBERG: Well, I do that anyway.

SNYDER: Yeah, I know, but the press has a leadership complex.

WATTS: Oh, they want to find the ringleaders . . .

GINSBERG: Yeah, they keep calling Gary my disciple . . . and they have me blowing his conch horn.

Who's in Charge

WATTS: . . . one of the four philosophical questions is: Who started it? And whenever the police or the press barge into a situation, they want to know who started it.

In other words, because they're still thinking about God and the first cause and they want to know . . .

LEARY: Who's in charge . . .

WATTS: . . . who started, who's in charge, and so on . . .

LEARY: Who gets the credit, who gets the blame . . .

WATTS: Let's get back to a fundamental thing. I think that what you are really—all of you—are having the courage to say, is that, the absolutely primary thing is that there be a change of consciousness in the individual . . . that he escape from the hallucination that he is a separate ego in an alien universe and that we all come to realize, primarily, that each one of us is the whole works.

Always

Each one of us is what is real and has been real for always and always and always and will ever be . . .

And although the time language may not be appropriate here, nevertheless, we are that, and to the extent that it can't be spread around . . . That's what you and I are, and we lose our anxieties and we lose our terror of death, and our own unimportance . . .

That this is the absolutely essential ingredient, which if we get hold of that point, all the rest will be added unto you . . . In the sense of, "Seek you first the kingdom of God and all these things shall be added to you."

SNYDER: Right.

WATTS: Isn't that what you're saying? I mean, isn't that absolutely basic? And even if this is only realized among a statistical minority (crash in background of photographer falling into woman's lap) . . . minority of people . . .

LEARY: That's a tender sight.

WATTS: Even if this is only realized by a statistical minority, nevertheless, it's *immensely* powerful.

LEARY: It affects consciousness.

WATTS: It affects everybody.

LEARY: I would add to practical step number two that more celebrations be set up all over . . . more Be-Ins . . . That April twenty-first, the solstice, be a nice time to try to arrange—in as many cities as possible, because that'll be spring in the northern cities where it's hard to have a . . .

And one thing I've learned in the last few months is that all of these experiences should be out of doors . . . What about April twenty-first?
SNYDER: Yeah, sure . . .
WATTS: And in Central Park, hah!
SNYDER: . . . and then in July with the Indians in New Mexico—the big gathering of the tribes.

Maha-lila

It just occurred to me, the practical details . . . The model of it is something like the Maha-lila. Like, you're asking, how's it going to work?

Well, now, the Maha-lila is a group of about three different families who have sort of pooled their resources, none of which are very great. But they have decided to play together and to work together and to take care of each other and that means all of them have ways of getting a small amount of bread, which they share. And other people contribute a little money when it comes in. And then they work together on creative projects . . . like they're working together on a light show right now for a poetry reading that we're going to give. And they consider themselves a kind of extended family or clan. When they went to the Be-In, they had a banner which said Maha-lila. Like, that was their *clan* banner.
LEARY: Yeah, I saw that . . . That's the model.
SNYDER: That's the model . . .

And the model for the time is that breaking out of the smaller family organization we work in slightly larger structures, like clan structures, in which people do work at various jobs and bring in whatever bread they can from various jobs.

But they're willing to pool it and share it and they learn how to work and play together. Then they relate that to a larger sense of the tribe, which is also loose . . . But for the time being everybody has to be able—from time to time—to do some little job.

But, the reference is . . . The thing that makes it different is . . . that you don't bring it home to a very tight individual or one monogamous family unit, but you bring it home to a slightly larger unit where the sharing is greater. I think that's where it starts.

Matrilineal Descent

LEARY: The extended family is the key.

SNYDER: The extended family is, I think, where it starts.

And my own particular hobby horse on this is that the extended family leads to matrilineal descent and when we get matrilineal descent—then we'll have group marriage, and when we have group marriage we'll have the economy licked.

Because with the group marriage . . . capitalism is doomed and civilization goes out. (laughter)

LEARY: Practical step number three (laughter) which I would like to see . . . I would like to suggest that June twenty-first, which is the summer solstice, we try to have an enormous series of Be-Ins in which . . .

GINSBERG: June twenty-first?

SNYDER: The summer solstice.

LEARY: April twenty-first we have Be-Ins in different cities . . .

WATTS: No, March the twenty-first is the spring . . .

SNYDER: The equinox is on March twenty-first, solstice is June twenty-first.

GINSBERG: What's an equinox?

SNYDER: That's when nights and days are equal.

LEARY: Wherever I said April, I want to take that back. I should have said March.

GINSBERG: Solstice?

WATTS: The sun's standing still at Xmas and midsummer . . .

SNYDER: Midsummer's night.

I think we should encourage extended families everywhere.

WATTS: Well, it's very practical to encourage extended families because the present model of the family is a hopeless breakdown. Because, first of all, the family is an agrarian cultural institution, which is not suited to an urban culture.

All the family consists in a dormitory . . . where a wife and children are located, and the husband, who engages in a mysterious activity in an office or a factory, in which neither the wife nor the children have any part nor interest . . .

From which he brings home an abstraction called money.

And where there are lots of pretty secretaries in the scene in which he actually works.

Bonds of Guilt

And so, they have no relation whatsoever to what he does, and furthermore, the awful thing about the family, as it exists at the moment, is
that the husband and the wife both feel guilty about not bringing up
their children properly, and therefore they live for their children . . .

Instead of living out their own lives and doing their own interesting
work in which the children would automatically become interested as
participants and watchers on the side.

As it is, they are doing everything, they say . . . We live, we work,
we earn our money for you darlings, and these poor darlings feel all these
things thrown at them and they don't know what to do with it . . .

And then they are sent away to school, shrilled off to school as Dylan
Thomas put it . . . to be educated for everything and nothing . . .

LEARY: By strangers.

WATTS: By strangers . . .

LEARY: Who are of dubious . . . aah . . .

WATTS: Who would teach them all sorts of purely . . .

LEARY: . . . moral, intellectual and sexual characteristics.

WATTS: Right. (laughter) Abstract formulations and things they'll learn,
and . . . the family has no reality. And the greatest institution today
in the American family is the babysitter. Someone just to take the children out of our consciousness while we enjoy ourselves.

VFA: And the *death* sitter, to take the old people out of their consciousness . . . and even *death* has been taken from the people.

Outside the Group

WATTS: And the *death* sitter, exactly . . . The courtesy of the morti-
cian, yes . . . A good death is no longer possible, practically . . .

SNYDER: I have a four stage thing . . . Uh, American Indian technologies . . .

WATTS: Practical now . . .

SNYDER: . . . meditation centers, group marriage, and periodical gatherings of the tribes.

LEARY: I don't agree with group marriage . . . We are a tribal people.
You cannot have infidelity in a tribe. Infidelity . . . ah, sexual freedom . . .

SNYDER: Infidelity is defined as going outside the tribe.

LEARY: . . . is anonymous, impersonal, anthill sexuality . . . Every woman . . .

SNYDER: Now, wait a minute.

LEARY: Let me finish . . . Every woman is all women . . . If you can't find all women in one woman it's *your* problem. Infidelity cannot be tolerated in a tribal, seed carrying . . .

GINSBERG: Who's tolerating!

SNYDER: Infidelity is defined as living outside . . .

GINSBERG: We're talking infidelity . . . What about homosexuality? We're . . . (laughter)

SNYDER: . . . is living outside the areas of your commitments, Tim. Anthropologically . . . and, actually . . .

GINSBERG: What's going to happen to me? (laughter)

LEARY: You're going to have nine children.

GINSBERG: What if I don't want them?

LEARY: You told me you wanted to . . .

GINSBERG: Sometimes, but not always . . .

SNYDER: No, here's what I was driving at . . . uh . . . Tim . . .

GINSBERG: But you're a Catholic . . . or something . . . (laughter)

SNYDER: Let me say this . . . Let me answer what he said there, Allen. (laughter)

LEARY: I'm an Irish Catholic . . . May I have the wine, please? (laughter)

GINSBERG: What Mario Savio said . . . (chuckling)

LEARY: What?

GINSBERG: That you were an Irish Catholic . . . (laughter)

LEARY: Well, the Celts, of course, have . . . a long history of . . .

GINSBERG: What should Mario Savio do?

SNYDER: I don't know . . .

LEARY: Drop out, turn on, and tune in.

WATTS: I think, Tim . . . you're being a little acceptive here. I do think it's possible for some of us to have found all women in one woman . . .

SNYDER: I want to get back at something . . . Just let me say something with him . . . [meaning Leary: Ed.] Infidelity means denying your commitments. Now, if your commitments are within a group marriage, then fidelity is being true within your group marriage. And infidelity is being untrue or dishonest outside of that.

Now there are some cultures in South America in which all forms of marriage are permitted. There are group marriages, polyandrous marriages, polygamous marriages, and monogamous marriages.

WATTS: By group marriages . . . Just a moment, let's get a question of definition here.

Group Marriage

SNYDER: Okay. A group marriage is where, a number of people—as a group—whatever the number is . . . announce . . . a marriage is a social announcement of commitment . . . announce that we will be responsible for the children we produce and for each other.

WATTS: Now in other words, all males and all females in this group can be in mutual intercourse with each other?

SNYDER: But not outside the group . . .

GINSBERG: You make rules to take care of that . . . You gotta bring in . . .

SNYDER: I'm not making rules. I'm just telling you what the anthropological precedences are in these things.

It happens that in this South American culture that the majority of the marriages are monogamous, but it also happens that there are some polyandrous, some polygamous and a few group ones.

I think that what we can allow is . . . people to combine in whatever combinations they wish.

LEARY: Oh, I would certainly agree with that.

Love Overcomes

vfA: Can I illustrate that? If my old lady wants to fuck anybody in the room here it's alright with me, but if she fucks . . . uh . . . J. Edgar Hoover, I'm going to get very upset. (laughter)

SNYDER: She should get a prize. She'd be doing something for the nation, baby.

LEARY: Yes, he'd be making love not war. (laughter)

WATTS: Well, you're simply saying that if she does that she's not at all the sort of person you thought she was. And that you've been deceived.

SNYDER: What you're saying is endogamy . . . Within the tribe it's okay, but outside the tribe . . .

GINSBERG: Why make rules?

FEMALE vfA: I don't think it's possible, in the first place, for anybody's old lady to fuck J. Edgar Hoover.

vfA: That may be the problem!

WATTS: Oh, that question is academic. (he laughs)

SNYDER: But I wasn't . . . You know, like your idea of fidelity . . . Fidelity is perfectly reasonable, but fidelity simply means: in terms of the areas of commitment you've established for yourself.

LEARY: That is a beautiful . . . a beautiful model . . . and I think it requires a little consciousness, which I hope will come quickly to the human race, Gary.

SNYDER: I think we've had it.

WATTS: No, but I don't . . . I don't think that you should talk about . . . When people, just as Lao-tzu said, when the great Tao was lost there came talk of duty to man and right conduct . . . and so when the essential idea of love is lost there comes talk of fidelity.

That actually, the only possible basis for two beings—male and female—to relate to each other is to grant each other total freedom . . . and say, I don't put any bonds on you, you don't put any bonds on me because I want you, I love you *the way you are!* And I want you to be that . . .

The minute you start making contracts and bonds and signing on the dotted line, you are *wrecking* the whole relationship.

And you just have to trust to the fact that human beings should be legally allowed to trust each other, and to enter into a fellowship that does not involve a contractual arrangement.

LEARY: I think we all agree with that.

WATTS: You know, because if you don't do that *you'll kill it!*

SNYDER: In primitive cultures marriage is not a contractual arrangement; it's a public announcement.

WATTS: Yes!

SNYDER: It's a relationship which is made public.

LEARY: What was your fourth point, Gary?

SNYDER: Occasional gatherings of the tribe . . . tribes! That wasn't a point . . . it was an activity . . .

Say rather that group marriage . . . extended families. Extended co-operation structures, in other words. American Indian technologies, meditation centers, extended cooperative clan type . . . or extended family type structures with much more permissiveness in the nature of the family structure than is permitted, say, in Judaeo-Christian tradition, and gatherings of the larger tribes periodically.

VFA: Gary, in a tribal situation, isn't it true that the tribe has a fantastic distrust of other tribes, and there is a whole set of magic rituals set up to protect itself from other tribes?

SNYDER: Not necessarily . . . No . . .

LEARY: I think that when Gary talks about tribes, he's not talking about . . . just the past . . . what we can learn from the past . . . I think that we can learn from the history of tribal relationships that there has been this neighborly antagonism . . . this territorial—distrust.

GINSBERG: The Jivaros . . .

SNYDER: What a beautiful trip.

vfA: We'll have a common enemy—for some time, which will make that . . .

GINSBERG: An enemy? Wait a minute . . .

vfA: A common enemy, in that, there will be people trying to destroy this concept taking place in actuality . . .

LEARY: All the German tribes got together to protect against the Romans.

Which will lead to practical step number five . . . I think that some thought should be given—to organizing a legal protection—for our co-religionists.

Now we want to avoid any sort of leadership, or tight organization, but there must be some way to work out models in tribal alliance . . . to defend ourselves—lovingly, against the legions of Caesar.

The model that we worked out, which our lawyers tell us, looks pretty good . . . is—that the tribe gets together and puts down on paper, its tribal code, its sacraments, its rituals, its center; and it states very clearly that it is going to worship—this way, in this place.

Specifically what that means is that any group of people can get together and put down on paper—how they worship.

Which, by the way, is a good exercise in seeing how centered the group is. Because it makes psychedelic sense as well as legal sense. And, then . . . The group is protected legally to worship . . .

I would like some practical consideration given to how we can provide—legal protection. The model that we've worked out—of a group getting together and filing papers, for what is essentially a license . . .

GINSBERG: How has that worked out so far? Martin Garvus, in New York, filed papers as an injunction against the FDA.

LEARY: We're waiting until I get back.

A Good Court Case

SNYDER: I don't know how this would work, but if one good court case, or a freedom of religion issue was won in the Supreme Court—that would solve the problem down the line just about, wouldn't it?

LEARY: No, it doesn't! Because we have to take into account, Caesar's anxiety about what we're doing. It's got to be done on a tribe by tribe basis.

That is, your tribe has got to file . . . Allen's tribe will help your tribe. You'll lose in California, perhaps, because the lower court judge was unsympathetic; but you'll win in New York State.

SNYDER: This issue will be won in the courts, though?

LEARY: Yes, we'll attempt to set up—an overall church hierarchy, but simply that . . .

WATTS: To put this down specifically, you are saying that small clubs of people, who are like minded, should incorporate themselves as non-profit religious organizations and should state their constitution, their by-laws, their liturgy.

LEARY: In every state, you can get a corporation form for a very small amount of money. If you want to start a bowling alley, with three of your friends, it's all down there.

You just fill out the places, in this mimeographed form, and file it . . . It doesn't cost any money to file it, and you've got a legally incorporated religion. It's so simple to do.

WATTS: Yes, but there needs to be spelled out the absolutely practical A-B-C legal terms in which this can be done.

Incorporated Religion

LEARY: Well, I suggest that the next issue of the *Oracle* carry a half page, or a full page—manual on how to form your own religion.

vfA: One of the steps there is that . . . in incorporating—there should be nothing in the rules of the corporation that is illegal—in the state of California. That means that if the group is going to use LSD or marijuana—it could not incorporate.

LEARY: . . . you don't worry about that. If five hundred groups form in California—and, of course, it's moot.

It's unsettled as to whether illegal or not, and immediately, there's your first case. If they say it's illegal, then you say, what's illegal? Holy marijuana—that's been in use for five thousand years? There's your first case.

Instead of being paranoid, and waiting for the police to bust you on Haight-Ashbury, let's take a loving-game move to clarify the situation, which *really* disturbs the police and it disturbs the San Francisco papers and it disturbs the San Francisco legislature. Let's take this first initiatory step towards them.

SNYDER: Well, the ACLU, Marshall Krause and Dick Wertheimer, are trying to figure how to get up a *good* grass case, right now. And move it through as a test case.

Unorganized Objectors

WATTS: Well, let's go back and take a certain historical perspective on this once again. For example, a parallel problem arises with regard to conscientious objection.

There are a lot of conscientious objectors who don't belong to any form of religion. They're not to say, Quakers or Jehovah's Witnesses, and their objections are based on philosophical grounds.

Well, *at last,* the government has been moved to give fair consideration to these cases.

Now, on the same principle, freedom of religion does not involve that you belong to a specific organization or that you have belonged to this religion for so long.

After all, supposing St. Paul had been challenged on the Damascus road . . . How long have you belonged to the Christian church?
LEARY: But practically, Alan, it does . . .
WATTS: Now, but this has to be argued . . .
LEARY: Because this case that was argued in Los Angeles last week was lost, because the fellow was busted and then he had to prove afterwards.

If he had simply filed a paper ahead of time, before he was busted, the strength of his legal argument would have been much stronger.
WATTS: Yes, but the thing is still unconstitutional, because the constitution does *not* say . . . that to exercise freedom of religion, you must have belonged to a group of x number of people for such and such a time in order to prove your sincerity . . .
LEARY: But practically, the judges want you to . . .
WATTS: It's your conscience.
GINSBERG: This case has to go on appeal still . . .
LEARY: Oh, I . . . I bless it and I hope that it does go on appeal.

The Anarchist's Credo

SNYDER: I have a very strong feeling about a lot of what Alan says here. An old left-wing political type of organization, namely the anarchists . . . blessed be their memory . . .

Good old anarchists practiced one thing, and that was they wouldn't use the courts.

And a conscientious anarchist, if robbed, and able to identify his assailant, would not turn his assailant into the police because . . .
LEARY: Why do that?

SNYDER: Because, he said, if I'm going to be an anarchist and deny that I need the state I'm also going to deny that I need to go to the state for protection.

And I feel very much the same way about . . .

LEARY: I think that's romantic, Gary. I see a situation . . .

SNYDER: I'm not going to go to a lawyer and ask him to incorporate me, you know. . . .

GINSBERG: Did you go to a lawyer to get married or divorced or anything?

SNYDER: Yeah, but I mean in terms of a religion.

GINSBERG: Yeah, because you can prove you're a big, formal Buddhist.

SNYDER: I can't prove it, actually, no. I really wouldn't feel like doing that, and I don't think the people at the Maha-lila feel like doing that.

LEARY: We're not telling anyone what to do. We're suggesting a way of dealing with this mutant revolutionary problem. I see us as in a dark ages.

We're little tribes getting together; there's feudal lords and barons and kings and dukes and so forth. And they own the land because they've got steel and we're under bayonet point.

SNYDER: That's too paranoid. We're on the verge of winning, really.

LEARY: Oh, no doubt about that.

Money Begets?

WATTS: Yes, because the people who are wielding the bayonets have no satisfactory life and they know . . .

You know, it's like producing all sorts of goods that are increasingly inferior, and you make lots of money, and then you've made the money, and what are you going to spend it on? There's only the inferior goods made by the other people who are in the same racket as you are . . .

LEARY: All right. Practical Step Number 6, which was suggested by Allen's last comment about conscientious objectors: once you start these little religious groups you automatically have a solution to the draft problem.

At Millbrook we formed our little religious group. People come to me all the time and say, "What should I do about the draft?" And I say, "DON'T JOIN IT! DON'T JOIN THE ARMY!"

And once you start your religion, since we are a belief that everyone is Buddha in the religion, everyone is either a guru or a monk or on the road, there's automatic protection against the draft which forces young seed carriers to kill other seed carriers.

Legal Solution

So that the tribal solution, to establish yourself legally as a tribe, as a religious totem tribe, not only protects you in your use of the sacrament, but it protects you in many ways—it protects you in the handling of money.

If you go out and make money, then you have to pay in income tax. The income tax then goes to support the war in Vietnam.

If you form a religion, the money that's taken in is used for the religion . . . the formation of the legal tribal groups . . . I don't think we should be *romantic* anarchists . . .

SNYDER: You're the one who said, "Drop out."

LEARY: This is the way to drop out.

SNYDER: But you're accusing us of being romantic if we say we don't want to use lawyers when we drop out.

LEARY: All right, fine, I admire you for dropping out farther than I am. (laughter)

SNYDER: Farther than thou. (laughter)

LEARY: I assure you, Gary, that as soon as I've done this little yoga bit of passing on what I've learned and what I've thought about, I'm dropping out too. I'm not going to spend the rest of my life . . .

GINSBERG: What would you like to do?

"Baby Hash"

LEARY: I'm going to go away to a beach and live on the beach. I'm going to take LSD once a week and I'm going to take hashish once a day at sunset and I'm going to have babies and I'm going to learn from our babies.

SNYDER: That's beautiful. What are you going to do?

WATTS: I'll tell you. I am trying to act as a pontifex, which is a bridge-builder, between two worlds: the world of the people who are anxious and concerned and square and think that they can use their wills to put things right, and therefore are asking what should be done and what should not be done; and on the other hand, the people who know that this is a delusion and a farce, and are dropping out.

And I'm going to stay *bang* in the middle and I'm going to learn the languages of both tribes.

SNYDER: What'll you do after that?

WATTS: This will take me the rest of my life. (laughter)

SNYDER: Tim was talking about what he was going to do after that.

LEARY: No, I want to comment on what Alan has done in the last ten, fifteen, twenty . . . I don't know how long you've been doing it . . . you have been living completely dropped out. And the tribute you paid Gary, I think should be paid to you. You've never collected your IBM check from the Establishment.

And you have influenced hundreds of thousands of people, millions of people.

WATTS: But that's only to say, Tim, that I've been in the position of somebody running his own private business. I'm my own employer, I run my own business, like somebody who runs a barber shop on the corner or . . .

LEARY: I wouldn't say that. I would say you're a wandering guru. You don't attach yourself to an ashram. You are, in the classic sense of the word, the perfect, effective, wandering mendicant.

WATTS: Yes, it's true I do that, but I also support seven dependents.

LEARY: Which is a trick that most gurus couldn't do.

WATTS: And therefore I'm concerned to stay in the bridge position between these two worlds.

LEARY: Well, suppose we had a tribal situation which would take over the support of seven dependents.

GINSBERG: I want my tribe card! What I want is to get some land and settle there, alone or with people, with enough money to support electricity and a large house, and fiddle around with manuscripts and go walking in the woods and then rush off and take a plane to India. That's what I'd like to do.

LEARY: What are you going to do in India?

GINSBERG: In India, just wander around and then apply for a visa to China . . . and find out how a tribal society does there, too.

WATTS: I'll tell you what I want to do after all . . . when I'm through with this bridge-building business, when I'm over seventy years of age, I'm going to retire to a small plot of land . . .

LEARY: Would you say "drop out," Alan? (laughter)

Psychedelic Herbs

WATTS: Well, I'll tell you. I'm going to cultivate an herb garden, and there will be three patches. They'll be very small, one for culinary herbs, one for medicinal herbs, and one for psychedelic herbs.

And alongside this little tiny garden, where the herbs grow, there will be a big wooden barn where they will all be hanging up to dry—in their little jars . . . (laughter) And I'll putter around there as an old man.

That's beyond my present ideal of trying to be an interpreter, of not only East to West, but of the squares to the underground.

LEARY: The young to the old.

GINSBERG: Yeah, but if everything were reversed properly, wouldn't the squares become the Bodhisattvas, really? What if we had a *real* revolution and we were all wrong?

Ground of the Universe

WATTS: Yes, but the squares are the very far-out people because they don't know where they started from.

You see, if by virtue of a psychedelic experience you know where you started from, you know that you are basically the Ground of the Universe.

But all these poor people *are* the Ground of the Universe, which has forgotten itself, and has gotten itself into a completely far-out situation, where it doesn't know where it started. And so you must say to them: "Congratulations."

LEARY: Practical Suggestion Number 6 is: I suggest that we have a series of Be-Ins starting in Europe in the middle of the summer, and that we continue to have Be-Ins across Europe, perhaps retracing the steps of the Crusades. We could call it a Crusade of Penitence or . . .

SNYDER: Children's Crusade.

LEARY: Yeah, the Children's Crusade . . . And that we have a series of Be-Ins . . . Not that all of us have to be there, but some of us could drop in and on, and work towards the East this way. Because, I'm convinced that what was started at the Human Be-In in San Francisco generated a momentum which must not be lost because of our particular predilections with our own fantasies. And, without tight organization or leadership, but cellular collaboration, I'd like to see this thing move as cells always move, or as clouds move, across this anguished and increasingly metallic planet . . .

GINSBERG: "Anguished and increasingly metallic!"

LEARY: Bad poetry?

GINSBERG: No, that was nice.

LEARY: So I suggest that we have meetings in cities April 21st. I suggest we have one national meeting perhaps June 21st, and that we start moving through Europe to the East so that we would, on September 21st, be on the door between India and China, with as many Indians or

Westerners or people that we've picked up on the way . . . I think that's the quickest way to end racial prejudice and the war in Vietnam.

Cross Cultural Purposes

SNYDER: Some cultures are not going to understand this; they're not ready for it.

GINSBERG: You're not going to get more than 20,000 people, and that was done anyway by Shankara-deo and he got stopped at the border of Burma. The Burmese let him through but the Chinese wouldn't let him through, and the Indians were upset . . .

SNYDER: There's a social-historical problem here: California is the only place that is ready for this, probably . . . Like, you couldn't do this in Japan.

LEARY: It's already done that. Why not?

SNYDER: No, but you can't do it yet. A great percentage of the world is going to have to move through the drama of Western culture and technology in some accelerated way, before they're ready for this.

America is the only culture in which a number of people have seen through it and are able to go beyond it.

Japan isn't ready to, for example. It would be incredibly eccentric for them. Nobody's ready to try it out.

Pepsi Degeneration

LEARY: I question that. I think that if you look at the spread of American ideology, France is just now starting its superdrugstores. You must not fail to realize that the authentic . . . deep American spirit behind this. And I think that if it's taken fifteen years for France to accept the superdrugstore, why not six months to accept the Be-In in San Francisco?

See, the way they spread drugs or Coca-Cola or Pepsi-Cola was, when Coca-Cola first showed up in the Grand Canal in Venice or Coca-Cola first showed up in Pakistan, it was considered eccentric.

But if Pepsi-Cola can do it, the energy and the cellular productivity which started here can move much more quickly because it's talking to deeper things in the human being than Pepsi-Cola.

I think this thing should start moving.

SNYDER: So many of these people in Africa and Asia are caught up in the drama of progress.

vfA: They want nothing more than to come to America and get a large apartment and a large car . . .

SNYDER: This is part of the paradox.

LEARY: We can tell them . . . I feel the same way about the problem with the American Negro. Does he have to become a middle-class white before he can then go on and leave that? I don't think we have to go through these historical periods, I think it's possible to move it faster and to jump . . .

SNYDER: Well, I hope it's possible to accelerate it but you can't take it around the world this year, or next year . . .

LEARY: Are you sure?

SNYDER: Yeah . . . I'm sure . . .

GINSBERG: If we all got together and tried we could.

Ten Men in a Drop-out

LEARY: I say ten people—ten men—who really would give to it can change this planet within a year. Ten men who would . . . drop out.

SNYDER: If we change America we are changing the planet.

LEARY: I'd like to have an electrician in my tribe.

vfA: Everything that's been said here tonight is in the air, in Haight-Ashbury, right now. There's a movement for people to set up small, organic cooperatives; not formal but small, organic cooperatives. There is a movement for people to move to the land, they want to get out of the city.

There's only one thing, this would naturally set up small religions on the land, and that's where they should be.

There is only one thing that I can see that is missing, and that is the land itself. If there is some way . . .

As you said, Tim, we can get together without getting structured, perhaps, to encourage people to set up small religious groups, perhaps we can get together in some way to make it possible for people without money to acquire a small amount of land and go and live on the land and work on the land.

I don't know if this is possible.

vfA: But the way to do it is by transferring information from people who already have done it!

You see, we're not creating anything. It's happening already, all we have to do is look at where it's happening and link those together—just as far as the knowledge and the experience of one group—and give that to those embryonic groups that aren't going already.

vfa: Just give them some legal status so that they can work the land . . .

In other words, so that they can pay rent for it or buy it. Because when you drop out, you don't have money and it's difficult to acquire land.

Alan can do it, but you know, Alan's got something going for him but the kids haven't. They haven't got money to acquire the land, and they're looking for land.

LEARY: That's ridiculous, OK . . . Suppose eight or ten or five couples or a group of eight or ten meet, in the Haight-Ashbury district, in one of those meditation centers we set up.

They say, hey, we want to get some land. Then they go to work maybe for six months. They all take jobs and they all live in one house. So instead of paying eight rents, they pay one rent, and in that short period they make enough money to get started. That's no problem.

GINSBERG: Yeah, but the conditions described here don't really obtain in New York. What do you do in New York?

LEARY: New York needs a tremendous amount of spiritual help and . . .

SNYDER: I don't think you live in New York.

GINSBERG: There's a lot of very beautiful people living in New York.

SNYDER: Well, if they all moved out of New York, they'd still be beautiful, and you could meet them someplace else.

GINSBERG: That's a possibility. You may have to go up to northern New York to . . .

SNYDER: No, the gathering of the tribes is the model of that. Cities are nothing but extended tribal gatherings which have become stabilized and made sort of semi-permanent.

Like, what were originally temporary markets, temporary dances and temporary gatherings. Except nobody goes away. They just stay there all the time.

Now, you go to New York because you want to see your friends and because the action is there. Now that's only about a thousand people, really.

If those thousand people were living in the middle of the prairie in Nebraska, you'd go to the middle of the prairie in Nebraska, you see? Instead of New York . . .

GINSBERG: Yeah, but I enjoy the beehive hum of New York.

SNYDER: Well, you're corrupt . . . You're a transitional figure, Ginsberg. . . . (laughter)

vfa: Do you think as well when you live in New York?

GINSBERG: Yeah, and slightly different thoughts.

LEARY: Allen is the mayor of one of the busiest, most populous precincts of New York.

A Deer Park

SNYDER: It's not an environment one would want to live in because the air is filthy . . .

GINSBERG: It's certainly interesting to figure out what to do with New York. But what are we going to do with seven million people?

SNYDER: Seven million people will be dead within seventy years.

GINSBERG: So you think the shells of buildings will be left standing and there will be a reduced population?

SNYDER: Why not?

LEARY: There will be deer grazing in Times Square in forty years.

GINSBERG: . . . Hell, possibly!

SNYDER: They'll just think of something else, and leave it behind. That's happened to many cities . . . Look at Angkor-Wat, they all left it.

LEARY: Rome, Jerusalem . . . Chichen Itza, Alexandria, etc. . . .

GINSBERG: Oh yeah, but where are seven million people going to go?

SNYDER: They're going to die.

GINSBERG: They're all going to die, and not have children?

SNYDER: Their children won't necessarily be there. Some may want to go someplace else.

GINSBERG: What are you going to do with seven million children?

SNYDER: They'll be someplace else.

GINSBERG: When? Seven million people take a lot of land.

SNYDER: No, they just spread out. (laughter) Like, what happened to the children of the people who left Angkor-Wat? They left it.

GINSBERG: Some got killed.

SNYDER: A lot of them got killed. A lot of people are going to die.

GINSBERG: Now, how do you think this is going to happen? People are just going to die off, or . . .

SNYDER: No, people are going to change their feelings. The drama is changing. What people are interested in is not things but states of mind. That is the cultural shift that is taking place now.

WATTS: Now, this is a very important statement.

SNYDER: We've turned a corner. It's a bigger corner than the Reformation, probably. It's a corner on the order of the change between Paleolithic and Neolithic.

It's like one of the three or four major turns in the history of man— not just culture—but man.

WATTS: Right. Now. An enormous number of people go into the heart of New York every day for no other reason than to shop.

They are to a large extent frustrated women living in those wretched dormitories. Their husbands are working, and the women go in in order to get some kind of a sense of existence, of being, by buying things!

Now suppose it happens that, instead of that, they change their state of mind; and instead of going out and getting goosed by buying something, they change their state of mind sitting where they are in the first place.

Then Bonwit Teller . . . everything in the middle of town, simply collapses! Lord & Taylor, and so on, have no more reason for existence.

It's like Market Street in San Francisco, where everything is slowly falling apart because it's so ridiculous to park there and you can't get at the place, anyhow.

GINSBERG: But where are people going to buy their Uher tape recorder machines . . .

SNYDER: Suppose they don't want them?

GINSBERG: Well, we all have them.

SNYDER: But we're transitional figures . . .

LEARY: We'll buy 'em from Vietnam . . . ?

SNYDER: We don't need them. I would be happy to hear Larry Bird sing his Corn Dance and I don't want to tape it. I'll hear it and that's in my mind for the rest of my life.

WATTS: Right.

GINSBERG: I mean, the problem here is there's a withering away of the state. In an advanced technology such as we are talking about you can imaginatively transform it into some Buckminster Fuller process, you know, and each individual tribe can operate and create whatever it needs. Other than that there is the technology as we know it now, like a large electronic network.

SNYDER: I think that the technology withers away as people learn to do it themselves. It's more interesting to do it yourself at home with your friends. Like, sit around and blow the buffalo horn and blow the conch horn and not turn on the television.

GINSBERG: That was like conditions that were possible when the continent held fifteen million Indians. But now the continent holds a great many more.

WATTS: The whole problem is reproduction. It's not only the reproduction of the species in a sexual way, but reproduction as we are now reproducing what we are saying on tape.

Because if, supposing this conversation were very turned on and far out (I don't know whether it is or not) people would say: "Oh, what a pity that didn't get recorded."

Because, see, "It didn't really *happen* unless it was recorded." And increasingly we're developing all kinds of systems for verifying reality by echoing it.

SNYDER: Well, trained minds remember and the words of the Buddha were all remembered by oral tradition. And they came down for two hundred years before anybody put it down in writing because people were paying attention to what he said.

vfA: Only then did they start embellishing it.

WATTS: But Krishnamurti would argue that remembering it was already a fallacy.

SNYDER: Well, he's very pure. (laughter)

That which is really worthwhile is what you remember. And if you've forgotten it, it wasn't that great. Or, like, if you can't remember it then that's too bad.

Part of what happens to us with civilization is that we lose the faculty of memory. In non-literate civilizations the capacity to remember and transmit songs and tales and myths is extraordinary.

Like, Melville Herskovitz, when he did his field work in Dahomey, found one raconteur who could tell 3,500 folk tales, all different.

vfA: Gary, in anthropology isn't it true that when you train yourself and learn an oral tradition, writing is not necessary and it's only when we start to use words that we've lost the oral tradition?

LEARY: Written words.

Self-Editing

SNYDER: The thing about the oral tradition is that it's self-editing and that which is not worth saving drops out. So you don't get this extraordinary accumulation of trivia in the libraries.

vfA: At the same time, we should realize the cybernetic civilization is taking place and that people disgusted with the cybernetic civilization are dropping away and becoming whatever it is . . . something else.

There is a division, because the children of the people who drop out, don't drop back in. Their tribal customs are different. They look different. The children follow the adults and so on.

GINSBERG: I don't think they are all gonna go out on a limb. I think they'll wind up dropping back in.

vfA: You have to be loving while this transition is taking place so that it doesn't get bloody. Because if it should get bloody, then you lose the core of the consciousness that's trying to come through.

Because if you have to resist evil on its terms, you have to take some of that poison into yourself and therefore dilute what's taking place.

So the loving attitude has got to be thought of constantly. People must be educated in that regard.

GINSBERG: What's interesting about that is that finally in Vietnam— what you do have is a collection of tribes being organized by various parties and finding themselves in the middle of a large-scale fight.

What do you feel about Rubin and Savio's concern with Vietnam? I saw Savio weeping about the Vietnam war . . . an image of the Vietnam war in his mind.

"Pot": Rebellion or Religion

LEARY: Well, that's a different thing. I respect his sincerity, but his tactics are part of the game which created the Vietnam war—power politics.

I want to suggest Practical Suggestion Number 99, and that is some way of reminding the young people who are being busted for pot that they are involved in something tremendously holy.

In India today the people who have the most respect, in some quarters, are those who went to jail for their principles during the independence fight. You can't be a politician in India today unless you went to jail with Gandhi.

I see the people being put in jail today for the possession of marijuana as being in a very similar position.

I would say that ninety per cent of the people in jail in the United States today (and there must be forty or fifty thousand of them) belong to three groups: they are either young, creative or they are minority groups.

There are very few *white, middle-class* Americans in jail for possession of marijuana.

I think it is important to give the young pot smokers and the young acidheads a sense of their historical meaning, that they're doing the most important thing that could be done, that they're not rebels. The choice is between being rebellious and being religious.

GINSBERG: Do you feel, for instance . . . I was talking about that the other day and someone mentioned the young cats who went south as activists for the Negroes—who felt that they had like an equal perception of reality around them and were like, really heroic, and were doing as much as any drug group for extension of consciousness and extension of relationships.

LEARY: I don't think so. You see, I feel very clear about this one issue, that you can't *do* good unless you *feel* good. You can't do right unless you feel right.

I think it's so easy to an American to go off to another place where you look down on a primitive people and spread the missionary zeal.

I think that many of the white middle-class intellectuals who went south during the civil rights movements were like Baptist missionaries, who went to far-out places to make themselves feel virtuous.

I don't think any good was done by that.

GINSBERG: You can say the same thing about anybody who's taking acid, to make themselves virtuous . . . So, if you go south with that sense, yes . . . But I'm impressed by the quality of the people that I met who have been south, or by the quality of their statements, or by the quality of their art.

vfA: If we are telling the kids they are doing something holy, to a certain extent we have to be a little bit holy. Holiness is giving and we have to learn to give.

The Diggers have said that, since the Be-In on January 14, thousands and thousands of kids—who don't really know where they're at, but who are attracted because they want to know where they are at, have come to the city.

But they come to the city and they don't know whether to be defiant; they don't know what to be. And unless they can become bridges for themselves, each person a bridge for themselves so they can show what they *have* got is something giving.

Yet the message doesn't get across.

vfA: We've got to become saints.

SNYDER: Which is not even a silly thing to say.

Meditation Centers

LEARY: They've got to be told that they're pursuing the holiest role.

Well, again, if we had these meditation centers in all cities there would be centers where the Gita would be read, where the ancient Sutras would be read, where they would be reminded. This is not teaching . . .

SNYDER: What we need is personal example all over the place.

LEARY: I would suggest that in these meditation centers there be some program of readings, not in the sense of educating or teaching facts, but just *reminding* young people and any person who drops out and turns on that they are a part of an ancient profession, the only holy profession.

The profession has kept the flame going and it certainly should express itself in pushing that Mercedes.

vfA: Do you think it's practical to try to get some sort of meditation in the public schools?

LEARY: No. Drop out of the public schools. The public schools cannot be compromised with.

vfA: Why say you can't compromise with the public schools if you're going to compromise with the technology?

LEARY: We're not compromising with IBM or General Electric. We're simply saying, as Gary has said, that part of man's karmic heritage is the ability to do incredible things with his hands and his analytic mind. But they should be holy things.

SNYDER: It's a question of right occupation or right conduct. It's not that technology is bad, or that schools are bad.

Joy and Delight

WATTS: Well, now look here. What are we saying when we say something is holy? That means that you should take a different attitude to what you are doing than you were, for example, doing it for kicks.

Now there's a curious thing here. I have noticed with Allen Ginsberg that when he chants Hindu sutras he doesn't do it in a pious way.

There's a *joyousness* and a feeling of *delight* to doing this chant that has more zip to it than anything we knew in the past as being holy.

Now when you were doing something holy in the past you had to put on a solemn expression of saying we are doing this but it hurts, but it's good for us. He is not doing that when he chants that.

He's not saying it hurts and therefore it's good for me. He's saying it's good for me because I enjoy it. It's gorgeous!

I'm going right in there and I'm going to say all these Om Hare Rama Krishna Rama Hare Rama Hare et cetera. You see?

LEARY: He's turning himself on.

WATTS: Right. I told some nuns a little while ago, when the mother superior came and they were all talking about the reform of the liturgy and how the Catholic church has gotten itself into a mess by translating the Latin liturgy into terrible English and all the magic has gone out of it. And I said you should come and listen to Allen Ginsberg chant the sutras because then you'd know how to celebrate mass properly.

So, when we are talking about something being holy, we've got to be very careful.

Gary, you were saying all right, people have got to be saints, and you said—well, that's not just a joke to say this.

But it's got to be saints in an entirely new sense. Not this masochistic kind of sainthood, whereby: "I am holy because I hurt and the amount of personal hurt that I've piled up is the *measure* of my holiness."

SNYDER: Well, that's the Judaeo-Christian idea that says, the Cross is at the center of the universe.

LEARY: Of course, what most Americans don't realize is that the Buddha was the greatest hipster of all, in the sense that he was the person that was teaching people how to up-level suffering and to turn on.

Krishna! Krishna! Krishna!

GINSBERG: So what do you think of Swami Bhaktivedanta pleading for the acceptance of Krishna in every direction?

SNYDER: Why it's a lovely positive thing to say Krishna. It's a beautiful mythology and it's a beautiful practice.

LEARY: Should be encouraged.

GINSBERG: He feels it's the one uniting thing. He feels a monopolistic unitary thing about that.

WATTS: I'll tell you why I think he feels this. The mantrams, the images of Krishna, have in this culture no *foul* associations. The word God is contaminated, so Tillich would say "The Ground of Being" instead of God.

The words: "Get down on your knees and be humble before your heavenly father." That gives everybody the *creeps*. It's just awful to say something like that, you see, because all these Christian images have horrible associations attached to them.

Whereas when somebody comes in from the Orient with a new religion which hasn't got any of these associations in our minds, all the words are new, all the rites are new, and yet, somehow it has feeling in it, and we can get with that, you see, and we can dig that!

And it can do something for us that it can't do in Japan. For example, in Japan, when young people hear the Buddha sutra chanted they think oohhh! Don't let's hear that thing, because they associate all that with "fogeyism."

Here in the Buddhist churches, in the Niseis, they can't stand it when the priests chant the sutras in Sino-Japanese language for the oldsters.

They want to hear: (singing) "Buddha loves me this I know, for the Sutra tells me so." (laughter)

They want to be as much as they can like Protestants because that's exotic to them.

GINSBERG: But what about India, where we do have a giant psychedelic community and many tribal groups and tribal gatherings which serve as a model for our own? What kind of a material system is that, and would that be acceptable to Mario Savio?

SNYDER: Sure it's acceptable. There's only one trouble with India and that's things like goats.

WATTS: Goats!

Ecological Ignorance

SNYDER: Because the goats eat the trees. As soon as you plant young seedling trees the goats eat them.

So India has for the last thousand years suffered from a blight of deforestation.

So again there is a kind of ecological ignorance that has plagued India for about a millennium now . . . water and land use ignorance. And that begins because they are far too removed from their primitive understanding and connection with things.

Like something really seems to go wrong when you get into agriculture. As soon as people get into agriculture they lose a sense of animals and of wild plants and they lose those connections.

Like I'm not saying what to do about that, but there is a very important thing there that's lost. Just like the whole use of natural psychedelics goes out when we enter agriculture.

The tribes, the peoples who knew what plants would turn you on, are generally primitive and non-agricultural.

As soon as you get onto agriculture you become concerned with cultivated plants and the whole knowledge of the use of wild herbs and wild plants drops out.

The Oracle Speaks

LEARY: Practical suggestion 99A . . . (laughter) We all put words down, but I think that each of us should contribute when we feel like it, perhaps the yoga of once a month, a few paragraphs or perhaps a page or two to the *Oracle*. We can use the *Oracle* as our means of sharing . . .

GINSBERG: Well, you see, that is already building a politics and an organization.

vfa: You don't have to call it an organization.

GINSBERG: We share the *Oracle* and the *Oracle* is distributed in nine cities. So that already involves us in dropping in again.

SNYDER: I don't mind that.

LEARY: I don't want pay for it.

SNYDER: This whole goddam dualism or whatever it is, this confusion bugs me.

LEARY: Allen is upset about my saying drop out. He's not ready yet; Allen, drop out when you're ready. Don't worry about it, drop out when you're ready.

GINSBERG: But I'm not worried, I'm having a good time.

SNYDER: I've never been in, what I'm interested in is building a new society.

GINSBERG: I think the whole thing of "in" and "out" is a mistake someway.

vfa: Well, we live with it. We live within the illusion, so being in or out is really absurd.

SNYDER: Like people say—"Beatniks are all conformists," as they said at one time, but that's irrelevant. Of course, you're conformists to a different order of things.

Hell's Happening

WATTS: Well, let's look at it in another way. Robert Oppenheimer is reported to have said, quite recently that, "Obviously the world is going to hell, and the only way that it could be stopped was not to try to prevent it from happening." (laughter)

LEARY: The guy who invented the atomic bomb. (laughs nervously)

WATTS: In other words, when there is a game going on that is on a collision course, and when this game is obviously going to lead to total destruction, the only way to get people out of the bad game is to indicate that the game is no longer interesting.

See, we've left this game and it bores us and we've got something going on over here which is where it's at, you know.

This is where it's at, and everybody is playing this game, you know, and they'll end up playing like YEAOOW on the mark and suddenly they realize that that's not where it's at.

So many people today are on the other side. Let's go out in the Haight-Ashbury and see what's happening over there because maybe something's happening!

SNYDER: Instead of the emphasis on the dropping out, and I think it worth the point to say there's something else going on.

GINSBERG: It doesn't sound alliteratively correct though. Tune in, turn on . . . there's something else by God! (laughter) Unless his language is interpreted in a way which is understandable and acceptable . . .

WATTS: Well now, look here Tim, in that thing at Santa Monica you made two points. One was: (a) you can't stay high all the time because when you finally come down from the high you realize that the ordinary state of consciousness is one with the high state.

This to me has been the most fantastic thing in all my LSD experiences. That the moment I come down is the critical moment of the whole experience. I suddenly realize that this everyday world around me is exactly the same thing as the world of the beatific vision.

Now, then, how do you integrate that realization with the drop-out?

Banned in Seattle

LEARY: Now, Seattle, you know, we were banned in Seattle. We went up there to talk about menopausal mentality and drop out. And at all the cocktail parties they said: "What does he mean?" drop out, menopausal, menopausal, drop out? I would agree to change the slogan to "drop out, turn on, drop in."

WATTS: Yes, there's always been the pattern. You have got to go alone into the silence, into the isolation, and then come back.

LEARY: It should be better, "drop out, turn on, drop in."

GINSBERG: The other one sounded prettier.

LEARY: Yeah, it's too easy, and youth should figure that out for themselves.

WATTS: But the thing is, that at the moment, it is strongly indicated that all the values which are creating the disturbance, that is to say acquisitive values, that of buying things, possessing them, holding on to property, etc, etc. Suddenly this has become of no interest to the people who are really with it.

GINSBERG: That's where the point of it is really; that there is an actual, empirical, cultural change.

SNYDER: It's not just in our heads.

WATTS: Now we've got to remember, that at the same time, and this has to sort of be stated for the record, there is always an illusion, which is referred to in the Gospels, ". . . do not pay attention to them when they say of the Messiah!" Now he is here, now he is there, now he is in the inner room, now he's in, you know, some little secret society that's going on, something special. *All* is the special thing.

Upaya

First of all it seems to be what some group has got that's out beyond you. But really, that's the donkey's carrot, you know, tied to a collar, dangling in front of him.

You'll never get it because you have it. Really, you have the thing that is where it's at in your self all the time, only it always looks as if it's out there, some group has got it.

But the thing is that the wise group of people who are in the know, these people who know that you have it yourself, in you, you don't have to go to East Village, to the Haight-Ashbury, to anywhere, Big Sur, etc. It's with you all the time.

But the group that indicates that it's in us, will seem to the others, as if they had it out there, and they'll become beguiled and interested. That is what is called in Buddhism, *upaya,* skillful means, a kind of trickery. (laughter)

LEARY: It's no question that we're suffering less, because we're striving less and that can't be underestimated in energy power. Anyone who came to the Be-In can see we're suffering less.

SNYDER: And you're suffering less if you learn how to accept suffering.

LEARY: When we're sitting around this table, we are suffering less.

WATTS: The thing that was so fascinating about the Be-In was that I . . . not having been able to be there, and having just read about it in the press . . . was that everybody was baffled as to what it was all about.

LEARY: No, just the press were.

A Need of Nonsense

WATTS: There must be something going on in every healthy culture which is, in a way, nonsense. If a culture cannot afford an area in itself where pure nonsense happens, and where it is not practical, it has no objectives, it was for no reason whatsoever . . . then this culture is dead.

Because, after all, God is the most useless thing in the universe.

But that God, you know, is in its own existence reality. The nature of reality is useless, it is not useful *for* something else, it is not a means to an end, it is not something that, when you look at it, you could say "So what?" Because it's *it!*

LEARY: I want to put in a plug for the old teaching.

WATTS: What do you think I've been talking about, Tim?

LEARY: You take these old things about the Bible and all the old prayers and just turn them in, instead of out, the mistake is always that . . . they have taken the internal fears of . . . "have no graven images before thee." That means don't get hung up on plastic plates. "Our Father who art in Heaven . . ."

WATTS: Don't get hung up on *that* Father bit . . .

LEARY: All the fathers and the mothers, you know: "Hail Mary full of grace." That's all it is, all the mothers, all the fathers. Great! As long as you center it inside.

Almost every prayer that has lasted more than two generations, cellular and mythic, works, if you address it within.

WATTS: In other words, when you get to the point in life when you realize that you're as stupid as your own grandfather, and therefore he no longer impresses you and you come to realize that you're out there just the same way he was.

SNYDER: My grandfather was an I.W.W. and he played a silver flute.

LEARY: I think it's important to know who everyone's grandfather was. Your grandfather was a "wobblie."

SNYDER: He was a wobblie, a homesteader, and he played a silver flute and sat in a black leather chair with a white mustache.

WATTS: My grandfather was private secretary to the Lord Mayor of London.

LEARY: Who is your grandfather?

GINSBERG: He was a black-hatted man with a black beard who came from Russia and walked down steps in Newark and said his prayers every day.

WATTS: Tim, who was your grandfather?

LEARY: Oh, he crawled out of a sludgy pool and learned how to breathe without gills.

WATTS: Oh God, I have another grandfather come to think of it. (laughter)

On my mother's side he was a bibliologer and I have, I don't know where they are now, they have disappeared, but I have wooden boxes full of all the books of the Bible in separate volumes carefully annotated, careful handwriting.

So we only missed one generation there.

SNYDER: It's just like the Indians. Like grandfather and the American Indians have their hair long and they follow the tribal ways.

The fathers have their hair cut short, they're Christians and they drive pick ups. The children are growing theirs long and they're joining the Native American Church.

LEARY: I have to leave now, and I want to make one motion, that we act upon every idea that was expressed tonight. (laughter)

GINSBERG: You were very clear tonight. Very clear. I would say a little . . . funky . . . at moments (laughter) but for practical suggestions, and for definition of drop-out . . .

LEARY: What were you tonight, Allen?

GINSBERG: The majesty of the law! (laughter) . . . just sitting here listening, and sort of reflecting my experiences in Berkeley.

LEARY: Yes, you've been very influenced by your turn-on session with Mario Savio. In addition to you turning him on, he turned *you* on . . . and you're concerned about him.

GINSBERG: Well, I sought him out.

LEARY: Yes, but still he turned you on, and you're concerned about him . . . and we consider him a tremendous energy center for good in this country, and that we want him to move along with us, dropping out, turning on, turning in and dropping out and dropping in and turning on. But he's got to keep turning on.

GINSBERG: Well, turn on to drugs necessarily? To marijuana or LSD?

LEARY: I mean get out of his game . . .

GINSBERG: He *is* . . . He lives without a telephone. He's less *gamed* than any of us.

And wondering whether the Haight-Ashbury people would survive because he's facing jail. As many are facing jail in the Haight-Ashbury, many are also facing jail there in Berkeley.

LEARY: Well, I'll give one message of reassurance to him: If anything will survive in the whole world, it's going to be Haight-Ashbury, because Haight-Ashbury's got two billion years behind it. I worry about Clark Kerr and Governor Reagan and the Berkeley activists, but one thing will survive, and it's what is going on . . .

GINSBERG: But there's some big weird fascist stomp-out, which is what he thinks about.

SNYDER: Yeah, but Tim is right. Weird fascist stomp-outs only last for a few generations.

GINSBERG: Now wait a minute!

SNYDER: Well, sometimes they last for a millennium.

WATTS: I suppose many people who are now in jail on charges of pot smoking and so on, will in a later age be regarded as martyrs and saints.

LEARY: Let's get away from martyrs; that's a messy game.

WATTS: Wait a minute . . . Aren't you playing that game?

LEARY: No.

SNYDER: Oh come on, Tim . . .

GINSBERG: That's a really good question. That's beautiful. Aren't you playing the martyr game?

LEARY: What! Don't you think I'm happier . . .

GINSBERG: It's whispered in all the urinals of Cornell that you're playing the martyr game. (laughter)

WATTS: Oh, you can be a happy martyr! But I do think that there may well be, in times to come, a second Saint Timothy. And I feel honored that you're with us this evening.

LEARY. We're writing our new myth . . . and we have to, in our sessions, relive the Christ thing, the Buddha thing, the Krishna thing . . .

WATTS: I know we do, right . . .

LEARY: We are creating a new myth, and we won't have saints.

WATTS: But we do it, everybody in his own way discovers the immemorial truth which has been handed down, and that's the only way you can get it.

Because you can't imitate it . . . you can only discover it out of your own thing, and by doing your own stuff you keep repeating the eternal pattern. This probably is the sort of situation we have.

LEARY: The seed-carrying soft body should not be embedded in steel, it does no one good, and I have no intention of going to jail, and I won't go to jail. No one should go to jail.

And I'm not going to provide any kind of model for people to go to jail for spiritual purposes.

WATTS: Well, that's gutsy; I like that. (laughs)

LEARY: That's cellular! Shanti, shanti.

WATTS: Shanti, shanti.

As editor and publisher of New York's East Village Other *for the last few years, Walter Bowart might seem uniquely unqualified to advertise the agrarian life. But his experiences with the so-called hippie renaissance in New York should be persuasive enough to deter those who still think that paradise can be found in an urban ghetto; as sociologists chart the population flow of movements like that of the hippies, the evidence suggests that many hippies are becoming converts to the Bowart philosophy. True, there will always be a New York, a San Francisco, and a Boston, but the best minds and the most creative life styles may be seen more frequently in New Buffalo or Taos. There is another incentive for the young in this migration; rural communities are often without phones ōr convenient airports, which has a certain charm if you're trying to escape.*

The Return to the Land

WALTER BOWART

While Congress cuts off the poverty funds and unrest grows in the "ghettos" of the poor in every major city in the country, and the head of the Department of Sanitation in America's largest city throws up his hands admitting that he cannot possibly keep the streets clean; while the air pollution grows worse and the coastline waters from Boston to Baltimore float more garbage, oil, and sewage than ever before with no sign of abatement; while another non-war is waged in Southeast Asia, making Brown and Root Company of Texas rich from constructing airstrips and landing docks; while the people gather in the streets for non-violent protests which are continually turned by police into violent demonstrations; while SDS and other political groups are thinking more and more of violence, unwittingly supporting a Fascist-Communist playoff as once occurred in Nazi Germany where the Nazis would not have been noticed if the Communists hadn't drawn the dialogue; while the President of a gangster government in a corrupt society reprimands the press and the demonstrators for violence started often by police following a carefully laid military plan designed to whip up and use a mob in accordance with the teachings of the late L. A. Police Chief Parker, and clearly explained by Canetti in his book *Crowds and Power*; while the newspapers and magazines publish scholarly psychiatrists'

The East Village Other, December 1, 1967

popular articles explaining from outdated Freudian positions why it's really the fault of parents that the kids are taking the LSD to which they will soon get addicted and nobody catches the lying or ignorance which is the main reason for "the generation gap" that is in reality only another "credibility gap"; while the outer-directed existential-nihilist remnants of the thirties are reaching a point of collapse and the cites teeter on ruin, many young minds are thinking of what it was that Moses did when he took his people into the wilderness for forty years.

Forty years is enough time for the old ones to die and the new ones to be born. If it is as Robert Graves and some other scholars think, the Jews had that magic mushroom, then it's easy to see that maybe Moses knew that old imprints could be suspended and new basic concepts of life imprinted during only one generation or forty years.

"After you take a little acid, you look around you in this city and see all the hate and fear and greed. The garbage in the streets can't be ignored, it's growing. And you see with your newly developed sensor that the air is brown and stale, and you begin to feel raw and yearn for a place where it's quieter and the energy radiation is softer," a tall sun-tanned young man just returned from the west was saying the other day in The City.

"I was born here in Brooklyn, but I've been living in Arizona for two years now, and coming back here is horrifying.

"In Arizona the landscape is great, the climate is perfect and there are only three million people in the whole state. I think that figures out to one person per square mile, and most of them are over sixty-five years old. Older people have learned tolerance, you know. I'm going back next week."

These casual words were uttered as the citizens of the largest city in the world's richest and most humanitarian country speculated and gossiped about a book, *Report from Iron Mountain* which was either a great work of satire or the gods-honest-truth; a report written in perfect bureaucratese proving beyond the shadow of a capitalist's doubt that world peace would be disastrous to the "free world's" economy.

As many prepared to leave the country the words of Horace Greeley came echoing back from 1851, "Go West, young man, go West."

The neighbors speculated about where all the hippies had gone as Californians, and Arizonians, and Okies, and Montanans poured into the east for the Washington Pentagon Exorcism, and many stayed and told stories, and many took back with them extra riders.

And the rumors ran that there was a plot afoot, to have in the "psychedelic free-American community" social, political, and economic power equivalent to at least the Mormons'.

Whispers spoke of taking over, by seeding, as had happened in Haight and Denver, a whole state which could then elect one or two Senators and some Representatives to go to Washington and ask some simple embarrassing questions or get censored or assassinated for at least being honest.

The Hudson Institute recently predicted that by the year 2000 we might possibly have an alternative "dropped out" country within this country. Meanwhile it is actually happening throughout the arid southwest.

In New Buffalo, about ten miles north of Santa Fe, it is often said, "When people come back to the southwest the rains will follow." Here in a tepee town local Indians are teaching city-dropouts how to build with adobe. The Pueblo Indians in the area have kept their life-style pretty much intact in the lonely New Mexico countryside where you can see over the sage from mesa to mesa nearly forty miles. The sixty-five pioneers at New Buffalo support themselves by working in nearby towns while they build their dream in the desert.

Taos, New Mexico, has for a long time been the center of much artistic activity. Outside of Taos a community of followers of the ways of Meher Baba has been established. This community has the financial means to build substantial buildings with plumbing and all the conveniences of a twentieth-century society.

More resourcefulness has been shown in Drop City, near Trinidad, Colorado. There refugees from the east are experimenting in putting into practice the concepts of Buckminster Fuller, building geodesic domes out of steel used car tops.

This past summer Timothy Leary toured the southwest visiting many of the "drop cities." The Denver papers rumored that Leary was thinking of establishing an ashram (a living-while-learning community) near Paradise, Arizona. Leary, while denying the report, strengthened a growing "new-age frontier" feeling by his visits to the scattered communities.

Meanwhile in many isolated towns throughout the southwest (such as Blin, located south of Albuquerque) individual "drop out" families are buying land at the going price of fourteen dollars per acre.

Unity comes in strange ways. Men are *forced* to move. Danger fosters the rescuing power. The two eternal forces, enlightenment and slavery, struggle on from yesterday.

There are no more frontiers. All terms have become inverted. The west has become east, giving birth to The Underground States of America.

As the boy scouts of the hip underground, the Diggers miraculously provide thousands of servings of stew a day, operate free stores, and offer community services. Disdainful of ideology, theirs is the dialectic of action. Diggers do, they say, and in spite of their predilection for burning money, they manage to substantiate the economics of free. Perhaps their anarchy is the source of their appeal.

Diggers Do

the diggers have been giving out, providing each other with free
FREE FOOD since the first week of October. and have never missed a day.
diggers have gone to jail for giving FREE SHOWS on the street.
diggers have gone to jail for suspicion of stealing
slabs of meat, sacks of potatoes, etc.
diggers have gone to jail for giving out free acid, grass, dope.
diggers have gone to jail simply because someone wanted them there.
but diggers have never gone to jail peace-fully-ably.

everyone tries to find out who sponsors the digger FREE FOOD. the
CP thinks it's in the SP, the SP thinks it's the CP, SDS thinks it's
PLP . . . they all know it's a conspiracy.
well the diggers despise conspiracy . . . the old left . . . the new left
. . . they're indifferent to their tactics and don't even bother talking
to them . . . (SDS NATIONAL COMMITTEE invited D I G G E R S to their
national conference: "no thank you, but thanks just the same. you
see. it's getting late. and well. the turnips. for chrissake
the turnips!"

d i g g e r s are street people: they just don't give a fuck! they
live their protest: they have nothing and nothing to lose. They
do their thing for free. and you can ask why? and how revolution?
and if you did this then maybe . . . but the diggers don't. no,
they really don't. and it's hard for me to understand, but it's
true. they're tough. they put down the psychedelic *fashion*
(revolution is killing people and taking their property away. if
not literally, then figuratively. but never asking them to buy . . .),

Inner Space #3, June, 1967

protesters (who keep their leftovers in DOW chemical baggies) guilt-
ridden gift-bearers (a favorite: a guy will come up to a
d i g g e r and say i think what you're doing is beautiful and sort of
palm a ten or twenty across and then have his stomach turned when
the throng is brought together to thank the gentle-man and burn
his offering to saint george metevsky who really hated all those
buildings he nicked with bombs for twenty-thirty years. all
anarchists have a strange fear of buildings . . .)

provos. . . . no, the d i g g e r s are not that. they're total
drug oriented mad ones, who are mad to live, mad to talk, mad to
be saved, desirous of everything of the same time, the ones who
never yawn or say a commonplace thing, but burn, burn, burn, like a
fabulous yellow roman candle exploding like spiders across the sky,
and in the middle you see the blue center light pop and "Awww!" people
who have ridden the crest of kerouac's bum's romance and slammed to
earth wailing love! and lady, they're wailing for maybes. maybe
two fingers can touch. maybe streets won't run into neighborhoods
any more. maybe there is something besides acid indigestion and
copsuckers and the gladly dead. just maybe.

The study of our social structure now requires an interdisciplinary approach. The economist who examines American society and concludes that "Marx was right" is not only half a century behind the times; he is also less valuable than one who has studied several fields, among them sociology and mass communications. But talk is cheaper than ever, and rational, abstract discourses on the market economy and its failures are of little help to those who suffer psychologically from poverty and impotence.

Unfortunately, it is more than a little difficult to construct an effective alternative to capitalism. One may get thrilling patterns from television sets, but there are also the banal commercials, which offer even the alienated tempting scenes of product lust. While hundreds of thousands of kids are trying to take themselves out of the consumer economy, their cultural patterning reinforces their dependence on that economy.

Sgt. Pepper's Political Club and Band

WALTER BOWART AND ALLEN KATZMAN

Labor unions struggled and fought in the leftist thirties for more pay and shorter hours and got them, eventually deteriorating into gangsterism. Today, in the face of advanced technology, the workers are obsolete, the fight, because of automation, is now for meaningful work-time which brings us back to the eternal answer—art.

Because of and during the linear industrial revolution (the last environment), the genetic pool on the side of the workers had increased and the pool on the side of artists had decreased; consequently today we have a large resource of people without manual dexterity and/or aesthetic conditioning being offered a role in a society which has left only the meaningful work of art. Sociologists seem to think that the current war development is God's answer to the depletion of the now superfluous worker class. This line of thinking entirely rules out redemption.

The East Village Other, July 1, 1967

The Psychedelics know about redemption. Rebirth, karma alignment and faith are major premises during ego loss.

She's Leaving Home

Danger fosters the rescuing power.

You know there is hope when you see the establishment completely uptight about the "hippies" and resorting to police tactics and thinking of internment camps. Soon the public will know.

Two thousand years ago some beatified rejects from the predominant tribe ran around the Mediterranean preaching love. For this they were persecuted and one of their leaders was hung on a cross by the Romans who thought they were a threat. History proved that indeed they were a threat to the Roman way of life which had become selfish and obsolete since a mythic (psychic) change had occurred in the collective unconscious. It proved that the Christians had the artistic vision to assimilate their mythic changes in the world's psyche and eventually marry the remnants of the Roman life. Eventually the mentality of greed which was the motivating force behind the Roman Empire took hold again and the "Christian revolution" was ruined—the Church became a land owner.

At an Underground Press meeting, the "hippies" (correlation of the early christians) sat around in a circle and spoke in turn, arbitrarily. No procedure was followed. Some spoke articulately, others stupidly and irreverently. Eventually the most articulate and intelligent were heard and evolved as natural leaders rising to meet the occasion. After the particular event had been dealt with they sank back to enrich the mass, so to speak . . . not consolidating power or looking to secure a selfish personal control over the group.

The difference between this "psychedelic" organic approach and the leftist/materialist concept is clear. Both left and capitalist groups see society organized in a linear class structure hanging over from the feudal concept. The left is trying to deal with it by emphasizing the "worker class" and dissembling, as much as possible, all class structure as a vertical thing with the rich at the top and the poor at the bottom. At best the left sees class structured as a horizontal phenomenon with peoples of different aptitudes and interests and abilities working side by side—on an equal basis—as one group mass.

Only the psychedelic "politics" realizes the truth of class as genetic. They have experimented with total freedom of choice and found that genetic heritage, the gift of the genetic pool, make for different roles where fluidity, predicated by the individual's ability in a certain area, is more or less dependent on his karma.

This new "body politique" is nowhere better expressed than in the present "hippie" phenomenon. They have dropped out of an obsolete society to find other alternatives. It is no longer a time of storming the barricades but of leaving them.

For in reality, "hippies are what hippies do," "lost bourgeois" who have taken up the highest ideal of the middle class—leisure time—and who wage the cool war. They are practicing what the government has already the money, the means, but not the desire, will power, or organization to carry out; a society based on the needs of the soul (creative time) and not of the flesh (work time) where machines (and not men) regulated by technicians turn out enough food, shelter and clothing for an entire nation, perhaps, in all probability, the world.

If this solution seems Utopian, one must remember that we still hold onto an age (environment), although obsolete, where we will fight to the death to keep what we have and that means using the ultimate weapon. From this point of view, as Dr. Shane Mage sees it, "Today we can be relevant only if we are Utopian." Looking at it from this perspective one is faced with the ultimate task of changing society from top to bottom: psychically, mythically and economically. How to bridge the gap from possession to non-possession, to insure that our new environment doesn't institutionalize and start the process of destruction over again, is a moot problem. But if we do not solve it humanity as we know it can no longer endure.

If then there is to be a change in man's condition through his mind and environment, the approaches must be threefold: 1) Drugs, Psychedelics, 2) Mass Media, Mass Communication, Education, 3) Cybernetics, Automation.

I Get High with a Little Help from My Friends

The best example of psychedelics in action can be found in the Haight-Ashbury district of San Francisco. Psychedelics, especially LSD, have spawned a generation of people readily aware of conditioned reflexes to their socio-economic and political past and present. This experiment in life style is not a controlled one and too often drugs limiting this awareness tend to corrupt and stagnate the possibilities that the "hippies" are experimenting with in Haight.

Many new relationships in living have occurred in Haight like the one described previously which took place at the Underground Press meeting. Another is the Diggers, anarchistic, communistic, who repudiate the present order by giving out free food, shelter, clothing and acid. They now have three farms outside the Haight district, growing and supplying food to the rest of the "hippie" community. And they do this without any reference to money or production of goods and services and without intent of sapping allegiance from the people they serve.

If the use of psychedelics shows us anything from this uncontrolled experiment in life style, it is the possibility that LSD can break old habits, especially "possession syndrome" left over from the old environment and ideologies, and integrate them into a supra-political situation where people recognize allegiance to a power higher than their own or Caesar's and not one of improving their own position of personal power:

> In Czechoslovakia there was a lot of experimenting by Dr. J. Roubicheck, who came to the conclusion that LSD inhibits conditioned reaction. This is very important in the Marxian, Pavlovian society, because what that means is that you have a way of wiping out brain-washing conditioned reactions.
> —thoughtfood excerpted from
> "What Allen Ginsberg Said to Dr. Fox"; INNER SPACE #3

A pilot study recently completed on the effects of continual psychedelic use on the social response and politics of ten people is extremely interesting in this context. I quote the results from the magazine of the psychedelic revolution, *New York Provo:*

> The new politics of the ten continual users studied, more than anything else, represented their reaction to their place in the American "Game." Three of the subjects were struggling against low socio-economic background and concomitant and educational drawbacks. They quit. Their politics represent, in spite of leftist sentiments, simple communistic anarchism, akin to the attitudes of the Diggers. Three others, of upper middle class background, were potential winners; they stayed somewhere in the middle class. Theirs are the politics of psychedelic non-involvement, to varying degrees. For two subjects with upper middle class backgrounds and extensive college, descent into the impoverished petit bourgeois came when genuine artistic activity supplanted regular occupation. One started as a rightist, the other as a leftist; both are now strictly Learyite in their commitment to non-involvement, their belief in LSD as a social panacea. For the two who in addition to upper middle class and college background had histories of Marxist activism, membership in the impoverished petit bourgeois intelligentsia is a badge of their place in the psychedelic revolution.

Illegality of psychedelics compounded the user's alienation. They tended to re-interpret the world in terms of their own experience, past and present; mass media and authority receded from their former pre-eminence as determinants. But however much alienation from capitalist society their political views expressed, in each case the user respected his socio-economic and political past and present. However modified by the psychedelic experience, socio-economic determinism still operates.

I Get By with a Little Help from My Friends

The problem of stepping out from a drug-oriented atmosphere into mass media is the next level of karma that the "hippies" have broached.

The fact that they have been much maligned as well as praised in the media has in any case left them open to manipulation from an outside force. They are combating this manipulation in three distinct areas, mostly primitive, some with a degree of sophistication.

A letter we recently received from the San Francisco *Oracle* demonstrates a method, though primitive, in breaking this response:

> My researches in television, triggered by Mr. McLuhan's researches, lead me to believe that television may be useful as a meditational tool and possibly as a meditational medium based on the analogy of sun yoga. The problem which presents itself immediately is the surplus of content transmitted by the "TV industry." By eliminating the content transmitted by the "industry" one can see the essentially stroboscopic nature of television, and familiar mandalic patterns are colored and formed by the retina of the eye in response to this stroboscopic light. That trance states can be induced by television is well known by the effects on epileptic inclined individuals when they get too close to their sets. Whether or not there can exist any feedback of mental impulses through the open channels of your TV sets is yet a moot point.
>
> Communication is faulty communion. Communion is the form toward which we strive. Perfect communion is communication without the intermediary of the world of forms—without formal analogs. Telepathy is communion in a primitive form or mode. Telepathy is becoming common.
>
> In concrete terms: In a darkened room, turn on your TV set. Find a full channel. Adjust the brightness control all the way to bright (to the right). Adjust the contrast control to minimum contrast (to the left). Adjust the vertical hold and vertical linearity

controls all the way to the left or right. Tune the channel selector to an empty channel. Readjust for maximum brightness as necessary—maximum retinal color results from maximum bombardment of the retina. Concentrate on sending your meditations out from your ashram to mine. Thank you. "We now return control of your TV set to you."

Remember that this is TV—TV is one of the essentially invisible forms—the color and shapes that you see in it are actually produced in your eye. In the future, there will doubtless be many more invisible forms with which to cope. Learn now.

Within You—Without You

The Provos (provocateur), a branch of the "hippie" phenomenon, and a word recently inundated in the minds and consciousness of people by the mass media, have their own way of handling media manipulation.

Provo, it must be remembered, is less of a political party than a theatrical demonstration. They use the street as their stage and their activity is an end in itself. They prick the bubble of our old environment and values through game play. Once the game is finished, another begins. Nothing is held onto and catharsis is realized through the pseudo-event which makes fun and absurdity of the real one.

The "Smoke-In," an event held in L.A. by the Hollywood Provos, demonstrates the futility of ever enforcing the marijuana laws. Under the guise of a fog machine on Hollywood & Vine, Provos smoked marijuana along with a lot of other pseudo highs, bananas, oregano, catnip, while the police were powerless to arrest the law breakers. The best they could do was to arrest a fourteen-year-old girl for dancing in the streets.

Other demonstrations, which were attacks on other aspects of society, were equally successful in baffling the police and the establishment.

The Provos in Amsterdam, where the movement originally began, became so successful that they were able to be elected to the City Council.

Recently they had to disband as a movement in Amsterdam with the head of the Provos giving up his position to become an actor; a kind of Ronald Reagan in reverse. The reason they gave for disbanding was "they had become too institutionalized, with offices and hired help, and that the decision would be in keeping with their original purpose. It's all a game and why possess it if it means the death of us all."

Sgt. Pepper's Lonely Hearts Club Band.

The most sophisticated method of the "hippies" and yet the least viable can be found in the newly formed Underground Press Syndicate. U.P.S. has almost fifty newspapers with a readership of close to a million. They speak essentially to their own people but they provide a platform to counteract the establishment's control and unify a group of people who long before this phenomenon thought they were crazy. The problems that they face are more deadly than the problems the Provos recently faced in Amsterdam, just because their approach is more sophisticated and therefore more subtle. The problem of becoming an institution possessing collective power as a minority, before utopia can be accomplished, can only be solved by our advanced technology, electronic and otherwise (drug). At best the "hippies" are pointing to that solution without the ability to initiate it. As Jacques Ellul points out in his brilliant book *The Technological Society,* "There are no more political solutions, only technological ones. The rest is propaganda." And so with "hippies," what they say and do, at best, is only propaganda and a stalling action. They do point to a solution but that solution can only be solved technologically.

Lovely Rita Meter Maid

If the problems of changing the values and ecology of an old environment through drugs, media and advanced technology are to be met head on, a new education system will have to be initiated. Such an experiment has already begun with astounding results.

Dr. Sheridan Speeth, of the Avionics Department at Cornell Aeronautical Laboratory, has been experimenting with "autotelic toys and environment." Autotelic toys are self-teaching toys. His results with a group of young children from a lower socio-economic group and similar intelligence quota have been fantastic to say the least. Dr. Speeth's conclusions are basic to his premise:

> If the stereotyping of responses and the suppression of novelty in the use of material are to be avoided, information should be taught with only so large a level of motivation as needed to maintain relevant activity. Both monkeys and men are motivated by curiosity and show continued activity as long as they have an effect on the surroundings. This is called playing or research in different contexts. It has been shown that by making an irrelevant reward contingent on performing some action which had previously been performed "for fun" one destroys its intrinsic ability to motivate. This suggests that the "educational" toy is preferable to the

irrelevant social rewards of the schoolroom as a support for the
early learning process. There are deleterious effects produced by
doing the right thing for the wrong reason.
> —"Toys That Teach" by Dr. Sheridan Speeth

In other words an autotelic toy and environment does not interfere
with a child's learning but even makes him more curious which is its
own optimum motivation.

Dr. Speeth also sees autotelic toys in relationship to older people as a
basis to a new creative time—spent by adults when their work-time jobs
are taken over by automation and also as a deterrent to a lack of quali-
fied people in the engineering field.

Given these results one wonders why the government hasn't picked
up on it yet. The reason is fairly simple. Dr. Speeth had initiated the
program, through government help, for the Haryou Act Poverty program. It was turned down not because it was too expensive or impossible
to put into operation, on the contrary, it was dropped by the government like a hot potato because teachers and the present teaching system
(another bureaucracy) would have been put out of work and made completely obsolete, not that they aren't already.

Here we have a simple case of "economic determinism" which could
be reduced to the simple observation that the transactions of any social
group—regardless of particular form or content—are largely transactions about the allocation of work and the resulting goods and services.
Norms like possession and control, institutional growths like the military-industrial complex, events like the war in Viet Nam—these are
functions of our present alienation from our economic interaction,
rather than consequences of technology or production and distribution
as such. Now every major socio-economic revolution (i.e., capitalism
replacing feudalism) has come with the implementation of a new
technology (steam engine, etc.) which enabled men to replace alienated
economic institutions with new modes of interaction with reference to
their economic environment. The steam engine was completely inimical
to feudal and post-feudal economic institutions. Today in 1967 it is
cybernetics, automation and our electro-magnetic society which could
enable us to create our new environment.

The government's refusal to recognize the new environment, as in
the case of Dr. Speeth, can only have disastrous effects. Granted the
government is not the only one holding onto obsolete ways but in spite
of them there have been some steps towards creating the new environment. Recently Kaiser Industries, in order to automate their plant, offered 1500 workers of the local union stocks equal in dividends to the
salary they were making, when they were laid off, for the rest of their

lives. These workers became capitalists. And it is not surprising that Wall Street, as reported in the *Wall Street Journal* of November '66, was recently thinking of pushing through legislation a law which would guarantee workers an annual wage of $5000 a year.

There can be no doubt that the more we hold onto the old environment and values, the more we are perpetrating our own destruction. Instead of using money and time wisely, we spend our lives in fruitless activities like war. In the field of cybernetics where much can be done to find ways to initiate the new environment we waste our money and brainpower on developing military cybernetical organisms for outer space and create robot soldiers to perpetuate a military caste after the holocaust.

If anyone is demonstrating the need for solutions to the human side of our predicament, it is the "hippies." What they are doing is much more relevant than a war in Southeast Asia or the Mideast. And for that reason alone they are dangerous to the government's hypocrisy.

I'd Love to Turn You On

IV. The Hippies:
Flowering of
a Nonmovement

Everything has already been said about the hippies; they
are the most overreported phenomenon of the last few years.
Like hula-hoops and the twist, hippiedom was a fad, colorful
enough to be splashed throughout the media, ambiguous
enough to allow any commentator to sound moderately well
informed. And if the hippies did not exist—and there were
many who bore the label who could not define its meaning—
they could easily be invented; with Vietnam and the blacks
out of control, the public needed some lighter news.

The influx of adolescents into the hippie world, insofar as
it can be determined, was more the result of this media exposure than its cause. Before the invasion of San Francisco,
before the standardization of bells, beads, drugs, and acid
rock as the prime commodities of hippie culture, the urban
communities were small enough to support their members.
But school vacations and the journalistic "silly season" combined to encourage the disaffected to leave their homes and
seek a better life with their peers. The rhetoric quickly became overblown, and the flight of the alienated assumed
the pageantry of a children's crusade. At its peak, perhaps

200,000 people grooved on their new freedom and each
other, but the triumph of a specious movement lasts only an
instant. The inattention of the press and the concern over
the next fad—the runaways—denied the validity of the hippies. That which could be artificially created could be similarly destroyed, but the cost was measured in real human
lives.

Suddenly the lexicographers had a new word, but no one could adequately define it. Innocent college students with long hair were asked about hippies, but they were as befuddled as the man in the street. True hippies, it is reported, refused to accept the label, but the "plastic" or pseudo hippies were only too glad to have a ready-made identity. Too much Eriksonian identity diffusion, or something of the kind. Unfortunately, the underground press couldn't resist the rather stodgy bait; as this attempt at definition indicates, not even those on the scene could isolate the components of hippiedom.

What Is a Hippie?

GUY STRAIT

It is strange and disturbing to watch the straight community's angry, sometimes violent reaction to the hippies. There are many reasons for this. The principal one is appearance. The hippies dress strangely. They dress this way because they have thrown a lot of middle-class notions out the window and with them the most sensitive middle-class dogma: the neutral appearance.

The straight world is a jungle of taboos, fears, and personality games. People in that jungle prey on each other mercilessly. Therefore to survive in any jungle requires good protective coloring: the camouflage of respectable appearance. The anonymity of middle-class dress is like a flag of truce. It means (whether true or not): "I'm not one of the predators." It is in the nature of an assurance of harmlessness. Unusual or bright-colored clothing, then becomes an alarm, a danger signal to the fearful and their armed truce with the rest of mankind. They see it as a challenge. They are fearful, unsure of themselves, and fear sours into anger. It is but a step to thinking that the anger is "good." The oldest fallacy in the world is that anything that makes you angry must be bad.

The sin of the hippies is that they will not play the straight game of camouflage. Their non-participation, in effect, exposes them as another tribe, whose disregard of straight taboos of dress makes them seem to be capable of anything, and therefore a danger. That danger moreover is felt clear up to city hall, that shrine of Squaredom. Why else, I submit, does the Health Department of this city have such a tender solicitude about the living conditions of human beings at the Haight when they have ignored the conditions at Hunter's Point, the Mission and the Fillmore?

Many people cannot understand the hippies' rejection of everything that is commonly expected of the individual in regard to employment and life goals: steady lucrative employment, and the accumulation through the years of possessions and money, building (always building) security for the future. It is precisely this security hypochondria, *this checking of bank books rather than pulses*, this worrying over budgets instead of medicine cabinets, that drives the youth of today away. It is this frantic concern with money that there will be enough of it, that the children start worrying about the always threatening future also drives the young into the Haight-Ashbury. They have seen their parents slave for years, wasting away a lifetime to make sure that the house was paid off, that the kids got through school in order to get "good" jobs so that they could join the frantic scramble, later on. The parents' reward for this struggle is that they wind up old and tired, alienated from their children and just as often each parent from the other. They have thought so long in terms of money and possessions, that they have forgotten how to think in terms of people. So they think of "my son," and "my daughter," and talk to their children as one would speak from a great distance to a check book.

"But you've got to build a future for yourself. If you don't support yourself, no one else is going to!" The tired, lined face argues to the young. "It's a hard world." And pray tell who makes it hard, participating in the scramble for material "security"? Who makes it difficult by insisting that everyone must participate in that scramble or suffer social censure? Listen to the tone of those who lecture about the "economic realities" of life. Are they presenting impartial facts? Or do they sound like someone expounding church doctrine? It is the latter. The conventional folk of our society, the "normal" people, so called, believe in the rat race. Competition is holy. Keeping up with the Joneses is a mandate from God. The requirement of keeping up a respectable front is the principal article of faith.

It has been demonstrated over and over again throughout history by the best possible people that very little is required for happiness. It is the fight for money and possessions and the prestige they bring that sets people at odds, and *that* is what makes the world hard. We are the richest nation in the world, with the highest living standard. By our own fond illusions about prosperity we should also be the happiest. Are we? Suicides, racial violence, and the exodus of the young from comfortable homes suggest otherwise. The terrible truth is that our prosperity is the bringer of misery. We have been brainwashed by the advertising industry into being the most dissatisfied people in the world. We are told we must all be handsome or beautiful, sexually devastating, and owners of a staggering amount of recreational gadgetry or doomed to frustration. The result is that most of us are frustrated. It is exactly this that the hippie avoids like poison. He wants no part of self-defeating goals.

It is very likely that the hippie will go hungry and suffer exposure, and perhaps freak out. But he considers these far less dangerous than the kind of dehumanization society tried to wreak on him before his rebellion. He has escaped from a culture where the machine is god, and men judge each other by mechanical standards of efficiency and usefulness. He sees a madness in the constant fight to sell more washing machines, cars, toilet paper, girdles, and gadgets than the other fellow. He is equally horrified at the grim ruthlessness of the men who participate in that fight.

Tuli Kupferberg, poet and member of the Fugs, a satiric rock group, is an over-thirty apologist for the hippie cause. His espousal of anti-Establishment activities makes him the living refutation of the generation-gap theory. He claims that in the mid-fifties, as a serious poet, "I was even squarer than you are now." Which may reassure those who are about to take the plunge into the underground.

The Hip and the Square:

The Hippie Generation

TULI KUPFERBERG

1. In the transition from hip to hippy the following perhaps occurred: The hippy (the new man) is a very recent phenomenon. The hip person, the "hipster" had to work for it. The hippy is to the manner born. He probably somewhere wonders incredibly what the fuss is all about. His times have solved (or in many cases: dissolved) problems the immediate past was obsessed with. The immediate past: incarnated in what is called the older (above 30?) generation is still obsessed with problems that have absolutely no reality for him. For example: the Black problem: namely & essentially: 1) shall we fuck beautiful black people? 2) shall black people partake equally of the benefits of American affluence? The hippy just fucks beautiful chicks (or men) of any color or nationality & just lives & shares with chicks & men of any nationality or color, naturally.

By naturally I mean without thinking twice. If differences are noted, they are perhaps praised & they are individualized. If one has to think in racial terms & really it is not that all necessary or useful & can be just as sociologically confusing at times as it is beneficial: for example: one fucks individuals not races, one must feed bodies of individual people, not of abstract groups—then in the new systems each group has its own superlatives—so that if the blacks are "different" even by the old standards they may come out different yes, but what if they're BETTER? (What now white cow?) BUT IN A JOYOUS, ABUNDANT SOCIETY

WHAT IS REALLY THE NEED TO CLASSIFY AND/OR RATE? There are enough emotional rewards for everyone. Then why classify or rank our brothers?

Hell (or heaven!) even the hippy dogs are friendlier, more beautiful, more lovable! The greatest, friendliest, most laughing-humorous dogs in the world walk the Berkeley campus. "I wd rather be a dog in Berkeley, than the mayor of Harlem." *

2. So here we have this sneaky hippy generation that suddenly appeared while we turned our back to have a chocolate malted. So here we have an underground press that emerges (worldwide) in one year to a readership perhaps in the millions & talks abt impt fundamental things of which the overground press was so terrified that it didn't want to even acknowledge their existence, or actually never realized existed at all.

& the rate of evolution (& the sometime generation gap) is so incredible that 2 yrs means a new generation, a new music, a new clothing, a new style or substyle.

The change is the massage. He who does not permit himself to keep fit runs the risk of spiritual death. No you need not accept it all—BUT YOU MUST FEEL IT ALL.

3. What is this new amazing generation that no one understands?

I dont know. I dont understand it myself. Maybe it does not understand itself. But my muscles or I myself dont know the formula of creatine or the amino acids or the energy paths of glucose metabolism either, & my fingers still write these words. Birds fly & know even less of the theory of flight that I do who cannot fly.

It is so new, it is so changing it is hard to grasp. Let us attempt some generalizations. Let us look for directions.

1) The change from hip to hippy was a change from hard to soft:

2) Tough leather towards nudity. Clothes reveal the body as a supple free instrument of beauty & joy.

3) Machine shoes to boots & sandals & to bare feet. Boots are elegant & they ARE masculine—& they can be "tough." The dammed up sadism exposes itself. When it works itself thru we see it again as rough love. After violence man becomes soft. The trick is to prevent the accumulation of uncontrollable deadly hate (murderous hate). The more man fucks, the less he beats, all other things being equal. Fuck however alas does not equal fuck. Some fuck with hate & not in love. Some achieve arousal & no satisfaction, no climax. Some fuck because it is expected of them. Some see it as proof of their worth &c. &c. "Are you fucking

---

* cf (s'il vous plaît) the old: "I wd rather be a lamppost in Harlem than the Governor of Alabama."

more & enjoying it less? . . . then why dont you fuck less & enjoy it more." The old are terrified of the frank dialog. The new say "we can work it out."

4) The music is free, dancy, inventive, moving, total, overwhelming.

The hippy is not afraid to be overwhelmed. He has more mystic (total) experiences in a week, than the old man has in a lifetime.

The music, art is not separate from life. He plays and/or listens to music everywhere. He will dance anywhere. He is not ashamed of his joy. His dance is a prelude to sex, or a celebration of his existence: not a substitute for sex, or a tease, or a ritualistic (unsatisfactory) discharge of sexual energy.

The dance has made him free. His freedom has made him dance.

The world is an artform. He will decorate his body as a work of art. He will bead it, paint it, clothe it in rainbows & the idiosyncratic style or mixture of styles of all times all place; there is no CORRECT way to dress, there is no correct way to fuck. Let a thousand bodies bloom!

5) The hair grows, yes it flows: look again: is it not beautiful! Head-hair kept its long growing capacity one might think only as an estheti-cally desired-able thing. What else is its function? Look at it, touch it, smell it!

Is it not beautiful!? Why do you cut your beauty every day, every week, every month? Your grandfathers were smarter than you!

See the miniskirts? See the beautiful legs. Yes they lead to the cunt! & these girls do not tease . . . they fuck. Can you take it?

6) There is a disgust with the cruel abstract, the fake, the phony, the rhetoric, the gas & lies of politicians, the neuroses of bureaucracy, the insanity of war & internal institutionalized brutality (ie the police & "justice" systems).

There is a mistrust of the written word—used to mystify & to oppress with meaningless dogma.

There is a mistrust of the phony sound, the bad poet, the lying, sneaking, power mad, murderous politician (often called: mayor, con-gressman, governor, president . . . formerly: king, dictator, commis-sar, pope . . . remember?)

There is an unwillingness to "play the game" when the game means disease, poverty, discrimination, boredom, murder (called "war" or "self defense"), enslavement to property (things), or many "ideals" (ofttimes meaningless abstractions like "nation," "country," "flag," "state," "honor" for which men are asked to die and kill—but which have their true reality only in the terrified emotions of greed, fear, hate, paranoid mistrust & "religious" belief in the foulness of man & of life itself, sexual frustration, unhappiness—distorted diseased perceptions

—so that friendliness is sometimes interpreted as guile—so that gratui-
tous love is sometimes rejected in fear because O Lord—if the world
is really loving then my whole life has been a terrible mistake and loss).

7) There is a movement of disgust with the entire old dying society
& an attempt to retreat, to drop out. There is an incredible seeking
out, testing & creation of new forms of living together & of raising
children: meditation, communal living, tribalization (a restructuring
of the old paranoid family whose main slogan was actually: "us against
the world"). There are new economic forms being contemplated: a
new "primitive" communism. There is a movement away from the
choked dying cities to the living countryside. There is a rebirth of
communal work, even in the egotistic arts. Works are appearing without signatures. The egomaniac artist sees his contorted face in the
mirror & starts to wonder just what his ego is all about. In a loving
world one doesnt need to always prove ones worth. In a joyful world
one does not need to retreat that much into a self contained world of
art.

In a world controlled by man for his own joy the difference between
art & object disappears . . . life becomes the work. The true work of art
is the infinite body of man moving in harmony thru the incredible
changes of his particular existence. When the body sings, the world
dances. When the world dances, the freed body sings.

He who cannot dance, dies.

8) Drugs are his magic. He uses them in 2 ways:
 1) to get him past the past
 2) to get him into the future
It is perhaps the nature of man to always want more. When the sat-
isfactions of this world are given (& a new 19 yr old, a 19 yr old hippy,
perhaps, has lived more than 98% of all people over 30. He has had
love-sex, travel, marriage, children. He has read more, absorbed more,
TV'd more, movied more, & intelligenced more than yes 98% of the
people over 30.) he goes on. & where is on? Some new country? Yes.
Some new familial form? Yes. Some new music or art? Yes. Some new
religion? Yes. Some new universe? Yes & Yes again.

& since this is a scientific & chemical & instantaneous age he uses
perhaps the old methods: fasting, meditation, music, fucking &c. but
he also is ready to & does use the chemical methods (do not be dis-
turbed by the word CHEMICAL: your body, your food are chemicals—
when the food you eat is powerful enuf it is called medicine—when
the medicine you take is powerful enuf it is called "drug.") Today the
foods & the medicines are powerful enuf. Today the powers are magical. TV & LSD: both are magical: that is instantaneous & overwhelming.

DRUGS BREAK PATTERNS, thats all they do. When patterns are broken, new worlds CAN emerge. They may be better or worse (good or bad trip) but they are new.

The new man is known by his readiness to embark into these new worlds. He is brave & of times foolhardy. These drugs have their dangers, namely the ability to permanently remove you from this plane of existence—either thru physical death or brain or body or genetic damage or "insanity."

We must all do everything we can do to make sure we reach new worlds & do not simply die out of old worlds: "A living ogre is better than a dead saint."

If I have but one life to lead let me lead it alive.

But the terror of the new, the irrational drug panic this country is now living thru is a sign of ITS disease, of its fear, of its terror. For all of these repressed desires shd come out: because they are beautiful, because they reinforce & add to & fructify & glorify life, because they strike joy into the universe!

If there was trouble with the term "hippie," there was chaos in the various attempts to pinpoint the concept of underground. "Hippie" sounded derogatory, but "underground," with its James Bond implications of intrigue, could be exploited by advertising, and everyone from magazine publishers to perfume manufacturers capitalized on its connotations. Avatar seemed to sense quite early in the game that underground was wherever they weren't.

What Is the Underground?

M. PRESTON BURNS

Since the beginning of civilized man there have been groups of subversive activists who have devoted their existence to the improvement or overthrow of the established norms in order to enhance the flow of culture's progress. Such groups have functioned within their restricted social systems in various manners determined by their obscure and sometimes radical philosophies. And always, these underground activities are either destroyed by the existing authority or, through their intellectual stamina, they build the foundation of future progressive movements.

Activists such as Plato, Christ, Alexander the Great, Hitler, and America's own founding leaders were members of movements to change or overthrow the presiding structure of the time. They, among numerous others, have left rewarding lessons to the history of man's attempt to grasp the Utopian ideals he strives for. Even today, such activist groups thrive within the system of man's present existence, with regional names and protected boundaries varying from national governments to outlaw motorcycle clubs. All of these groups shall oppose one another until they are destroyed or absorbed by another.

Today's underground, a social form similar to the Impressionist movement in France at the turn of the century, and not too unlike the Christian movement of two millenniums ago, follows the pattern of time's flow and repartition to further the greater pattern of man's quest for a unified existence within the natural structure of evolution, a quest towards peace and knowledge for all men. Today's subversive movement is part of the progressive flow established when man realized that there

Avatar, June, 1967

were many directions from which he could further the ideas of his civilization and continue his involvement within the structure of his social system. Any individual who opposes any portion of established authority, whether for constructive reasons or not, is a subversive element within that authority. Any group with ideas to improve or destroy the established authority is a subversive element within that authority. With the added strength of numbers, these become the underground.

Who is the Underground?

You are, if you think, dream, work, and build towards the improvements and changes in your life, your social and personal environments, towards the expectations of a better existence.

Who is the Underground?

The person next to you on the street car, as he proceeds to be where he wishes to be and do what he wishes to do.

Who is the Underground?

Think—look around—
    maybe in a mirror
        maybe inside . . .

As soon as parents admitted their inability to understand the young, they were mercilessly baited for their total deviation from true morality. The logic was a bit perverse, but so much the better; if the fogies couldn't understand the barbs you threw at them, you could craftily pin the guilt on them. After all, they did drop the bomb on Hiroshima, right? Because they could not blame themselves—the innocents-in-a-world-they-never-made gambit— the young accepted the obvious alternative: the tyranny of the old. It wasn't true, but the average age in America was twenty- five, which made untruth profitable, and anyway, as they say in the overground press, it makes good copy.

The Morality of the Immoral

ALDO GIUNTA

There is a new morality in America, and with it, a new hope for our sal- vation. There is a new coming of age in this country, and it serves its own notice. Old men, aged by formulas and made cynical by incestuous agreements to keep silent or to freeze the world into a shape they can understand, who trumpet dull explosions of clichés they call speeches . . . These do not understand that there is hope for us now.

A powerful burst of energy has been released onto the American soil: youth has found its voice. Everywhere, evidence abounds. In Berkeley, in the great rash of protest demonstrations across the country, and now in the great "Draft-Card Debacle." The American student body has at last come of age, and probably, with it, so has America. Until recently, there had seemed to be a prevalence of apathy in the community of young American intellectuals: in Europe, in Asia, *certainly* throughout the history of Western Civilization, the student bodies have traditionally been quick to raise their voices in wrath at unpopular edicts or dicta of Governments, while in the American university there was silence. No one questioned the silence: indeed, it seemed to be a sign of content- ment, an indication of satisfaction with everything American, and a complete acceptance of authority.

. . . But now, a tiger is loose, and the zoo-keepers are nervous. Gov- ernment has a case of the jitters, the national press quotes President,

The East Village Other, October, 1966

Congressmen, Senators, Educators and Churchmen as reflecting the reprehensibility of the actions of youth: everyone is looking for the national bogey-man, Communism, at the bottom of the woodpile; accusations ranging from "treason," to "cowardliness," to "irresponsibility," to "subversion" spew from mouths with the heat of vituperative lava, and the Federal Government has already shown that it will brook no nonsense regarding draft card destruction . . .

The Administration is not so much annoyed by the New Voice of America, as it is puzzled. It does not understand how young people, how intellectuals, can stand against *its* decision to wage war in Vietnam. Nor does it understand why there isn't *complete* accord on Vietnam, and it is made uncomfortable at the *violence* of the disagreement. After all, it reasons, we are all Americans, are we not? And what is good for many Americans, *must* be good for all!

. . . It is a question, sirs, of moralities. There is an essential dichotomy of moralities in America, on the one hand of Caesar (*where Caesar commands, we obey*), and on the other of truly modern, flexible man (*I will not, until I have questioned*). Students, who are perhaps closer to history texts than leaders of states, and whose heritage from their instructors, from the current literature predominant in every bookstore, and from the constant reminders of movies, television, et al., cannot forget as easily as statesmen the lesson of Nazi Germany in the thirties and forties, where the morality was unequivocally, *where Caesar commands, we obey*. In the Nuremburg trials, almost every defense was predicated on the premise that *Caesar* had commanded, and as good German soldiers there was no choice but to obey. . . .

In America, now, in the 1960's, students are demanding their right to *question*, before it is too late. Once a man is inducted into the Armed Forces, he waives his rights as a citizen, and becomes only an instrument of some higher commanding body, or invisible influence. Men are shot for disobeying commands under arms. The most basic tenet of this democracy is that men have the *right* to disagree. And American youth is *not* taking that guarantee lightly. If the young men of our country find it within their consciences to refuse to fight a war, whether on religious, political, or ethical grounds, the Government is *morally obliged* to honor their decision, and more; it must guarantee their *constitutional right* to that decision, for *that* is what democracy is all about, and *that* is why a democracy is such a difficult undertaking. And anything short of that guarantee subverts the *meaning* of democracy.

We are either complete wards of the State, *or* a nation composed of individuals *in* the State, which therefore *is* the State. Either the State towers over us as an independent monolith, *or* we are the atoms that compose its firmament. If we are the property of the State, then no man has the right to disagree with the decisions of the State. And, as the numerous statesmen, educators and churchmen have told us, dissent is treason, disagreement is irresponsibility, queries are cowardly, and any form of individual assertion is subversion. But in that case, *what precisely* is the difference between the United States and totalitarian China or Russia?

If all the gentlemen who thump their bellies in rage and wave flags stood for a moment in silence, with their fingers up their noses, and contemplated a bit, they might see something, or hear something of value. The new breed of university student has a message for them, if they will only listen. It is that there are all sorts of wars, and that the more ferocious, and deeper-thrusting wars are not always conducted on the battlefield, with bullet and shell. There are moral wars, and spiritual wars. In America there is now a new, vigorous, healthy spirit. Young men and young women seek a voice all their own, for they have a new vision that perhaps older men do not quite understand. Their heroes are not generals, but peace-makers. Their gods are not George Pattons, but Mahatma Gandhis. There, perhaps, lies the key to much that the Administration does not understand.

Ralph Gleason is one of the few writers over thirty who have enthusiastically embraced both the new music and the new life styles. A highly regarded jazz reviewer, he praised the rock ballrooms so extravagantly in his San Francisco Chronicle *columns that the city was forced to discontinue its unofficial policy of harassment. By the time the repression machinery was back in gear, the ballrooms were firmly established.*

It is impossible to dance and hate at the same time; this revolution marches to singularly unmilitary drummers. Gleason has helped it along by cosponsoring the Monterey Pop Festival, the prototype of all rock festivals everywhere, and by founding a weekly journal of rock news, Rolling Stone, *which is equally distinguished by the soundness of its criticism and its unique literacy.*

The Power of Non-Politics or the Death of the Square Left

RALPH J. GLEASON

Joe MacDonald is a folk singer, a guitar player and a political activist. Or he was.

He used to get his songs published in *Broadside,* the magazine of protest songwriters; and when they wanted musicians to play along the line of march of the Vietnam Day Parade to Oakland they called in Joe MacDonald.

Now Joe MacDonald has long hair, wears beads and sometimes war paint, plays an electric guitar, and leads a rock group called Country Joe & the Fish who record for Vanguard.

Late last spring, Joe went to a meeting in Palo Alto, the creamy rich suburb and intellectual elephant graveyard of the San Francisco Bay Area. The meeting was political and the people at it wanted to talk to someone from the New Youth, the Love Generation—a Hippie.

"No one wants to listen to speeches," Joe MacDonald told the stiff politicos. "We had the groovy anti-war march and then the speakers rapped away with the same old political bullshit. The revolution is now. It's happening on the streets."

Evergreen Review, September, 1967

"Politics and social activity have to be entertaining, rather than boring," MacDonald said later. "When the left wing does things, there's no energy. But when the hippies do something, there's energy and the radicals are beginning to realize this."

It's not "flower power" to Joe. That's just a slogan on a button and no more to be taken seriously than "Make Me High" or "If It Moves, Fondle It" or any number of other silly slogans the button entrepreneurs are marketing.

"What Joe told them," says Saul Landau, co-author with Paul Jacobs of *The New Radicals,* a friend and associate of C. Wright Mills, and a veteran politico himself, "is that if they want to make politics, make it groovy. When one of them asked him what his political program was, Joe thought for a moment and answered: 'Free music in the park.' 'What about the social organization of the society?' another one asked him, and Joe snapped back 'Fuck it!' "

The trouble is that radical politics in the United States has demonstrated its bankruptcy too openly now to have any real attraction for youth anymore. If you postulate—and no one operates on any other basis—that armed revolution in this country is an impossibility, then there is no hope in radicalization of politics. Without guns the radicals are powerless to make any fundamental changes because politics does not now and never really has made the machinery go in the U.S. of A. What runs this country is money, as the steel companies demonstrated when they socked it to LBJ and told him where to go.

The increasing attraction of the long-haired Haight-Ashbury hippies is in the obvious fact that what they do generate is power. You may call them flower children, call them The Love Generation, call them mindless LSD idiots, call them anything you please, they are the most powerful single social movement in the country amongst Caucasians. They generate psychic force; they accomplish things and they have created a community that is effectively functioning, surviving the guerrilla attacks made upon it by the Establishment, and within the ordinary society. And, as the hard reality of white politics is revealed to youth—the Free Speech Movement never had a chance and its leaders are in jail this minute, not for revolting against the stodgy University of California administration, but for trespassing; i.e., threatening property—more and more of them are simply turning away from the traditional forms of dissent because they find dissent meaningless.

"Turn on, tune in and drop out" is widely read as meaning drop out completely from society, which is what the beatniks did. This is not at all what is going on with the hippies. They are doing something else, much more constructive and much more meaningful and infinitely creative. They are, in effect, the first creative social movement in decades among white people in the U.S.

The hippies are dropping out of the Madison Avenue, LBJ society in which a Hubert Humphrey can publicly put his arm around Lester Maddox and say there's room for him in the Democratic Party. They are dropping out of a society which condones napalm (and from the radical intellectual society which condones it in one country and condemns it in another).

But they are not just dropping out into Limbo or Nirvana. They are building a new set of values, a new structure, a new society, if you will, horizontal to the old but in it.

Plato said that forms and rhythms in music are never changed without producing changes in the most important political forms and ways. One recent night outside The Matrix, a San Francisco rock 'n' roll club which is non-alcoholic (more on that in a moment) the lead guitarists from two groups featured that night found out they both had been in the Sproul Hall FSM sit-in at Berkeley and that the drummer in one of the groups was also involved. None had known of the others' background until that moment.

Thus old politicos. From the FSM to rock 'n' roll. And, as the Supreme Court appeal was refused and the jail sentences loomed a couple of weeks away (the University of California and most of the rest of the educational establishment has been talking about educational reform for two years now, thanks to Mario Savio—and Clark Kerr is a martyr for being fired and Mario is in jail), one defendant said: "Man, I got to get that bread! I can't afford the fine, but I really can't spend two months in jail now. The group needs me. We're just getting going."

Now the point of that is that the rock groups and the Diggers represent communal, low-pressure-on-the-individual organizations in which the whole of the Haight-Ashbury hippie world operates, as opposed to plastic uptight America.

Communes, handcrafts, survival in the wilderness, farming, and other similar activities are a part and parcel of the movement. Maybe the Luddites did have a bad press, as E. J. Hobsbawm has suggested, and we may have to go back to them or even before, to take up the thread of history and straighten things out.

But the fact of the matter is that these people are trying, by demonstration, to show the world *how* to live now.

In a communiqué distributed on Haight Street this spring by a group of Diggers, the statement is printed: "Enlightenment, described in many tongues and in many ways, teaches, among other truths, that truly to feel the unity of all men that is love requires the giving up of the illusion of game-playing abstractions. A perfection of inner self, sometimes attainable through LSD-25 or other psychedelics, reveals the failure of all political games . . . the failure to LET IT GO. Do you want to SHOW people a groovy way of life, or do you want to TELL THEM HOW TO LIVE, and back it up with bottles, bricks, boards and even bullets?"

This is where the hippies are at.

That all this should gestate in the San Francisco Bay Area is no accident—the anti-HUAC demonstrations and the spectacle of the San Francisco police hosing the non-violent students took place here. So did the Chessman vigils, the Palace Hotel sit-ins, the FSM, the Vietnam teach-ins, and the troop-train demonstrations.

And the same freedom to dissent, which allowed all those movements to rise and to evolve (the existence of the anti-McCarthy newspaper, *The Chronicle;* the free-speech non-commercial FM station, KPFA; Harry Bridges' radical-turned-respectable union, the ILWU), allowed the hippies to turn on, tune in (on life), and drop out of the games.

It's no accident that *Ramparts*, the muckraker of the Square Left, was born in San Francisco's foggy climate, even though its existence was made possible by the abandonment of their responsibilities by the mass media, from the *Times* through TV to *Time*. But *Ramparts* is only the white hope of the Square Left, just as its managing editor, Bob Scheer, became the white hope of radical politics. He polled forty-five per cent of the Berkeley vote in a race with Democrat Jeffrey Cohelan for Congress last fall.

But congressmen don't run the country, and it made no difference whether or not Scheer—who soft-pedalled his legalization-of-marijuana plank, trimmed his beard, got married and began to wear a tie, button-down collar, and a vest when he became a serious candidate—was or was not elected. If Wayne Morse can't do anything, what can a congressman do?

This is what the hippies understand. And this is what the Square Left can't dig in any way. And this is what Stokely Carmichael knows, too. The kinds of change that need to be made in this society cannot be made by electing congressmen. Short of guns, they can only be made by changing the heads of man, and the hippies are quite openly and definitely and consistently going about just that.

Not everything they do is laudable; not everyone who looks like a hippie is one. "Long hair doth not a hippie make, nor scraggy beard a knave," says an Ancient Irish Proverb (invented by me to illustrate a point). This generation of cultural dropouts has invented its own Bohemia. It is not the old Greenwich Village or North Beach, the

Greenwich Village of San Francisco. They went out and found a new place. And, intuitively or, as is the case of the Diggers, intellectually, they realized the truth of the *Catch*-22ish idea that any attempt to deal with the system makes you a victim of it.

A word on the Diggers. This is a loose group within the hippie society which takes its name from the seventeenth-century British communal group which took possession of land after the Civil War, tilled it in the name of the people, and gave the food away. The Diggers abolished money a year ago. They have been feeding anyone who shows up every afternoon at four at Oak and Ashbury in the Panhandle of Golden Gate Park with a perpetual picnic. "Take it, it's yours, it's free," they say.

There are no Digger leaders. Only spokesmen. "I may be a spokesman tonight and somebody else is a spokesman tomorrow," says Emmett Grogan, who is, if not a leader, one of the principal figures within the group. But think of that fact. There are no leaders ("don't follow leaders, watch your parkin' meters," I seem to hear Louis Simpson's favorite poet singing). And the fact is that there *are* no leaders either of the Diggers or the hippies. They read Alan Watts, they read Allen Ginsberg. They dig Michael McClure and Tim Leary and Ken Kesey. But they don't follow them and when any one of them makes the mistake, as some have done, of telling the hippies what to do, it just doesn't get done.

The Diggers are the monks of the Haight/Ashbury, some observers say. They are certainly the self-appointed conscience of the community. And they are attacking the very basic principle upon which this society is built: It is more sacred to make money than to be a good man. The Diggers began during the week last summer when a San Francisco policeman shot and killed a young Negro who was running away from an auto the cop suspected had been stolen, property being more valuable than human life. The Diggers refuse money. You can give them food and you can do things for them, but they will burn your ten dollar bill if you offer it. Their philosophy, Grogan once said, is accepting the futility of either fighting or joining the system.

In planning how to keep the people off Haight Street and thus avoid confrontations with the police, Digger elements and other interested hippies such as a group called The Summer of Love, organized or rather prepared the way for a series of free afternoon concerts in the Panhandle with rock bands.

"We have discovered the power of music, when played for free, to remove the hostilities of crowds," says Peter Cohan, another Digger. At the Great Be-In in Golden Gate Park last January 20,000 people, at least, gathered and spent the afternoon listening to music, digging themselves and one another, and there were only two cops in evidence.

The Digger *modus operandi* is "do your thing." A University of California professor, a good and honest and gentle and liberal man, genuinely concerned about the necessity of providing food and housing for the summer invasion of flower children, came to a meeting and asked "for an inventory of your needs." A Digger told him, "No, man, you know what we need. You see something we need and you get it. Do your thing, man. That's all. We need whatever you think we need."

"I don't care too much for money, money can't buy me love," The Beatles sing and Bob Dylan says, "Money doesn't talk, it swears." Roy Ballard, another Digger, observes that maybe these artists don't even know how seriously the youth is taking what they say. But the point is that youth *is* taking it seriously.

The experimental colleges, the Free Universities which have sprung up all over the U.S. in the past two years, were born in the corridors of Sproul Hall that grim December night when the students felt the armed might of the State risen in the defense of property. The Diggers' free food and abolishment of money has spawned other organizations in New York, in Los Angeles, in Berkeley, and even in Cleveland. One can, with logic (but aren't we all in some sense the prisoners of logic, as Malvina Reynolds points out?), say that one swallow doesn't make a summer and that the Diggers won't change the world. But there remains something strongly attractive to the idea of money being no good. Free food has come to the Diggers from as far away as Texas and New York.

Maybe the Diggers won't change the world. But they have certainly changed the heads of those they have touched. What other cauldron has so altered the young in this society as to cause any of them to abandon money?

"The Haight is a subsistence community, living on a fringe of surplus never before present . . . in this or any country and creating a new culture based on a radically different sense of human and social priorities," observes Michael Rossman, one of the FSM leaders (currently in jail) and now a close student of the hippie culture.

"Just do your thing, man, it'll be all right." Hang loose. "It's all right ma, I got nuthin' to live up to." We have raised this generation in an emotional pressure cooker and they are saying to us, hey there, you with those achievement stripes, that logic in your head, those meetings and those plans and those proposals. IT ISN'T WORKING.

And we know it. That's what has frightened the daylights out of all the older generation faced with the long hair. The youth looks peaceful and content and at ease. It has dignity. It is not hustling and it is not, so very obviously not, striving for the same values its parents strove for.

Cleanliness is no longer next to Godliness and logic is not sacred. It is all right to have fun and the human body is not a thing to be ashamed of ("if the merchandise is offensive, complain to the manufacturer," Lenny Bruce used to say).

It is perfectly okay to smoke pot. Everyone who really knew anything at all about it, in contrast to the professional, Parkinson's-law narcotic fuzz and the bluenoses, always knew this but didn't expect to operate on it. Liquor is the real enemy. An outstanding characteristic of the be-ins, the dances, and the other happenings in San Francisco ever since the hippies began to congregate there is the absence of drunks. There are no fights at the dances. None at all. And no booze. Beer sales are off in some territories, including Northern California, and the night-club business, which depends on hard liquor for its real profits, is in deep trouble. Is it true that Schenley and a tobacco company have merged and does it mean what the hippies think it means?

If we can accept the idea that black pride is not racist, then white pride is not racist either, and a characteristic of this Bohemian group is that they are not ashamed of being white. A SNCC worker, a young man who was arrested in the Oakland *Tribune* picketing, a young veteran of civil rights, saw no evil in the dance poster from the Avalon Ballroom which showed, in full blazing color, a very black, very old woman with a red bandana wrapped around her gray and grizzled head. "We've got to get past the old images. If it's a groovy picture, it's a groovy picture."

The Beatnik world of the fifties was an interracial world first and foremost. But an interracial world based on a white assumption of innate black superiority. The hippies' world is quite different. The stereotype black stud from *The Dutchman* is discovering that the hippie chicks don't get uptight when he tells them "you won't make it with me because you're prejudiced." This, too, is changing.

Hippie groups, including the Diggers, recently put on a two-day free festival with free food and music and balloons and sundry goodies in the *Black Orpheus*-style ghetto of Hunter's Point and they called it a Muhammad Ali Festival in honor of Muhammad Ali's stand on the draft. There are no leaders in the Haight, just people who do things, one of them said. And they just went ahead and organized this event.

The hippies simply disregard laws that they do not approve of, most of the time. They now hitch-hike with one foot usually on the curb to keep from getting busted on a state law, but they blow pot when and where they feel like it in blissful disregard of the reality of the law. And many don't register for the draft or report for induction.

"We know something has got to be changed about the draft law," said a parole officer who visited me on a case where I was listed as a reference. "We can't put them all in jail. The law is inflexible and unjust and inadequate."

When the Bob Dylan film *Don't Look Back* was shown in San Francisco this summer, the hippie audience applauded the line "I don't read *Time* or *Newsweek* to find out what's going on." They know the truth of that. They *do* read the underground press. Some magazines. A few people. But basically the radio is the communications medium because it is instant. In the Haight, the society is back to the broadside. Sheets appear on the street three, four, and sometimes more times a day in runs of five hundred to get the message out to the people on the street.

The hippies, represented by various groups including the Diggers and The Summer of Love people, had been bugging the city authorities all spring about making plans to feed and house the summer invasion.

"They're begging the city, they're dropout middle-class kids and they're asking for things the Negro kids would never ask for, because they've had things given them all their lives," a critic said. That is quite true. But the point is that they know that what they need is possible to get and that the State is there to serve the people and a public servant is a servant of the public. So they step up and they say it, loud and clear. And this causes the city and the authorities to explain and explain but it also makes everyone, old and young, re-evaluate the concepts. When the San Francisco City Board of Supervisors adopted a resolution that said, in effect, we don't want the hippies here (which is what it *did* say, later denials to the contrary), even the *Chronicle* had to speak out against it. Willie Brown, the Negro member of the State Assembly from San Francisco, pointed out in a public statement to the Supervisors (one of whom is Terry Francois, a long-time leading Negro civil-rights leader) that discrimination against one minority opens the door to discrimination against others.

The hippie culture is a drug culture, too. I suppose one has to say that. But in saying it, it should be pointed out that the entire American culture is a drug culture. "Mother's little helpers," the Rolling Stones sang, and Grace Slick of the Jefferson Airplane in "White Rabbit" sings of the pills that make you tall and the pills that make you small "and the ones that mother gives you don't do anything at all."

Between the use of tranquilizers, alcohol, and other drugs (even excluding tobacco) the majority of the people in this country are on one thing or another. LBJ has been on tranquilizers since 1955, James Reston reveals.

So what is pot? So what is LSD? They may freak out those unfamiliar with them and, surely, the society has made official LSD research all but impossible and you are punished more severely for possessing marijuana than for drunken driving. Who's worse off, the alcoholic or the guy on a bum trip? Something is wrong here. Psychiatrists don't know how to handle LSD bum trips, but the hippies know, and the first thing they do is try to keep the guy on a bum trip out of the hands of the cops and the psychiatrists.

"What should we do when a kid makes his defense on a marijuana charge temporary insanity and we know he is really sane?" a reputable psychiatrist asked me.

"Lie to the cops, if you're trying to save people rather than be Adolph Eichmann," I told him and he gasped, "It's against my code of professional conduct!"

Like the hippies, I fail to see the distinction between that and hedging on your income tax report or telling a traffic cop you were only doing thirty mph when you know you were doing forty.

The sacredness of authority. The sacredness of logic. The sacredness of money. In fact, almost all of what our history has been built on is being questioned.

And why the hell not? Look where it all has got us in 1967?

That these kids are operating from a childhood spent gazing at TV Westerns in which right is right and wrong is wrong may put them on a TV Western trip in buckskins and beads, but Executive Suite, Adlai Stevenson, John Kennedy, and Hubert Humphrey got us backing General Ky in Vietnam.

"For the reality of politics, we must go to the poets not the politicians," Norman O. Brown says. And the truth of the matter is that Allen Ginsberg has more illuminating things to say about the American condition in his *Wichita Vortex Sutra* than all the SDS literature of the past four years.

The youth is having none of the ideology of its parents. The radical line that folk music and Woody Guthrie were where it really was at makes no more sense than anything else the Square Left has said.

"We have the chance to change the world," one of The Byrds said on TV recently. And I was reminded of the night that Kennedy instituted the blockade of Cuba. I was in the audience at a Nelson Algren talk at the University of California in Berkeley. He was speaking on Hemingway and he interrupted himself to look out at the audience and said: "I would regard a United States invasion of Cuba as a violation of everything I have been taught as an American."

Later, at a party, a member of a well-known folk-singing group, himself a radical of lifelong standing, said, "What courage that took! We never can say *anything* when we have 5,000 people out there!" And Algren smiled and quietly said it didn't take courage at all.

And that's the way the hippies are going to change this society. It doesn't take the kind of courage we have been taught to believe it does. What it takes is men like the Diggers and the rock musicians and the rest "doing their thing."

We may not live to see the complete change. We may be blown to bits in the meantime. It may well be too late. But precinct politics are not going to stop that, if the anti-war demonstrations don't mean anything we are truly helpless.

Money is losing its power to buy and thus its power to corrupt. Conformity is being lost in the Dylan ethic of "Dig yourself" and the Digger ethic of "Do your thing."

The revolution, as Country Joe MacDonald says, is already happening in the street. Radicals had better get with it if they can (most of them probably can't unless their kids can blow their minds, somehow, possibly with pot).

Everyone remembers the feeling of mutual understanding and love and the blessing of a common cause, from everything from the Free French to the Stevenson campaign. The hippies have it all the time. "I came here because of the psychic energy. I get recharged," said Arthur Lisch, a painter who is now a full-time active Digger.

And the release of that psychic energy is what will change the form of American life. The beginning has already been made.

Even before the murders and the publicity about hard drugs, the more sensible of the underground papers realized that there was no very cogent argument to be made for living in an urban ghetto. Slums lose their appeal rapidly, even for romantic young idealists who are predisposed to like any place that isn't home.

Lionel Mitchell avoids the misrepresentation that is almost calculated to build a population of transients. He knew, far before the experience of a dozen cities proved it, that no one can live indefinitely on love, and that communities consist of more than a dozen psychedelic shops. One senses that the time to make the New York scene was several years before the mass influx; almost nothing remains of the spirit Mitchell cherishes.

Look at Down Here

LIONEL MITCHELL

At Avenue A and Tenth Street, a marvelous phenomenon exists. There is a vacant store undergoing renovation. There is the parachute-decorated "Cave." There is the PSYCHEDELICATESSEN, and there is the Leather Shop, a Puerto Rican enterprise. This phenomenon is at once a symbol or embryo of the whole East Village, because it is more or less typical of the many scenes, cultures, and antagonisms that push their way to the surface in our lives here. Looking upon the scene, one is struck by the fragmentation. This is deceptive and superficial, because there *is* a unity that runs undercurrent. The hitch comes in the difficulty we all have in admitting just what the unifying element is.

A plump woman walks through Tompkins Square Park, leading a ridiculously under-sized dog on a gaudy chain. "Too many freaks, too many freaks," she crows.

A Polish man answers in the heat of argument, "No . . . the police do not beat me . . . no . . . not in *this* country."

We hear, knowing that America played a cruel joke on us all, and in particular, on the tender Beat Generation. "See," she smiles wanly, "I can do it better." No one was told that the most ferocious tensions are the basic premise of life in this country, and that when the game gets too rough, all heads are cracked for good measure. No one understands that, in order to be conservative or compassionate, it is best, first, to be rich. If it appears that the many fragments of the East Village are at each other's throats, then, that is because we find it so difficult to individually and lovingly admit the truth of our common situation.

The Village tourist buses have been re-routed to include in their route the St. Mark's area, to cruise past the Dom, and to bring tourism, money, and MacDougal Street East. Not only did the West Village experiment fail, but the failure became expensive, and no one wants to remember why. Having devoured the so-called Beat Generation, society digests its masticated fragments, to the sole benefit of society. Our slum is a merry-go-round with no memory, but at least it is alive. It is the confrontation of these various lives that seem to us ominous. The hippie maintains some poignancy here. The student gets an introductory course in life here. The Puerto Rican enters our dreams, and forces us to use them. I am saying, through contrast, that society, as personified by the West Village, is decadent, not because it has no morals or bad morals, but because it has no manners, and because it is redundant.

Part of the issue for the East Village, then, is courage. We discovered this in a solemn ritual, a bloody prelude to truth. We have already been over the old grounds, where death, and death alone, gave us our ultimate definition. Beyond death (so we discovered) there was nothing. On the side of the inadequacy of definitions, there stood life. Must the same discoveries be quixotically re-discovered? Perhaps a litany is in order. To be afraid to die is to be afraid to live, because life and death are on the same cycle. To be afraid to live just so happens to be a kind of death in itself. In other words, if one is going to be raped (or better still, if one puts oneself in that position) then be revolutionary enough to plunge into it without squirming.

Avenue A is a montage of truth. Here, we see scenes existing together which do not have a common history or a common growth. Superficially, they have nothing in common. The truth of the matter is that every single inhabitant of the East Village has, in his or her own way, heard the flickering voice of disquiet, saying in its own tones, "Something is wrong . . . something has gone wrong." There is profound hatred in the assumption that our tools (our acid and our police troops) can do our living for us. The specific form of hatred underlying this very, very American prejudice, is hatred of self, lack of self-confidence, feelings of self-unworthiness. The unifying factor of the East Village is that every one of its inhabitants are, in fact, drop-outs, if in no other area than that of the escape from high rents. Not one of them could honestly live strictly legal, true-blue, red-blooded American lives. Anyone who wishes to disprove this assertion may try. One only wants to laugh, or cry, or both, when one sees the grotesque extremes people will go to rather than admit the truth of why they are here. People are here in the East Village because they could no longer make it in Harlem or Poland or Russia or Eastern Europe or Suburbia or Puerto Rico or what have you. And perhaps one of the main reasons they could not make it where they were is that they couldn't accept it or believe its truths, as truths for themselves. Part of their misery they packed-up and brought with them. This, then, is the part of the cruel American practical joke that they play on themselves (ourselves, if you wish). The truth is whole, and it does not depend on our diversions for existence. The East Village is a place where everybody is in the same boat. We can make it into a paradise, or we can go on importing hell into it.

There are not enough women in the East Village. Men are naturally conservative. Left to their own devices, they tend naturally towards boredom. Oscar Wilde declares, through a character, in *A Woman of No Importance*:

> "Women are a fascinatingly wilful sex. Every woman is a rebel
> . . . Men marry because they are tired; women because they are
> curious. Both are disappointed."

I propose certain remedies. (1) The institution of a series of girl happenings or "girl-ins," designed for the fairer sex, openly recruiting the fairer sex. (2) A new league or committee, to handle the welcoming of females to the East Village. This league may take as its cry the preservation of human sexuality under adverse circumstances. It may adopt a crash program geared to the needs of the East Village, recruiting at girls' colleges, finishing schools, stenographers' schools, and the like. Finally, it need not be anti-anything, excepting VD. (3) I propose the remedy of an "honesty badge": the I AM HORNY button. This would take the "make" out of making-it and the "cruise" out of cruising. It was once said of Jean-Paul Belmondo: "He may not be beautiful, but at least he's vulgar."

In short, the restoration of the sexual revolution to the East Village may arouse it from its sloth. A sexual revolution (just like an un-sexual one) cannot limit itself merely to new photography or agitation against obscenity laws, while ignoring the complications, absurdities, and wastes present in human relationships.

> ". . . A revolution is not a dinner party, or writing an essay, or
> painting a picture, or doing embroidery; it cannot be so refined, so

leisurely and gentle, so temperate, kind, courteous, restrained and magnanimous . . ."

(Mao Tse-tung, Selected Works, Vol. 1, p. 28.)

There is an intrinsic narrow-mindedness in people who want to love and don't crack a smile. The same is true for people who are full of gripes against society but are left in trembling anger when their apartments are robbed or their girls molested.

There is a touch of Don Quixote in the black revolutionary who is ready for the race war but who cannot talk to or does not know a Negro not in the Village scene.

The curious, amusing charm of America; its accidental honesty is magnified in the East Village.

Example: A few black kids run up to the door of a few Polish apartments, knock on the door, and scream, "Death to guineas!" That seems minor enough since they couldn't tell an Italian from an Eskimo. Go to! This is America where fear is our most important product. Law and order trembles and a few days later efforts are made to organize a vigilante committee to oppose "rioting, looting, raping, and Mau Maus."

It is lewd and in the poorest taste for a man living in a world rapidly realizing seven women per man to publically admit that he cannot hold his own woman without extraneous and irrelevant aids.

Let us push further.

Much by way of negativism can be said of what Claude Brown has called "the Village Negro." But the Village Negro, so-called, has rejected the stance of "universal man" through hard knocks and because he grew weary of going it alone. He watched too many of his beatnik friends get married, go home and get rich instead of dropping out. The Powell case taught him most recently that there is neither freedom nor individuality, nor security outside of the tribe. Not only is Uncle Tomism impractical and restrictive, there is absolutely no profit to it. The Village Negro lived similar to lumpen proletarians, that is to say, with hope, a hope that has slowly been shattered. He becomes nationalistically inclined not strictly by choice but by force of circumstances. He felt hounded and hunted off the West-side. No "Spade" making the West Village scene of several years ago is without his memories of violence that seemed to spring from the shadows as he stumbled home with the principal ideas of the day in his head after hob-nobbing with the main literati or culturati of the epoch. Imagine a hipness, a scene where one had to appear "cool" and where the very price of that coolness meant that one couldn't make any mistakes. The black hippie retreated East where he is raising a family and where he learned the word "brother" with a vengeance and where for the first time this soul who ran from the small towns and the ghetto has put down roots. It is so difficult to understand, especially with an expanded consciousness, why he laughs cynically when one says to him, "love"?

After all, he is not being hostile just for the sake of being hostile. He believed in the ideas and premises of the Beat Generation and he came, in time, to realize that he was a mere guest there too. When he was not betrayed outright, he and his new found idealism were left defenseless. If only he had heard the Marquis de Sade tell Marat, "Compassion is the property of the privileged classes."

Black nationalism is whirling through its stages at record pace. In the East Village the egotistical stage is already over. There are still bad vibrations but TCB is the order of the day. True, the profound ethical revolution implied in the autobiography of Malcolm X is being neglected. The "spades" are just learning to call each other "brother." They haven't tackled all the implications of that word yet. They soon will, of course. But nationalism is as creative as it is destructive. Time and freedom are inextricably bound up with this particular "ism." In the matter of freedom, one must be careful not to be tricked. Monsters are not free, however phallic they are able to be, only man has the possibility of freedom.

No discussion of the East Village can ignore the coming Age of Love. Love? The word is old, the cry is new, perhaps, and the answer is acid. Gertrude Stein was asked as she was dying, "What is the answer?" Her last words were, "What is the question?" Is love a fond hallucination remaining as a verbal residue after a brought-down acid consciousness —a memento mori? If love is so passive, so slogan-like, how can it have meaning in the hellish instants of reality? What does it mean in tenements and brickpiles and police stations and racial antagonisms and among those who have no other choice but to be exploited? The approaching Age of Love does not seem to be a very expressive one. It shows no such passivity in the production of put-downs for the rest of humanity, that is . . . taking Timothy's adjective for consciousness he doesn't approve of . . . "menopausal minds," for instance. Where does one draw the line between this new love and the old, ordinary, intolerant, Auschwitz variety with its exclusive, banal, horrific results? Leary in the article with Watts, Ginsberg, Snyder . . . also had narrow references . . . had to be cautioned against anger . . . had to be reminded that human beings are human beings whether they had acid consciousness or American Gothic . . . His models were much too MIT professors with the money to buy farms at Lexington, white collar workers and students with the relatively nice problem of whether to drop out or not. Still the psychedelic happening produced the Diggers or men who believe that love is an *act* with which to fill every instant of existence. No skeptic can stand before an act. Only cynics can do that. When love becomes *action* and when the only obstacle to this action is the number of tiny, tiny instants wherein it is impossible to act, logic is made poetry. Against poetic logic there is no defense, there can be no skepticism, and a very, very little cynicism. In this sense Diggerism is Revolutionary. It can change and create. It can move and it can shake moral, political, ethical, economic, and spiritual consciousness.

I quote from St. Paul, the man who said . . . "It is better to marry than to burn" . . . but who is most lyrical on the question of love:

"Though I speak with the tongues of men and of angels, and have not charity, I am become as sounding brass, or a tinkling cymbal.

And though I have the gift of prophecy, and understand all mysteries, and all knowledge; and though I have all faith, so that I could remove mountains, and have not charity, I am nothing.

And though I bestow all my goods to feed the poor, and though I give my body to be burned, and have not charity, it profiteth me nothing . . ."

(Apparently, "menopausal minds" have not lost the poetic touch. More interesting is the fact that Paul, writing in New Testament Greek, used the word agape which combines eros and total responsibility. The royal translators of King James used the Latin word charitas, from which our "charity" comes. Agape is that love of God which can only exist in our human love for each other. A recent article describing Haight Street lists rape as common and characterizes the experiment as a small scale domestic Vietnam and traces the blame to psychedelic commercialism. I take the liberty to substitute the word "love" for charity in the remainder of this quote.)

Love suffereth long, and is kind; love envieth not; love vaunteth not itself, is not puffed up,

Doth not behave itself unseemly, seeketh not her own, is not easily provoked, thinketh no evil;

Rejoiceth not in iniquity, but rejoiceth in the truth;

Beareth all things, believeth all things, hopeth all things, endureth all things.

Love never faileth; but whether there be prophecies, they shall fail; whether there be tongues, they shall cease; whether there be knowledge, it shall vanish away.

For we know in part, and we prophesy in part.

But when that which is perfect is come, then that which is in part shall be done away.

When I was a child, I spake as a child, I understood as a child,

I thought as a child: but when I became a man, I put away childish things.

For now we see through a glass, darkly; but then face to face: now I know in part; but then shall I know even as also I am known. And now abideth faith, hope, love, these three; but the greatest of these is love.

I think that every man, however hung up, looks out of his own inferno at various times and dreams and cries out for a better way. All great faith is predicated upon this anguish. Paul's statement is comprehensive and goes further than anything to be heard so far in the debate on love. In the East Village I have seen that at least part of the time flowers can be given out with a terribly cold-blooded condescension, that love can be twisted into a euphemism for hate, guiltless selfishness, and snobbery. The work of love lies before the brave and there is much, much room for it to expand into. Since the East Village is not Haight, it has a chance to abstract and take only what it needs from that experiment. The Digger influence is already being felt here. A visit to the Head Shop or the Psychedelicatessen will show that already a cult of love has developed a new style from the old, hostile bohemianism that was characteristic of the fifties. They reach out to the newcomer and look him straight into the eye, and hipness, that neo-elitist cult, is no longer all important. They give food. They want to do away with the dealer, a measure which is sure to disarm society and shows they mean business. I always wondered in the late fifties how people who called themselves dissenters against capitalism could so freely engage themselves in the burning and hoodwinking of not just mere strangers but their closest friends too. Feverish activities are afoot to provide free clothing and food at many points in the East Village. I have heard of some Diggers being arrested for distributing food on the Sabbath. If the reader is interested in one man's opinion, some way must be found to restrain the false piety of the law. Efforts must be made to prevent New York from becoming the first city in history to make breathing illegal or to impose its taxing power upon air consumption. Love is an act, most holy, most lyrical, and most sublime!

Courage, truth, and love are the things to be expanded in the East Village. All other problems will fall before these three. And what is the result of this expansion? It is not even necessary to prophesy. The East Village is so fertile, so rich in energy and creativity that once it transcends its fragmented lies the results are plain to see. It is already on the verge of ceasing to be a slum without the bulldozing away of the indigenous population. Only a massive combination of energy and faith will suffice to do this. Courage, truth, and love; these are its greatest needs at the moment. It already has the cohesive qualities that will stand with integrity against MacDougal streets and news reporters. Moreover, it is large enough to contain great diversity without the importation of extraneous hang-ups which are absurd, wasteful, and destructive when applied here. It has no economy at present. But there are signs of one developing. This is to say, if the scene is not blown, it will be possible in a few years through a cooperative effort for most of the inhabitants to gain their support without going too far from their familiar surroundings to find it. The reality of the East is unique and there is nothing but buncombe in the attempt to bring stances and problems which do not apply when there is so much to be done right here. If one were asked what is the East Village, the answer must undoubtedly be that at present it is the most fertile and wasted potential in terms of communities on the North American continent.

Drop City is the oldest of the rural communities, and its success is celebrated whenever a news magazine wants to show seminude hippies against a backdrop of geodesic domes. It squats in the Colorado wilderness, located far enough from civilization to insure the dual benefits of cheap land and privacy. This isolation— Drop City's almost total break with modern life—is both its strength and weakness; distance has fortified commitment to the community while it encourages a kind of cultural solipsism.

The experience of its citizens reminds those who plan similar communities that it can be done, though not without hardship. And unlike most tribes, success has not weakened Drop City's structure; the inhabitants have not succumbed to mindless viewing of daytime television as an escape from the problems of natural existence.

Drop City:
A Total Living Environment

ALBIN WAGNER

It is impossible to define Drop City. It fell out a window in Kansas three years ago with a mattress and a balloon full of water and landed in a goat pasture near Trinidad, Colorado. At first Droppers lived in tents and tarpaper shacks. And then others began to see the same vision and began making things. Geodesic domes. Now there are sixteen to twenty Droppers living in ten domes and as many different ideas of what Drop City is as there are Droppers.

We have attempted to create in Drop City a total living environment, outside the structure of society, where the artist can remain in touch with himself, with other creative human beings.

We live in geodesic domes and domes of other crystalline forms because the dome shape is easier to construct. We live on a subsistence level and almost entirely scrounge the materials for our own buildings. All materials are used. Car tops, cement, wood, plastic. The cheapest and least structural of building materials are structurally sound when used in a true tension system.

We can buy car-tops in Albuquerque, N.M., for 20¢ each. We jump on top of a car with an ax and chop them out, stomp out the back glass, strip off the mirrors, and pull out the insulation. All of it can be used to cover a large dome for the small cost of about $30.

We have discovered a new art form: creative scrounging. We dismantle abandoned bridges by moonlight. We are sort of advanced junkmen taking advantage of advanced obsolescence. Drop City was begun without money, built on practically nothing. None of us is employed or has a steady income. Somehow we have not gone hungry, or done without materials. Things come to us.

America, the affluent waste society. There is enough waste here to feed and house ten thousand artists. Enough junk to work into a thousand thousand works of art. To the townspeople in Trinidad, five miles away, we are scroungers, bums, garbage pickers. They are right. Perhaps the most beautiful creation in all Drop City is our junk pile. The garbage of the garbage pickers.

Drop City is a tribal unit. It has no formal structure, no written laws, yet the intuitive structure is amazingly complex and functional. Not a single schedule has been made, and less than three things have come to a vote. Even though Droppers rarely, if ever, agree on anything, everything works itself out with the help of the cosmic forces. We are conscious of ourselves and others as human beings.

Each Dropper is free. Each does what he wants. No rules, no duties, no obligations. Anarchy. But as anarchistic as the growth of an organism which has its own internal needs and fulfills them in a natural, simple way, without compulsion.

Droppers are not asked to do anything. They work out of the need to work. Out of guilt or emptiness the desire to work, hopefully, arises. It is no longer work, but pleasure. Doing nothing is real work. We play at working. It is as gratifying as eating or loving. We are based on the pleasure principle. Our main concern is to be alive.

Droppers come in all sizes, shapes, colors: painters, writers, architects, panhandlers, film-makers, unclassifiables. Each has his own individual endeavors and achievements. These perhaps tell what we are doing more than anything else. But they cannot be enumerated. They have to be seen, read, touched, heard. They speak for themselves. But we do all have this in common—whatever art we produce is not separated from our lives.

Droppers have painted the Ultimate Painting. A rotating infinite sphere, a circular geodesic structure loaded with spatial paradox, complete with strobotac. A painting to walk up the stairs into and lose your mind by. The Ultimate Painting was done by five Droppers, to make it five times better. The Ultimate Painting is for sale for $60,000.

The Droppers have printed a comic book called The Being Bag. We welcome the feds and postal inspectors who come to harrangue us about its content. Our poet looks forward to the inspectors and their reading of his work.

Droppers make movies, black-and-white wind poems, flickering TV beauties with all the subliminal delights of pulsating Coke ads, the crystal-molecular good sense of a dome going into time-lapse, and the grunting goodness of sex. We have two movies on Drop City for distribution.

The second weekend in June we held a Joy Festival. The First Annual Drop City Festival and Bacchanal Post Walpurgis and Pre-Equinox Overflow and Dropping. Over 300 people attended. It was a freakout in all media, 96 hours of continuous mind-blow.

We want to use everything, new, junk, good, bad, we want to be able to make limitless things. We want TV videotape recorders and cameras. We want computers and miles of color film and elaborate cine cameras and tape decks and amps and echo-chambers and everywhere. We want millionaire patrons. We need the most up-to-date equipment in the world to make our things. We want an atomic reactor.

Drop City is the first attempt to use domes for housing a community. Buckminster Fuller gave us his 1966 Dymaxion Award for "poetically economic structural achievements." We hope to buy more land, build more Drop Cities all over the world, the universe. Free and open way stations for every and anyone. Living space and heat can be made available to all at a fraction of the present cost through application of advanced building techniques such as solar-heated domes. Already Drop South is firmly established near Albuquerque, N.M.

Drop City is Home. It is a strange place. An incredible webbing of circumstance and chance, planning and accidents, smashed thumbs and car-tops. We are not responsible for what and where we are, we have only taken our place in space and light and time. We are only people who want love, food, warmth. We have no integrity. We borrow, copy, steal any and all ideas and things. We use everything. We take things, we make things, we give things.

Drop City pivots on a sublime paradox, opposing forces exist side by side in joy and harmony. A psychedelic community? Chemically, no. We consider drugs unnecessary. But etymologically, perhaps. We are alive. We dance the Joy-dance. We listen to the eternal rhythm. Our feet move to unity, a balanced step of beauty and strength. Creation is joy. Joy is love. Life, love, joy, energy are one. We are all one. Can you hear the music? Come dance with us.

Bowart's view of San Francisco, one of the earliest reports of the western mecca to be published, captures both the reporter's sense of the Haight and the insider's sense of the future. Bowart is really describing the condition of participatory democracy in San Francisco, a barometer of community health that was to fluctuate wildly as the influx of runaways destroyed the area's internal communications and its native economic resources.

This is a portrait of the Haight on the threshold of the migration, with most of the characters who were so frequently to be quoted present and on the stage. The city officials, the hippie leaders—they are all there, draped in paranoia excessive even by contemporary standards, the spokesmen endlessly denying their own clear impulses toward self-aggrandizement.

Gropings and Fumblings

WALTER BOWART

In the late fifties and early sixties after the "beat generation" had been incubating for ten years, it stuck its head out of its cloistered womb and ran into the ominous status quo. The Health, Police and Fire Departments, acting on the advice of a sensational press, representing a frightened and lost power structure, launched what appears in retrospect to have been a carefully laid plan to harass the beatnik communities in New York and San Francisco.

Inspectors scurried over MacDougal Street issuing summonses for infinite "violations" which had previously remained undiscovered. Artists were thrown into the streets when they were discovered living in lofts—places which because of their condition could not be rented to commercial establishments, yet were not ramshackle enough to be condemned.

In New York the exodus began from Greenwich Village, which had become a political plum for the Village Independent Democrats, to the unaligned, undesirable Lower East Side where the rents were still cheap.

In North Beach, gangster elements took over as the beatniks moved out, leaving today a quieter craftsman's community surrounded by topless joints.

The East Village Other, April 1, 1967

Like a cue-ball scattering the opening shot, the establishment broke the cluster and spread the beat generation across the country. It took the seeds carried by poets, painters, and psychedelic holy men ten years to flower into the gigantic minority of gypsy drop-outs currently imploding from the middle-class vacuum.

Now thousands of hippies have come together in the Haight-Ashbury section of San Francisco to experiment with a new world of design, to offer alternatives to an established order of profiteering, usury, and greed which is leading the noble American experiment on to a vulture's perch at the edge of an empire.

Built on seven lush hills, San Francisco is the Rome to a future world founded on love. Enter Haight-Ashbury as the love-guerilla training school for drop-outs from mainstream America.

The squares are frightened. They are afraid of love! They are so practiced in paranoia and suspicious that when confronted by large groups of long-haired friendly children, as free as the wind, they react with hostility.

Once again there was the same old crisis brought about by sensation-seeking newsmen, who couldn't (with their professional cynicism) know anything about love. Good news is always violent.

And once again there was the same old reaction from the police, fire and health departments. Harassment.

A Digger communal house was recently ransacked by police with a warrant reading "for suspicion of possessing illegal deer," which in fact an officer of the Forestry Department had given them.

But this time, ten years later, the confrontation is taking a slightly different beat. The squares, by harassing the Haight-Ashbury hippies, have taken on the entire one-half of the United States which is under twenty-five years of age. These children of the two-car garage are adopting the beatnik style, turning on and dropping out, and experimenting with utopian living and papa wants 'em back into his authoritarian rut.

An ocean of acid laps at the shores of Haight Street. Long-haired, spangled battalions dot the main street, even at noon on Wednesdays. Incense and perfume waft among the tell-tale body of acid-induced "schizophrenia."

It's the new Jerusalem, they say. The second coming is coming, they say. And by now it should not be alarming to recognize that a common acid vision is the flying saucers.

The philosophy of love is practiced. In Haight-Ashbury it manifests itself in a warmth and friendliness and sense of community not found on such a scale in any other city in America. There is a renaissance of folk-art.

Grass and acid are so prevalent that even the police are having a hard time taking it all too seriously. Everyone from Marin County to Sausalito to Chinatown is a pot-head.

Magic is everywhere and everyone talks in tongues. The Indians, it is said, left good vibrations in these hills where the top-forty radio show is called "Lucky Zodiac Show," with the idea that you can phone in and have your sign read over the air.

The only official Haight paper, *The San Francisco Oracle,* in only seven months of existence was printing 120,000 copies containing poems, esoteric discussion, and trips while the establishment papers, *The Chronicle* and *Examiner,* blare banner headlines and sensational stories:

(March 22—*S.F. Examiner*) POLICE CHIEF WARNS HIPPIES

"Police Chief Thomas Cahill today stood four square behind the Recreation and Park Commission in its resolve to prevent Golden Gate Park from becoming a 24-hour haven for hippies.

"Cahill took his stand in the face of a clergy-sponsored resolution calling upon the commission to relent on the hippie sleeping ban because of an anticipated influx of some 100,000 or more hippies this summer.

" 'Any encouragement through the mass media tending to attract still more undesirables to the problem areas of San Francisco is a disservice to the community,' Police Chief Cahill said."

(March 24—*Chronicle*) MAYOR WARNS HIPPIES TO STAY OUT OF TOWN

"San Francisco's city government began putting the slow squeeze on the Haight-Ashbury hippie land yesterday in an effort to discourage a summer influx of perhaps 100,000 more hippies.

"Police Chief Thomas Cahill conferred with Health Director Dr. Ellis Sox about providing better liaison with police in handling hippies who 'freak-out'—become psychotic—while on LSD trips."

NAVY ADMITS DRUG INQUIRY AT LEMOOR

"Officials at Lemoor Naval Air Station in Kings County confirmed that an investigation was under way there into the use of LSD and other drugs.

"But they denied a petty officer's claim that peace symbols had been painted on warplanes.

"The news came as the petty officer, Allen Weisenmuller, was released from Oakland Naval Hospital, where he had been held for psychiatric observation.

"While confined there, he told the Rev. Lyle W. Grosjean, assistant pastor of All Soul's Church in Berkeley, that he'd lost all his war-like notions after taking LSD last year."

Day after day these stories fill page after page in the San Francisco dailies. We must remember that in the old days it was a *Chronicle* writer that coined the term "beatnik." It's no wonder then that two to three hundred thousand more hippies are expected this summer.

Daily the underground Communications Company sends forth its hastily mimeographed instructions and broad-sheets advising the hippies how to act, how to clean up, where to buy health food, and what to expect next from the ugly square humorless community represented by Police Chief Cahill.

Easter Sunday, while New York was having its Be-In in the Central Park Sheepmeadow, and Los Angeles was holding its giant Love-In, Haight-Ashbury had an Easter Parade described by the papers as a "mill-in" which later turned into a riot when square entrepreneurs over-sold a benefit dance.

The Easter Mill-In was perpetrated by the mis-management of S.F. police who, when discovering the heavy tourist traffic along the six block stretch of Haight Street, blocked it to vehicles. Without the cars driving in the usual creeping line, bumper to bumper down the street, the hippies rejoiced in spilling over the crowded curbs into the roadway. For a few minutes there was dancing and frolicking but then the blundering blue-boys began driving the hippies out of the street, and then tried to thin the overflowing sidewalks.

Diggers spontaneously started performing their "Barn Dance" an erratic diagonal intersection crossing. When the cars were allowed back on the street again, to clear them of people, the diggers started sweeping under the tires of the gawking motorists.

The roof tops were lined with overjoyed spectators. One man fell off a roof while wearing his flying cape. He was not hurt, and after being released from the hospital was booked for disorderly conduct. Several arrests were made by the police, though the seven paddy wagons and twelve patrol cars were never filled.

The radio from five o'clock that day until eight thirty gave regular bulletins as to the progress of the Mill-In. Motorists hearing the reports on their car radios locked their doors and drove directly to the scene.

Protestant clergymen showed up to be a buffer between the kids and the cops, but it was easy to see that the clergy were fully on the hippie's side.

Rev. Durham from Glide Memorial Church offered a square radio reporter a flower and explained to the microphone that, "Citizens Alert has been notified of the arrests and lawyers and bail bondsmen are already getting them out. The police have learned a couple of things here this afternoon. They realize that the less they are seen the less trouble there is."

The crowd chanted "The streets are for people," as a sergeant at a phone box reported, "Things are getting hot. The traffic is heavy. I think we'll leave the scene."

The next day a press conference was held at All Saints Episcopal Church by the hippie leaders. All elements of the community were present except the police, who were not invited. What went down that day might have been a synopsis of the whole traumatic situation existing when change comes too fast. The fifty people sitting around in a circle searched their hearts for a rational strategy, a point to fix their charts from, and desperately groped for some communication with the square community.

The press set up their cameras on the other side of the room, outside the circle, representing the mass media's role as outsider, and provocateur.

A Digger named Ken began by saying that since he had this microphone around his neck he was the chairman: "For three days we've been hearing in the press about an exodus of two to three hundred thousand hippies to Haight Ashbury this summer. The mayor is scared. The Health Department is coming around flushing toilets and getting paranoid. The establishment is making war on us. We are under siege. We are at war.

"Anyone who is thinking of coming to San Francisco this summer should know that the mayor, the toilet flushers, and even the Parks Department are against them.

"The facilities of the establishment have been refused us. We say we don't need your facilities. We don't need you. We don't need old forms. We've proclaimed new forms and we're going to live by these new forms.

"I would like to invite all of America to come to San Francisco and learn these new political methods. America is hardening into an Empire, dominating the world. We are not going to pay for the trip of the American Empire."

Michael Bowan interrupted the speaker and said that he did not think that one should talk in such violent terms.

Peter Berg of the Diggers interrupted Bowan: "The media digs the idea of having an enclave of alienated people to harass. The abacus of media is working overtime on this thing. Someone is really cooking up a brew of bullshit. Someone really wants to start a riot.

"The media really loves desperadoes. I saw Allen Cohen on TV and up until that time I thought he was a softie. Allen said something like 'let's love—' and the announcer said, 'That's Allen Cohen, editor of the San Francisco *Oracle*, a radical dope fiend' and he looks all hairy and fierce like a rabbi and the media loves it.

"We've been set up for a fall by a military strategy laid out years ago on a wide scale. We've been set up."

Allen Cohen interrupted softly: "Instead of seeing the police as an enemy, let's look at them as someone blinded, someone scared and confused. The police have aroused a war. We have the choice of participating in it or renouncing it and creating models of intimate human relationships."

Poet Peter Gleason of the Dream Theater carried on: "The establishment has permanence and structure and a disregard for order. The next step for us, I think, is real events and dream-theater. We must show the squares the absurdity by putting life up against the establishment.

"We'll have a Drip-In, beautiful chicks in wet bathing suits at city hall; a Goo-In, kids in syrup covered clothes; a slow speed accident, two cars creeping slowly down the street into a head-on accident, one car full of whites and the other full of blacks who after the slow motion crash get out and then re-enter their cars and speed off.

"We'll set up an invisible government which will invisibly take over the city and issue statements. We'll have a 24 hour war with bulletins and then we'll win and take over and set up a welfare state distributing all necessities including fresh air, but we'll never give anyone quite enough.

"We must take political action and at the same time apologize for taking it. There's no reason we can't be Malcolm X and Uncle Tom at the same time.

"There's a tremendous revolutionary potential in Suburbia. The kids will come a long way to blow the scene. The more the city fathers get up tight the more the scene will be blown."

Peter Berg interrupted: "I think we can turn any potential riot into a celebration. I think we should live on the roofs and communicate with mirrors. We should put artificial paper boundaries everywhere."

Peter Gleason continued: "It's true that people are coming here because we're offering an alternative that's better than what they have been offered by the squares.

"It's possible that the kids will come here in a retaliatory mood and trouble may begin. We can do something about the war the establishment has declared. We can turn their war back on itself by real events, formalize their games, and make their rules beautiful and give them back as play.

"We must do all our plotting out in the open, just like this."

Michael Bowen chimed in: "The machine on Haight St. is still a problem. What are we going to do about all those gawking tourists in vehicles? I say make Haight Street into a mall."

A Digger named David elaborated: "Put a sign DO NOT ENTER, YOU'RE GOING THE WRONG WAY, NO RIGHT TURN, NO LEFT TURN, STOP, etc., at the entrance to Haight. The cars will stop in confusion and begin to jam up, then we can turn them over and fill them with dirt and make planters out of them."

Roy Ballard, described by some as a Black Muslim Digger, took the opportunity to announce his candidacy for mayor: "I'm running on the platform of turning things back to people. The police chief in my administration will have to be a man who knows the prison system from the inside."

The TV cameras whirred away. Peter Gleason warned, "The news media is going to take things down and edit it anyway they want and have us say anything they want to edit into it."

An ugly man from CBS grinned evilly.

Peter Berg grabbed the mike: "We have captured the station. *You are free!*"

Lovebook poet, Leonore Kandel, added, "This is a recording."

Dr. David Fisher, Research Associate of the National Institute of Public Health, finally spoke up from the back of the room. "Dr. Ellis D. Sox, the Head of the San Francisco Health Department is a weak man. He recently dropped his middle initial D. You know why. He is not an evil man, he's just a weak man. He has raised the specter of bubonic plague and venereal disease in the hippie community. His office is being used to push you around. After he made the health scare announcement last week, the inspectors came down in droves and so did the tourists.

"You don't get bubonic plague or cholera from rats or flies. You get bubonic plague from fresh shit, and that's the only thing issuing forth from the Health Department."

William Fortner summed up most aptly what it is that is happening in Haight-Ashbury: "When you find yourself in the situation of existing in a sub-culture which has dropped out of the mainstream, at that time you cannot pursue your values truly if you continue to ask the mainstream culture for welfare, government, or justice."

The gropings and fumblings of the Haight-Ashbury hippies may not reach the fruition of a true utopia, which the world has never seen, but one leaves San Francisco with the feeling that it is here and now where the new world, a human world of the 21st century, is being constructed.

In the words of Walter Rathenau: "Even the most troubled epoch is worthy of respect, because it is the work not just of a few people but of humanity; and thus it is the work of creative nature which is often cruel but never absurd. If this epoch in which we are living is a cruel one, it is more than ever our duty to love it, to penetrate it with our love till we have removed the heavy weight of matter screening the light that shines on the farther side."

V. The Ascendancy of Agape and Its Abuses

If their parents could personify pure evil, the young might represent pure good. The complexity of reality, the sheer brainwork necessary to produce profundity, the willingness to tolerate the unknown—all these were lost in the mathematical equation of love with goodness. Like lobotomized Gandhis, the beads-and-flowers set dominated; armed only with a sense of mission, they swamped the underground press with their love ethic. Addicted to the beat of love rock, unable and unwilling to earn a living wage, they pushed love to the limit. How can you arrest us, they questioned policemen, when we love you? Can I have a quarter, man—I'm looking for a place to crash.

The more elevated the ideal, the harder the bringdown. Lovers starved, passed cold nights huddled in doorways, and, finally, begged drugs to escape the realities of love. Always in motion, eyes trained only on the place ahead, the girls with braces and their gangly male companions abused their temporary hosts with a moral obtuseness that belied the emotion they claimed to represent. Love gives, and in the act of giving is fulfilled; when the true lovers had given their all, the loving had to stop. And when the murders proved that not everyone loves a lover, fear and hatred widened the range of emotions by two.

When starvation, addiction, and disease could no longer be ignored in the Haight, people began to take the Communication Company's leaflets seriously. Publishing whenever there was something to say, ComCo was the news center of the San Francisco underground. Its spokesmen were angrier than most, less likely to get suckered into nonreciprocal love pledges, and as a result, some of those who planned a pilgrimage to the Haight decided differently after reading ComCo bulletins in their local papers.

Haight / Hate?

Pretty little 16-year-old middle-class chick comes to the Haight to see what it's all about and gets picked up by a 17-year-old street dealer who spends all day shooting her full of speed again and again, then feeds her 3000 mikes and raffles her temporarily unemployed body for the biggest Haight Street gang bang since the night before last.

The politics and ethics of ecstasy.

Rape is as common as bullshit on Haight Street.

The Love Generation never sleeps.

The Oracle continues to recruit for this summer's Human Shit-In, but the psychedelic plastic flower and god's eye merchants, shocked by the discovery that increased population doesn't necessarily guarantee increased profits at all, have invented the Council for a Summer of Love to keep us all from interfering with commerce.

Kids are starving on The Street. Minds and bodies are being maimed as we watch, a scale model of Vietnam. There are people—our people—dying hideous long deaths among us and the Council is planning alternative activities. Haight Street is ugly shitdeath and Alan Watts suggests more elegant attire.

The Oracle, I admit, *has* done something to ease life on Haight Street; it's hired street kids to peddle the paper. Having with brilliant graphics

Communication Company, August, 1967

and sophomoric prose urged millions of kids to Drop Out of school and jobs, it now offers its dropouts menial jobs. That's hypocritical and shitty, but it's something. It means that a few dozen kids who can meet the Oracle's requirements can avert starvation whenever the Oracle comes out.

Groovy.

And why hasn't the man who *really* did it to us done something about the problem he has created? Why doesn't Doctor Timothy Leary help the Diggers? He's now at work on yet another Psychedelic Circus at $3.50 a head, presumably to raise enough cash to keep himself out of jail, and there isn't even a rumor that he's contributed any of the fortune he made with the last circus toward alleviating the misery of the psychedelphia he created.

Tune in, turn on, drop dead? One wonders. Are Leary and Alpert and the Oracle all in the same greedy place? Does acid still have to be sold as hard as Madison Avenue still sells sex? What do these nice people mean by "Love"?

Are you aware that Haight Street is just as bad as the squares say it is? Have you heard of the killings we've had on Haight Street? Have you seen dozens of hippies watching passively while some burly square beats another hippy to a psychedelic red pulp? Have you walked down Haight Street at dawn and seen and talked with the survivors?

The trouble is probably that the hip shopkeepers have believed their own bullshit lies. They believe that acid is the answer and neither know nor care what the question is. They think that dope is the easy road to God.

"Have you been raped?" they say. "Take acid and everything will be groovy."

"Are you ill? Take acid and find inner health."

"Are you cold, sleeping in doorways at night? Take acid and discover your own inner warmth. Are you hungry? Take acid and transcend these mundane needs."

"You can't afford acid? Pardon me. I think I hear somebody calling me."

I don't know what they'd say to the little girl that got gang-banged. They might not even believe it, since it's part of their religious creed that acid makes everybody automatically BEAUTIFUL, and therefore nobody would do that to a little girl. They might (as The Examiner certainly would) say that since the little girl had the clap before she was gang-banged at all, but went through the whole ghastly business willingly, as if that made a real difference.

They would never believe that they were guilty of monstrous crimes against humanity. They won't believe it this summer, when the Street reeks of human agony, despair and death death death.

Because few underground papers can pay their writers, most of their articles are written by dedicated and overworked writers and by those who Want To Write. On one level, this provides a greater opportunity for personal communication; on another level, it means that would-be philosophers are proliferating like wild mushrooms.

The catchwords change from year to year—one year, it's love, the next, revolution. Attacks on this cultural faddism are most persuasive when they come from within, and this piece of criticism effectively destroys the monolithic solutions that are a constant danger to movements whose followers share only the same neuroses.

Is Love Obscene?

JOHN KELSEY

There's no future playing one-two-three-O'Leary, even though it's fun. The hippie doctrine rests on let's all close our eyes and love each other, for then all the bogies will go away—or if they stay, they'll become loving too.

It doesn't work. The hippies are useful in a manner similar to the way Hitler tried to use the Social Democrats in Germany—a lessening, liberalizing force to sweep away later. I've nothing against hippies, but I think there are better things to do, and I can't see dropping out of a fight that must be fought. The doctrine of love has little meaning for a Filipino Huk, who's seen the CIA and Suharto kill about a million neighbouring Indonesians, and who knows that if he doesn't keep his knife sharp, he's next. He could turn loving, but then he'd starve even faster than he might now—because US imperialism owns him and his country. Love doesn't fill bellies or make better lives or eliminate storm troopers.

Storm troopers don't love back, see, they just walk on your prostrate, flowered face.

The world, unhappily, is filled with storm troopers in many guises; sometimes they're Marines in (god forbid the word)   , maybe they're cops in Los Angeles, or perhaps northern affairs officials in Inuvik or maybe even parliamentarians in Ottawa.

Canadian Free Press, May 26, 1967

Look at the Diggers in San Francisco. Hippies with a difference, who exist to give things away. The things they hand out so freely are the drippings from a sick, obese society, and their parasitic relationship with it provides suburbia with laughs and the Diggers with food.

The shock will come this summer, when teenyboppers from all over North America stream into Haight-Ashbury to discover starvation with love; the Diggers don't understand basic economics. You don't have to understand when you are hungry.

Sure, it'd be better if everybody loved one another with glee and stuff. But don't dream that Lyndon Johnson will love you. He doesn't and he won't; you're just a non-consuming pimple on the face of the real great society. If society accepts the hippies and the drug bag, that's fine, their struggle will be a part of the struggle of mankind, the struggle for liberation around the world. All societies in the world are linked by a bond of humanity first and by a bond of empire second. The empire should be of men, not money. We want to keep the first and fuck the second. I'm convinced the future is with those who are subjects of the American (and increasingly the Soviet) empire. The revolution won't come here until it comes in all the exploited countries around the world, but it will come, it must come. Old Marx was right, capitalism contains the seeds of its own destruction. Trouble is, the hippies aren't seeds of anything but wasted time. Dropping out does not change the nature of an evil social order; only naivete assumes those who control will also drop out.

Hippy love and Leary exist in an ideological vacuum, precariously balanced on ground that's been plowed under before. Anarchy, the usual hippy creed, gives way to syndicalism, the Digger creed, which when understood properly sways to communism and the withering away of the state. But that implies political action to make it so. Marx had a vision too, a vision of a society and a world free from material need. His manifesto says mostly you don't have to be hungry anymore to all the hungry people in the world. After Marx, philosophers like Erich Fromm and psychiatrists like R. D. Laing have correctly diagnosed the schizophrenia in society that doesn't allow hippies to exist, and does allow around the world brown men to slave their lives away for the sake of affluent, corpulent white men in North America.

It's a combination of things, closely related to economics and class and racism and fear and liberalism and often plain stupidity. It boils to this, for hippies: Society won't let more than a small percentage of its members drop out, because if it did, profits would drop through lack of consumers, the factories would close, and the men who own the world go broke. Besides, hippies make damn poor cannon fodder in empire-building wars that require young men by the thousands for said fodder.

Tuning in to the flowers and to love and turning on to acid is very nice, but it's schizophrenia just like the suburban kind. The book of the dead doesn't do anything about murderers—they don't read it and won't listen to you.

The overwhelming problem with true Christian charity in this world is the enormousness of the commitment; those who are in need always seem more plentiful than those who are able to help. When traditional values are reversed, and young adults— who have age and a certain predisposition toward achievement in their favor—consistently assume the role of the needy, the result is confusion and anger. Liza Williams is appropriately furious; the pseudo hippies tagging along for the ride were virtually elevated to the rank of scenic wonders in Los Angeles.

Flotsam and Jet Set

LIZA WILLIAMS

OK so you are wearing beads, and your hair is long and from the back you might be anyone, and from the front your face isn't too different either, your expression, is it an expression, is non-attendance, and your style is all I ever know of you. Style, it's all style and not much content, but what is the definition of decadence? Is it the substitution of style for content? Is that why so many love children smile a lot and score off you for everything they can get, cigarettes, hey man, lay a cigarette on me, or another ploy, anybody got a match? OK, now who's got a cigarette to go with it? Or you walk into an underground paper office where there is a big sign on the wall that says "Don't make magic, Be magic" and "Love" and you ask about something and receive cold indifference, they are too busy manufacturing love to give away any samples.

Hippiebums, dirty long-haired hippiebums with nowhere to go and nothing to do and they spend a lot of time using your daylight and your floor doing their nothing so that if you have something to do it is impossible. Who's that bunch of hippies out there in our garage-way mending their shoes and dancing and inviting the man to come and bust us, while we stand at the window and worry, from inside our tenuous safety, where we just got through with a lot of cleaning up after a departed hippie community, washing, wall painting, and removing piles of animal shit from under the refrigerator?

Split, that's what it's come to, a big rift, hippies and hippiebums.

Los Angeles Free Press, October 13, 1967

Upstairs the acid freaks are screaming and shouting and beating each other up and chasing each other around in lace dresses and the child who lives there sits at our table asking for food and wondering where her mother is, only not too hopefully.

Hippiebums give you presents, like dirty feathers or one bead or the clap. Hippiebums tell you about mystical experiences while they finger your breadbox. Hippiebums start off on your floor and make it to the couch and then eye your bed. When it gets tight for them they split, but they let you keep the feather or bead or the clap as a souvenir. You're materialistic they mumble at you as they drag themselves out your door, their pockets stuffed with peanut butter sandwiches.

Hippiebums write bad poetry and draw ugly pictures and make you look at them. They sing dull songs to one chord change and tell you how it is, letting you in on the secrets of life. Hippiebums hitch rides with you and roll joints in the back seat leaving seeds on the carpet. Hippiebums are just leaving for San Francisco or have just come back. Hippiebums use your telephone to call Chicago or Great Falls and three friends in New York; they pass the time on your phone. Hippiebums are always there at mealtimes but can't wipe dishes; hippiebums bring their friends over but never tell you their names.

Hippiebums come from middle-class homes and want you to be their parents, want you to pay their rent, want to make your world their high school. Hippiebums believe in the abundance of the Great Society, and want you to supply it. Hippiebums are predatory but wear a disguise of love. Hippiebums serenade you with their bells and dance for you, stepping on your feet.

I used to smile at everyone with a button or a bell or a flower, I used to think how beautiful it was all becoming, how rich it was, how sweet and good. But it's fantasy time, that's what it is, fantasy time in the twentieth century and style is where it's at, and only a few maintain content, and content, in the end, is really what creates a good world, and love, and being together with people and doing and making peace and feeling love and sustaining energy. So don't feel bad if you can't love every long-haired flower-bell child in the road; things aren't always what they seem.

At the age of twenty-three, Richard Goldstein has written more about modern rock music than any other critic, outdistancing his competition weekly in his columns in The Village Voice *and* The New York Times. *Refreshingly, he has not been overwhelmed by the glitter of the recording studio or by his own power. Rock for him, as for his audience, is the artistic expression of the lives and experiences of its creators.*

But music, with its "love vibrations," is best enjoyed when the societal vibrations are good; if the community is plagued with violence, hard drugs, and paranoia, the rock experience is almost worthless. The publicity that followed the murder of "Groovy" Hutchinson and Linda Fitzpatrick, while revealing just how bad the vibrations can be, has done little to alter the reality of New York's Lower East Side. Winter arrives, and hippies are as cold as Bowery bums. Meth is dealt to pay the rent or just to guarantee oblivion, while angry articles appear and parents worry for their children. Nothing has changed, except, of course, for the victims.

Love: A Groovy Idea
While He Lasted

RICHARD GOLDSTEIN

We are all victims of symbols. Events breed their own ritual. Maybe that is why the murders of James Leroy Hutchinson and Linda Fitzpatrick read like Act Three of an off-Broadway closet drama. The truest theatre of the 60's lies spiked across the city desk, slugged "slay."

What happened at 169 Avenue B happens all the time. A man and his woman are hauled or lured down to the boiler room, where amid rags and ratsmell she is banged senseless, and both are stomped dead.

Such crimes become incidents. We never hear about them unless the woman was pregnant, mutilated, or both. But Groovy and his girl were slaughtered right on page one of the Daily News. Journalists made pilgrimages to Tompkins Square and its adjoining shrines. Even Mayor Lindsay took note. When he called the murders "a tragedy" he was

The Village Voice, October 19, 1967

speaking not about the crime but its particulars. The tragedy in what went down on Avenue B is who went down, and not who did the felling.

Some crimes seem to apotheosize an age. This time, only the corpses make it improper to write off victims and villains as an allegory staged by some playwright-deity. We would have waited in line to see it in the theatre, specifying alternate dates and all the rest, while on a stage set as a boiler room masked hippies and black militants dance a stylized ballet, feigning death and delight respectively. In quiet Phil Ochs voices, we would inquire of the stagehands: "Have you got a picture of the pain?"

Photos were plentiful. "His own weird world turned against him," crooned the Daily News. In centerfold obituaries they immortalized Groovy as a speed-saint, guru-clown, lover-dealer. Crucified by gangster-Romans, he became a true martyr. As a reformer of meth swindlers, his arrest for possession of a deadly weapon seemed irrelevant. How well he personified the love ethic, and how much more perfect he was as a symbol than he must have been as a man.

He and his girl were buried last week in their respective cultures. Linda's velvet-draped casket was carried down an Episcopal aisle while the minister chanted from the Book of Common Prayer. She rode to her burial in a gray Cadillac. Groovy's funeral was conducted in a Baptist minister's parlor. As a eulogy, Galahad played the harmonica that was part of his friend's costume.

Neither coffin was notably arrayed with flowers, which was appropriate. Both were victims of such symbolism. They were beautiful people, and beautiful victims. They followed their supposed assailants into the basement, exuding love and groove. And they died near a pile of their clothing, not merely rubbed out, but smashed faceless.

The News eulogized Linda Fitzpatrick as "a pretty fair-skinned aspiring artist who clung to the fringes of hippiedom, terrified of the denizens of that accursed land, but fascinated by them." Gone are Linda's beads and bangles; the papers were filled with straight rich-girl snapshots. She too lost her personality to allegory. Her swirling stares and speed-chatter were buried in a reserved coffin. To the News and its audience, she was not high but afraid.

That fear is all over the East Village today. The murders were too plausible to be ignored, the suspects too real to be dismissed. No one escapes the media, including its antagonists. Everyone knows that Groovy died in a mandala of his own blood. And suddenly, everyone remembers why. Other killings come to mind; not the publicized ones—like the fatal stabbing of Walter Coey on his stoop on East 11th, or the bizarre ones—like the Central Park mugging of Bruce Mantel, "the poet," and the rape of his 15-year-old "flower bride." They remember the casual murders (five or six since the early summer, some claim). Accounts of unreported rape abound, and hallway muggings seem to be a rite-de-passage east of Tompkins Square.

It is a slum; Groovy's death seems to have awakened that realization. And hippies, they mutter, are the new niggers. "The odds are incredibly stacked," they say. "There is opposition from every corner." "Flower power was a summer vacation," they hiss. "In San Francisco, they staged the death of the hippie. Here, we got the real thing."

The mindblower is not that love is dead in the East Village, but that it has taken this long to kick the bucket. Flower power began and ended as a cruel joke. The last laugh belongs to the media-men who chose to report a charade as a movement. In doing so, they created one. By the thousands, the real victims of flower hype poured into the slums of both coasts. LifeLook filled its pages with technicolor testimonials, to the young drop-outs living the love ethic their leaders were wary of. The hippies tried to warn their suburban following through the underground press, but the copy poured thin, like Digger stew. Through it all was a bizarre camaraderie between the fourth estate and the fifth dimension. Aspiring scenemakers quickly mastered the art of journalistic posturing; one façade, they discovered, was better than a thousand words. Every daily paper picked its own hippie spokesman. The Post latched onto Abbie Hoffman, and in their tradition of prophetic misprints, called him a "Bigger" and his followers "Happies." The Times found Galahad, and made him the East Village Lawrence of Arabia. Reluctant, willing, or both, these men too became symbols, and hired killers. They found they could mainline their pronouncements into the American blood-stream through the press. The price they paid for being culture definers was their sacred anonymity. Those who accepted the new definition became their ultimate victims.

The flower children, high on love, brought their material feast to areas of constant famine, and then went on a hunger strike. Even in rags, they seemed wealthy. Even destitute, they knew their rights and privileges. The attention they won from the press, and the police, made reprisals inevitable. "The hippies really bug us," a young Negro East Sider told the New York Times, "because we know they can come down here and play their games for awhile and then escape. And we can't, man."

Only now, after Groovy's murder, is there talk about the madness of counseling large-scale settlement of the ghetto by drop-outs from the middle-class. Only now are flower children wondering why anyone would sleep in Central Park, or offer flowers to a raging madman. And only as the Summer of Love chills into a violent harvest, is there talk of getting out. Like generations of Lower East Siders before them, the Group Image wants to move to the country. Abbie Hoffman wants to split for San Francisco. In supermarkets and psychedelic shops, a rash of neatly printed notices has appeared, offering cash and gratitude for the return of a son or daughter. The old folks are scared, but so are the kids. Those who cannot change may claim their own rewards.

Groovy's legacy is a new slum-hippie. He lives in the ghetto and he acts like it. He sees his scene for what it is. "The mystique has worn off," he says. "People are beginning to admit the ugliness of it now. The myths are peeling away, like bad paint, man. Take the drug thing. This is an amphetamine scene here. Part of your flower power survival kit is meth. It's ugly, and it's real, man. And it was here all along, for anyone to see who felt like it."

The new hippie is on the scene already, even as the media-ministers whisper "dust to dust, ashes to ashes" over his saint of an ancestor. Galahad helped usher him in when he told the Daily News: "Just give me ten minutes alone with whoever did this to my friend Groovy." The word has gotten around that some Diggers in New York and San Francisco carry guns—and intend to use them. The flower child, now a veteran of violence, is toughening up. Did we expect anything else? For a long time now we have been glibly informed that the most logical way to cope with the culture of poverty is psychosis. Dare we demand sanity from the slum-hippie?

"I respect those who respect me," he says, with a passing glance at the east side of Tompkins Square Park. You ask about the mood on the streets and he smiles. From beneath his corduroy robes he produces a wooden shaft painted in dayglo swirls. It snaps open to reveal an erect steel blade.

"Love," he mutters, "was a Groovy idea—while he lasted."

VI. The Radicalization of Hip and the Reportage of Empathy

No one speaks for an age, or even a generation, but it does not seem too unfair to argue that we are now almost without hope. The future, that shining time when we would prove ourselves useful to ourselves and our society, is just another enemy. Marked for death by a war machinery we never authorized, daily insulted by political parties that offer similar solutions to social unrest, and condemned even by our parents—surely, this is not the normal history of the process of manhood. If we absent ourselves from an acquisitive society, we are called morally subversive, and if we attempt to change the system through radical politics, we are called politically irresponsible; damned if you do, damned if you don't.

"Oh for a man who is a man, who has a bone in his back which you cannot pass your hand through!" There are some who fulfill Thoreau's definition, who do not choose to be processed through our moral and political computers. But, unlike the hippies, they live with fewer illusions about human nature; it's Us and Them, and They can no longer be superzapped with love. For the knowledge of The Way Things Might Be directly threatens The Way Things Are, and every act is therefore political. Long hair and underground newspapers in the schools, peace marches in the streets, free speech without fear of censorship—if we are increasingly distrustful of adults, it is because they seem to have forgotten that these are rights, not privileges.

It is no longer acceptable for adults to claim that they only know what's printed in the papers. Whose papers? we demand, and what interests do they represent? If they perform no other function, the underground papers provide the other side of the political stories we instinctively disbelieve in the mass media. And if we are increasingly cynical about the way men operate, and increasingly militant in our protests, it is because the disparity between popular journalism and the underground reporting—between appearance and reality, as some would have it—is now too great to be endured silently.

Revolutionaries are dangerous to the system when they possess more strength than they think; they are dangerous to themselves when they imagine their strength to be growing while their numbers are actually diminishing. What is one to think of these self-styled revolutionaries, who claim to be enacting major social change where no change can be seen?

The revolution, then, remains internalized—to nobody's surprise. Perhaps that's why Orwell's dystopians invented thought scanning; until we arrive at that point, or until the revolution manifests itself, Stokely or Ho or even Che may be riding on our buses alongside the stodgiest matron.

Revolution

KURT ABRAM

Like revolution, the old forms crumble, the old forms have to go. So we attach ourselves, or some have attached themselves, too strongly to the forms without and will not see them go. But there's a revolution afoot and nothing stops, no thing stops this revolution, so we detach our selves from many forms, many many attractive forms, and some have never been very attractive at all.

And the revolution goes on. You can't write about it or label it, for you write about things past. You can intellectualize it and shelve it, but you can't kill it, you can't touch it . . . so the revolution goes on.

The revolution is like many things. In fact, every thing is in some way like revolution. A stone is like the revolution in the perfect order it promises; or the explosive energy present in its tiniest grain. Man is the object of this revolution; his forms, the forms he has thought into being.

So catching a rumor of the revolution I listen . . . *It* listens, that which presents a vehicle for the revolution.

The rumor tones more than hope. It tones promise . . . and then the work begins.

The dualities descend and purge the system. It's no good projecting the revolution. It has taken seed within; it has taken seed and threatens to destroy. All forms. All relationships. It threatens to destroy as it purges the system. . . .

Many in the battle are scathed, many killed. With each death a promise is made. The man whose mind has split—a kiss on his lips. And those cut and dismembered—we sleep with each corpse.

And the revolution goes on. The work of one's self continues. One learns there is no glamour or glory in revolution, not when the system is stripped and treacherous elements and delusions uprooted. Of course, myths about and for one's self have been conceived in the process, but they must go if the work is to go on.

The depths are sounded. And in giving over one remembers what a promise has been made . . .

Now is the revolution to begin? Now the real work?

So catching a rumor of the work of the revolution it listens . . . and the rumor deals in symbols that even the word cannot touch. And response is due . . . so the revolution goes on.

One sits down for the first time since the seed was sown to work methodically in mundane fashion for the revolution.

Pamphlets are distributed. Soft words are sent forth.

Meetings are arranged.

Numbers are tallied.

The question of power is discussed.

The power of love.

The power of vehicles that love.

And the revolution goes on.

The revolution permeates the world. One of the goals—unity. In the realm of ideas the revolution deals with synthesis. In human relationships the revolution deals with integration and love.

Things to be dispersed are:

NATIONALISM, by reason of its separative nature.

GLAMOUR—building the haze around the personality, the glamour of occupation, the glamour of many friends, the glamour of fine taste, the glamour of belonging to this or that group, the glamour of being avant garde, the glamour of revolution—all this has to be dispersed.

MATERIALISM, accumulation and attachment to these things, for obvious reasons.

SEPARATIVE THINKING of every kind eventually has to go.

The revolution begins with individuation, in order to make one fit for revolution, because revolutionary activity denotes first power and then sacrifice. The process of individuation, therefore, must take place first that power will not corrupt and eventually destroy the vehicle itself. And only the individual is capable of significant sacrifice.

The revolution permeates all levels, all classes, all outer departments. There is no voice proclaiming revolution. There are many voices proclaiming many aspects of the whole revolution.

So we can become less separative in our thinking and work with groups and individuals from many levels.

Love is difficult. We see it now as a necessity in the world. Therefore, we see it now as the will to love.

It deals with a shift from personal possessive to impersonal all-inclusive. The word "impersonal" falls hard. It denotes detachment. It denotes not bearing the usual fruits—like lovers and friends who say good words. Impersonal is a no-strings-attached "free" love. A love that gives . . . a very quiet love that gives courage to do the work oneself.

The outward form of the revolution in the time of shifting forms is difficult. Most of the forms are old forms. Most of the forms have to go. Before new integrating forms are built, old forms must be destroyed.

How to be occupied among the old forms?

How to be occupied with meaningful activity?

No life's plan among the old forms can be charted. At best the immediate step is known. We work in the dark. Though the way is lighted. We move within without the forms, being not too attached to any one thing. And the revolution within, the inner development is silently noted.

Outward organization is difficult. It deals with quality groups and creative thinkers. It deals with united purpose and sacrifice. It deals with short, concentrated, focused group effort. Then the group is dispersed and other groups take form.

The battlefield of emotional desire is projected outward and confounds the revolution. Emotion and desire, once thought the very breath of the creative nature, are now seen as hindrances. With great effort one by one the illusions we vitalize with desire are relinquished, dispersed, smashed.

And the revolution goes on. . . .

On one level, prose this vague doesn't really tell you anything. But its ethereal qualities, its somnabulistic rhythms are deliberate; Eben Given, like the Avatar's *other metaphysician, Mel Lyman, writes more for Those Who Know than for the uninitiated.*

The underground is rich in mystical prose that doesn't mean anything, but the Avatar *has weeded out the would-be gurus to publish only those with enough "soul" to meet biweekly deadlines. Ultimately, the strongest testimony for writing of this kind lies in the lives of its authors. From the success of the* Avatar *community, Eben Given's work assumes a stature that it might never gain from the hardened skeptics who read papers that appear one week and fold the next.*

Secrets of the Heart

EBEN GIVEN

There is a time that each of us knows that comes without warning. Suddenly it comes and so silently and it descends upon us like a net and like a light. Indifferent to our plans or our hour it falls on us, and however our time was allotted and conceived the plan fades away under that light as though the lines were written there in pale ink. No fact remains. What was so pressing and hard to bear seems suddenly thin and very small. And one by one the actions and conversations, the words of praise, the held angers—all melt together and their colors blend and at last there is only an indifferent shade and we cling even to that.

But in the light we begin to see—not with the eyes of our mind but with an eye behind our mind we begin to see. And we do not see with that eye so much as *feel* with it. As though we saw into the surfaces, not that they were hard, but instead, unkind—not soft, so much as gentle. We hear our own voice speaking and the words become thin and transparent and suddenly it is as though we were behind them at the place from where they came and they are like things floating.

—falling, rushing, upon a wind like leaves or like rain and it is the wind's voice that we hear—the voice behind our voice.

And faces come before you and expressions. And you see that the faces are talking even as the words and you see that all of the face is brought together only for you and there is nothing else besides. And the mouth moves and opens and smiles and the eyes look at you and sometimes they are saying what the mouth is saying and sometimes they aren't any way saying that, but something else or nothing or anything and you are asking and no answer comes but a lie comes.

And we see ourselves and our actions, even as we walk or sit or eat. And we see each attitude, each gesture is developed in us only for expression of who in this world we are, and we watch ourselves from away behind and we are walking or sitting or eating and it is as though we were stringed puppets hung in a place where there were vines and wires and kite strings and we were hung too close together. That when one is pulled or moved all the strings are shaken and we jerk and twitch and drop our plates.

And sometimes the words ride on that voice and are like it and are at one with it, and sometimes they are nothing at all like it but confute it with every syllable and the sound that is all around you is the sound of a hundred liars.

And in that light these things are heard and seen but they are seen not from without but from within.

—From a place where there is no distinction of words or of actions but only a discernment of *Feeling* and in that light it is not feeling that is regarded, because all that is done with feeling melts and dissolves in the light that is all about you—but what is regarded is the *Lack* of Feeling.

For your ears and your eyes are suddenly become the entirety of all that you have ever felt from your heart—

and the feeling is shallow, and thin and so, so empty.

and then nothing remains of your own image but gaps and empty places and in no instance will you see how much there is of you that you cannot feel anywhere there, nor see at all—nor hear nor anyone else.

At one point, there were so many reporters in San Francisco that one thought the World Series was in town. One paper predicted that pseudo hippie Life staffers would soon be interviewing pseudo hippie Look correspondents. But those who were sincere about dropping out caught on to the public relations racket early in the game. Emmet Grogan, the mythical or real leader of the Diggers, appeared simultaneously on television shows in several cities. Others burned money publicly, and every week end cameras filmed the hippie equivalent of the Easter Parade.

The dichotomy between sensational reality and overly sensational news coverage culminated in the "Death of Hippie" ceremony, complete with mourners and coffin. Whether the hippies were actually dead became, in its turn, the topic of the minute for at least a few minutes, much to the delight of the planners of the event. The funeral proved newsworthy, the public seemed to enjoy the put-on, and there was no sense to be made of any of it.

The Death of Hippie

OCTOBER SIXTH NINETEEN HUNDRED AND SIXTY SEVEN

MEDIA CREATED THE HIPPIE WITH YOUR HUNGRY CONSENT. BE SOME-BODY. CAREERS ARE TO BE HAD FOR THE ENTERPRISING HIPPIE. The media cast nets, create bags for the identity-hungry to climb in. Your face on TV, your style immortalized without soul in the captions of the Chronicle. NBC says you exist, ergo I am. Narcissism, plebeian vanity. The victim immortalized. Black power, its transcendent threat of white massacre the creation of media-whore obsequious bowers to the public mind which they recreate because they too have nothing to create and the reflections run in perpetual anal circuits and the FREE MAN vomits his images and laughs in the clouds because he is the great evader, the animal who haunts the jungles of image and sees no shadow, only the hunter's gun and knows sahib is too slow and he flexes his strong loins of FREE and is gone again from the nets. They fall on empty air and waft help-lessly to the grass.

Broadside distributed in Haight-Ashbury, Fall, 1967
266

DEATH OF HIPPY END/FINISHED HIPPYEE GONE GOODBYE HEHPPEEEE
DEATH DEATH HHIPPEE

death 1. the act or fact of dying; permanent ending of all life in a person, animal, or plant. 2. (D-), the personification of death, usually pictured as a skeleton in a black robe, holding a scythe. 3. the state of being dead. 4. any ending resembling dying: as, the death of fascism. 5. any condition or experience thought of as like dying or being dead: as, it was death for her to have to see him again. 6. the cause of death: as, the atomic bomb was death to thousands. 7. murder or bloodshed. 8. (Obs.), pestilence: as, the Black Death.

EXORCISE HAIGHT/ASHBURY CIRCLE THE HASBURY FREE THE BOUNDARIES
OPEN EXORCISE

exorcise 1. to drive (a supposed evil spirit or spirits) out or away by ritual charms or incantation. 2. to summon or command (such spirit or spirits) 3. to free from such a spirit or spirits.

YOU ARE FREE. WE ARE FREE. DO NOT BE RECREATED. BELIEVE ONLY YOUR OWN INCARNATE SPIRIT. Create, Be. . . . Do not be created. This is your land, your city. No one can portion it out to you. The H/Ashbury was portioned to us by Media-Police and the tourists came to the Zoo to see the captive animals and we growled fiercely behind the bars we accepted and now we are no longer hippies and never were and the City is ours to create from, to be in. It is our tool, part of the first creation which the FREE MAN creates his new world from.

BIRTH OF FREE MAN FREE SAN FRANCISCO INDEPENDENCE FREE AMERICANS BIRTH birth 1. the act of bringing forth offspring. 2. a person or thing born or produced. 3. the act of being born; nativity. 4. descent or origin. 5. descent from nobility. 6. the beginning of anything as, the birth of a nation. 7. an inherited or natural inclination to act in certain ways: as, an actor by birth.

DO NOT BE BOUGHT WITH A PICTURE, A PHRASE. . . . DO NOT BE CAPTURED IN WORDS. THE CITY IS OURS. YOU ARE ARE ARE. TAKE WHAT IS YOURS. . . . TAKE WHAT IS YOURS

THE BOUNDARIES ARE DOWN SAN FRANCISCO IS FREE NOW FREE THE TRUTH IS OUT OUT OUT truth 1. the quality or state of being true; specifically, a) formerly, loyalty; trustworthiness. b) sincerity; genuine-ness; honesty. c) the quality of being in accordance with experience, facts, or reality; conformity with fact. d) reality; actual existence. e) agreement with a standard, rule, etc.; correctness; accuracy. 2. that which is true; statement, etc., which accords with fact or reality 3. an established or verified fact, principle, etc.

WE HOLD THESE TRUTHS TO BE SELF-EVIDENT, THAT ALL MEN ARE CREATED EQUAL, that they are endowed by their Creator with certain unalienable Rights, that among these are Life, Liberty and the Pursuit of Happiness—That to secure these rights, Governments are instituted among Men, deriving their just Powers from the Consent of the Gov-erned, that whenever any Form of Government becomes destructive of these Ends, it is the Right of the People to alter or to abolish it, and to institute new Government, laying its Foundation on such Principles, and organizing its Powers in such Form, as to them shall seem most likely to effect their Safety and Happiness.

October 6, 1967

The use of the term "alienation" as a catch-all label to explain the revolt is yet another form of societal overkill; it fails to suggest that some of the alienated have specific ideas about revamping the country's societal and economic structure. Among these is Paul Williams, who left Swarthmore to found Crawdaddy!, *the most prestigious and literate magazine of rock. At the age of twenty, with two years of semiregular publication behind him, he has become a perceptive commentator on the rock renaissance and the social change it inspires.*

The Hippies Are Gone.
Where Did They Go?

PAUL WILLIAMS

Everyone can see the handwriting on the wall, but nobody knows what it says.

Take this whole Groovy story. It's being played up as a big moral lesson, right? Don't stray from Greenwich. Don't trust niggers. And above all don't carry flowers when everybody's *sick* of flowers.

But it's just another murder. A hippie being killed is just like a housewife being killed or a hoodlum being killed. None of these people, notice, are persons; they're labels. Who cares who Groovy was; if you know he was a "hippie," then already you know more about him than he did about himself. And news isn't about people any more, it's about labels; the journalist sees the world as a big political cartoon, a guy in a tall hat with "U. S." on his back, a tough-looking guy with "hawk" on his back, and what-have-you. A dove does what he does simply because he's a dove; a taxpayer because he's a taxpayer; a bureaucrat because he's a bureaucrat. Don't confuse me with individuals.

Hell, if this guy in this other murder trial says he took *acid* as well as some methedrine and two pints of wood alcohol the night before, what more do I need to know about him? Those hippies should be locked up.

But you don't have to worry any more, folks. The hippies are gone,

The Village Voice, October 26, 1967

and it wasn't the murder or the methedrine that did it. It was a surfeit of attention. Hippies are no longer good copy.

See, it's hard to explain to a lot of you what a hippie is because a lot of you really think a hippie *is* something. You don't realize that the word is just a convenience picked up by the press to personify a social change thing beginning to happen to young people. And when somebody says, "The hippies are gone," you only think: "Where did they go?"

Abbie Hoffman was on the David Susskind show a little while back, and about when it was beginning to get dull, at the start of the program, he let the duck out of the box. The duck had a little identifying plaque— HIPPIE—and it squawked and ran all over the place and finally vomited out in the audience. Susskind didn't want to run the segment. "But you said it was okay . . ." "Yes, Abbie," said David, "but the duck freaked out. You let him get out of control."

That's what you get for miscasting.

The point is, it *is* a hippie if it has the sign around its neck. That's what hippie is. It's a word for the people who read about hippies, and talk about hippies, and fret about hippies; it isn't anything real enough to hang a string of beads on.

As everybody who writes for *The Village Voice* seems to know, this country is crazy. Freaked. Out of touch with reality. Nothing that goes on in the U. S. can be put in perspective, because there's no framework left. We've built up a system of irrelevancies based on misinterpretations based on inaccuracies, and we can't get back to Start to try again. Every day's newspaper is funnier than the last, because it's all serious reporting in a ridiculous context. The persecution and assassination as performed by the inmates, etc. We pretend not to notice the bars on the windows.

And every now and then we look around at our society and say, "This place stinks. Next week I've got to start doing something about it." This has gone on for a couple of hundred years, and now we're beginning to get kids saying: "This society stinks. I'm getting out." Quitters? Well, would you repair a building if eighty per cent of the wood in it was rotten? Or tear it down and construct a new one? While you're making up your mind, you might at least get out before the place collapses on your shoulders. . . .

So the kids started dropping out. And they wore long hair and beads and all so as to be different from the world they left behind, yeah, but they did it even more so they'd know they weren't alone. Every long-haired kid was another friend to support you when you felt like a That in a world of This. And if there would only be enough of us—and there seemed to be more every day—maybe soon we could feel secure enough to go out and start building our own thing in this world full of strangers.

And the media coverage? A drag, but a good thing—all those teen-agers reading *Look* magazine, and we need all the recruits we can get.

So what happened? Nothing important; don't worry, nobody's drop-ping back in. Nobody who meant it in the first place. But the "hippie" is gone, or going, because the hippie has been overexposed. He's received so much attention from American society that he—the label—has be-come a part of that society. Gotta get a new label. Or none at all, this time.

Consider an actor, sick of his part, sick of the melodrama he's stuck in. I'm getting the hell out, he says, and he walks out the stage door onto the street. He's just about gone a block when the curtain starts to fall and he hears applause—he realizes the stage was larger than he thought, he's still in the play, his part is The-Disgruntled-Guy-Who-Walks-Out.

So we've got a problem. How do you drop out far enough, without geo-graphically leaving the country you were born in and love? Easy, friend: drop out inside—not on the cover of *Time* where the world can see it, but there in your head where you decide what the world is and how to relate to it and what you want to do with it. Drop out inside, and run things your own way for your own benefit, and don't get hung up on the System.

As for saving the world, looks like we gotta find another act. Some-thing that'll do more than show our contempt for this nuthouse. Some-thing, maybe, that'll show people the reality outside the nuthouse, the real world we could all be working to achieve.

Bring back reality! But not as a goddamned slogan. We don't need another label—but you can be sure that's the first thing we'll get.

"Well, flower power didn't save Linda and Groovy." This was the accumulated wisdom of a New York Timesman who had spent several weeks reporting the significance of the death of hippies, both real and symbolic. The truth of the matter, judging from the reactions of the so-called hippie papers, was clearly less precise and probably less profound as well. If anything, media coverage of the death-of-hippie only confirmed the underground's "devil theory"; "they" gave life to the phenomenon, and when too many people began to take the idea seriously, it had to be destroyed. The cynical reporting of the underground press echoes the bitterness of the summer of love, when magazine covers served more to increase sales than to stabilize an already overloaded community.

Autumn in the Haight: Where Has Love Gone?

DON McNEILL

FUNERAL NOTICE
* * * * *
HIPPIE
In the
Haight Ashbury District
of this city,
Hippie, devoted son
of
Mass Media
* * * * *
Friends are invited
to attend services
beginning at sunrise,
October 6, 1967
at
Buena Vista Park.

The Village Voice, November 30, 1967

The season changed, and the moon thrusts of the Autumn Equinox preoccupied the many people in Haight-Ashbury who chart by planetary movement. Others participated in the Equinox celebration, a pleasant event which has become a tradition here in the past few seasons. This celebration was of special note, because two traditional American Indian medicine men decided at the last minute to attend. The medicine men, Rolling Thunder and Shaymu, came to the Straight Theatre on Haight Street and helpers hurried to the street with handbills reading "QUICK INDIANS WANT TO SEE YOU." The natives came, and, in front of the Straight, Rolling Thunder met Shaymu, and Shaymu said, "Let us adopt these people, who are called hippies, as our children. They have been disowned." Rolling Thunder agreed, and the Indians and many of their new children went to the country to dance all night around a fire on a beach.

The vast majority of the younger residents of Haight-Ashbury just hung around the street, aware of neither the Equinox nor of their new family. Most were unaware because they didn't care. They had more pressing problems: to find some bread to get home, to find a place to crash for the night, or to find some speed so they could forget about the night. Haight Street was lined with people with problems.

Most of the tourists were gone, and with them their funny money, which really didn't matter because they only clogged the streets and not much of the money filtered back into the community anyway. But the community was certainly short of bread. The Haight-Ashbury Medical Clinic, which had given free medical treatment to 13,000 people since June without any financial or moral support from government or foundation sources, finally closed its doors, defeated and depleted, on September 22. The Digger Free Store was in debt and the proprietor threatened to split to New York unless the $750 in back rent materialized. The Switchboard, which maintained a volunteer legal staff of thirty lawyers and had found crash pads for up to 300 pilgrims a night, was doing fine until it received some contributions. They spent the money before the checks bounced, and needed $1000 to survive. Most of the communes in the country still depended on outside support, and even the free food in the Panhandle, which began to resemble a bread line, threatened to fold without more funds.

Haight-Ashbury had survived the Summer of Love, but it seemed mortally wounded.

It could have been worse. Estimates in the spring had doubled the estimated 50,000 saints and freeloaders who came to the Haight seeking the love and free life that the papers had promised. The subdivided flats in the bay-windowed houses—the rule to Haight-Ashbury as tenement apartments are to the East Side—stretched to accommodate guests. There were no hunger riots, and the now defunct free medical clinic kept the threatened plague and pestilence in check. The pilgrims were fed and housed—with occasional free music and drugs thrown in—and the panhandlers on Haight Street were still asking for quarters in October.

As I arrived, there were kids on many corners with packs on their backs and thumbs stuck out trying to leave. The people I met, many of whom had been here before the Human Be-In and the Summer of Love (some of whom had coined the words), were exhausted and dejected, rather like a bartender counting unbroken glasses after an all-night brawl. Yet they were counting broken spirits and their few veteran friends who had not yet split for the sanctum of an unpublicized commune in the country. They were the hosts of the Summer of Love and now, after the Autumn Equinox, it was time to clean up.

There's not much reason now to go to Haight Street unless it's to cop. The street itself has a layer of grease and dirt which is common on busy sidewalks in New York but rare in San Francisco, a film that comes from bits of lunch, garbage, and spilled coke ground into the cement by the heels of Haight Street strollers. It is not a pleasant place to sit, yet hundreds do, huddled in doorways or stretched out on the sidewalk, in torn blankets and bare feet, bored voices begging for spare change, selling two-bit psychedelic newspapers that were current in the spring, and dealing, dealing, dealing. The dealing is my strongest impression of Haight Street. The housewives with their brownie cameras miss the best part of the show.

It's not hard to cop in the Haight. If you look remotely hip and walk down the street, a dozen anxious peddlers should approach you to offer their goods. It is something that may happen once a day on St. Mark's Place. Here I am asked several times on each block whether I want to buy, or occasionally sell, grass, acid, meth, kilos, lids, matchboxes or, in the case of one ambitious (and, I think, mad) merchant, "Owsley tabs, mescaline, psilocybin coated grass, or anything, anything you want." The merchant was young, fat, owlish-looking, perspiring and unshaven. He had an entourage of several pre-adolescent kids swathed in Army blankets. "I know the stuff is good," he said. "I try it all myself."

The pace of dealing picks up at night, when the dark provides some protection. Walking down Haight Street at night, the offers are whispers in the shadows or in the crowds. Mostly it's acid. But street acid is usually a combination of a taste of acid fortified with anything from methedrine to strychnine. There have been a lot of bad trips here lately, because there has been a lot of bad acid.

Even in October some new stores are opening, latecomers for the leftovers of the poster and bead market, but it should be a rough winter for the bead game, with no assurances that next summer the circus will come to town again. Enlightened natives have spread out all over town from Haight-Ashbury. Anyone curious about hippies can pick up a hitchhiker or find some on his own block. Unlike Greenwich Village, the shops are not an attraction in themselves. The same goods are sold in more attractive shops all over town.

I did find one merchant who wanted nothing to do with the psychedelic market. I needed some matches so I went into a liquor store on Haight Street off Clayton and, rather than hassle the thin, white-haired man at the counter, I bought a pack of cigarettes, which he gave me with a pack of matches. Then I asked for an extra pack of matches.

He eyed me severely.

"You got matches, right here," he said, tapping the pack of matches with the nail of his index finger.

"I'd like an extra pack," I said. "I'll pay you for them."

He shook his head. "No," he said, "you got matches right here. One pack is all you need. One pack of cigarettes. One pack of matches. What do you need more for?"

I pulled out my other pack of cigarettes. "For these," I said. "That's what I came here for."

"What happened to the matches you got with those?" he shouted triumphant with the evidence, finding me guilty of all the dope-fiend-marijuana-puffing sins that the mind of a liquor-store keeper could imagine. Even after the hordes, he was holding his hill. He was doing his bit.

The street is the heart of the Haight. It is where everyone first realized that they had company on their trip. It is reality—a hard fact to stomach when you're fifteen and strung out on meth and it's midnight and you've got no place to crash except a doorway. Without the coffee houses and bars of the beats, the street is the scene, a hell of a scene, with tourists and runaways and dealers and burners and the holy Angels with their bikes and the gaudy stores as a backdrop.

A schism exists between the street and the elite in Haight-Ashbury. The same is true in New York. The elite of the Haight-Ashbury scene are even more aware of it, and they have occasionally tried to bridge the gap, without much success. Chester Anderson began the Communication Company over a year ago, hoping to keep the street in touch and control with an "instant newspaper" of enticing handbills. The handbills fascinated the fringes but bored the masses. Anderson was finally purged and split several months ago for Florida. The Diggers tried harder, attacking the needs of the neighborhood with free food and free stores and free theatre and free thought. They convinced Jay and Ron Thelin, pioneer proprietors of the Psychedelic Shop, to forsake free enterprise and just be free. The shop became a lounge for the street and finally died October 6 with the proprietors in debt, in love, and enlightened. On that day, the elders decided to put an end to it all.

The idea was kindled at a meeting earlier in the week at Happening House, a beautiful Victorian mansion just off the Panhandle on Clayton Street, which opened at the end of the summer to serve as a community center. The idea was to have a three-day funeral for the death of hip—of the death of the Haight—and most of the meeting was spent trying to determine just what had died. But all agreed that a funeral was a good idea. "The idea of a few people going down Haight Street," sighed *Oracle* editor Allen Cohen. "The idea, the symbols, go through walls, through windows, through air, through mountains. Through the media, it will hit millions of people." The media giveth and the media taketh away.

"I'm going to be driving the truck all day," a Digger said, "and I'm going to be talking to people."

"What are you going to tell them to do?" someone asked.

"I'm gonna tell them that everything's out of control. That they're free."

And then someone read the surrender speech of Chief Joseph of the Nez Perce and the meeting was adjourned.

After the meeting I walked with several of the talkers to the house of the Grateful Dead, where Rolling Thunder, the Shoshone medicine man, was staying while he visited Haight-Ashbury. It is a four-story Victorian townhouse, glowing with stained glass windows, which clings to the hill on Ashbury Street and houses the Dead, their entourage, and the offices of the Haight-Ashbury Legal Organization. Rolling Thunder was sitting in the parlor.

Had it not been for his turquoise headband and heavy necklaces, which he said were given to him since he arrived in Haight-Ashbury, Rolling Thunder would hardly have looked like an Indian, let alone a medicine man. His skin is light and his face bears the hard lines of the harsh weather in the country of the Western Shoshone, which is Eastern Nevada. His hair is short and combed back and he wore the simple clothes of a rancher. He is soft-spoken, with a slight Western drawl, and loves to talk, making him the most candid prophet one could ever hope to meet.

Rolling Thunder, who is chairman of the traditional Tribal Council of the Western Shoshone Nation, came to San Francisco to join thirty-two traditional Indians who were about to embark on a caravan to circle the country to protest a bill pending in Congress which will allow Indians to borrow money on their lands. He believes that the bill is a trick to deprive the Indians of their remaining land.

But the real threat of the bill before Congress, Rolling Thunder explained, is that it endangers the lands of the Hopi, which have always remained intact. "The Hopi are the keepers of our religion," he said. "As soon as we found out that the white man was taking everything, our sacred tablets were hidden with the Hopi.

"I was praying for my people," he recalled, "and I had a dream. I was in Kiva. I saw a fire—blue and green—in the dark at the far side. I knew it was a presence. I know it was the supreme being. He was covered with eagle feathers. He had a beak like an eagle and a body like a man. He said to look to the left. I looked and saw stone tablets with pictographs. He said, look there and you'll find the answer.

"A few days later I was in Hopi land, and they brought out the stone tablets, and I read them.

"They said, in the last days, the Hopi would be the last to go. That's happening now, so we know the time is close."

The caravan is intended to fulfill the prophecy which speaks of two stars in the sky. "For hundreds of years," Rolling Thunder said, "the large star followed the small star across the sky. And the Great Spirit said, when the stars reverse, the time is right. That happened two months ago. He also said that we should go out and meet people, to see who is true and who is not true. And that is what we are doing."

The prophecy also speaks of destruction, that after the stars reverse a "gourd of ashes" will fall from the sky, destroying the people who are not true. "It's written on the rocks," Rolling Thunder said, "and when that comes people will come to the wilderness to seek refuge with the Indians and they'll try to buy their way in, but their money will be of no value. We will know who is true and who is not true."

Thelin explained the idea of the funeral. "We're really trying to sabotage the word hippie," he said. "It's really fucking us up. It's not our word. It has nothing to do with us. We'd like to substitute 'free American' in its place."

Rolling Thunder smiled and nodded. "That free American term sounds a lot better," he said. "I've asked several people what they call themselves, and they couldn't give me an answer. Now maybe they can give me an answer."

The medicine man sat on a large desk, and a dozen people sat around him on the floor. "I saw this before it ever happened," he said. "This is a direct prophecy from myself. I wondered if the white man could ever live in this country and eat the food and still remain a hashed-over European. And I saw these people with the long hair. These people will be the future Americans.

"What you people are going through is the same thing that we've gone through. You're just getting your training. We'll help you in any way we can.

"There will also be people among you who will be medicine men. He will know protection. He will know what areas will be safe. There's one among you already. He doesn't know it. I've talked to him and he will be coming to my country to learn. But, until you have your own, you can borrow one once in a while.

"It's going to be rough," he warned. "It's going to be violent, especially in the cities. The spirit told me to stay away from that violence. I think that might be good advice for you people. Violence is not the way. There's something more powerful than that.

"In the last days, they will throw everything at you to destroy you, and that's what's happening now. And now the medicines are coming back. When those stars reversed—that is when the power of good took over from the power of evil. Many young people are becoming medicine men. So now your people, who are living like Indians, you see what you've let yourselves into.

"They may prosecute and jail people. They may do everything because they are fearful. But they won't succeed."

Someone asked about the Shoshone way of facing death.

"Death?" the medicine man asked. "There is no death. But if you kill yourself, you displease the Great Spirit, and you may be reincarnated as a worm."

Rolling Thunder's daughter, who was with him, said that she was walking down to Haight Street, and asked if there was anything she could do for him.

"I'll tell you one thing you can do," he said. "You can go down to the Psychedelic Shop and get some of those 'We Shall Overcome' buttons. They'll be very popular up in our country. Can we get them wholesale?"

"They might for you," someone said. "They should know you."

"Then I guess I'd better walk down myself."

The next day was a day of preparation and press conferences. I walked into the Psychedelic Shop in the late afternoon to find CBS News waiting in line behind a local television station to interview Ron

Thelin in his tiny office at the back of the shop. A tiny enameled American flag hung from Thelin's freshly pierced ear.

The funeral notices had been printed. They were small, stiff cards, bordered in black, reading "HIPPIE. In the Haight-Asbury district of this city, Hippie, devoted son of Mass Media. Friends are invited to attend services beginning at sunrise, October 6, 1967, at Buena Vista Park."

Saturday morning the little windows in the parking meters up and down Haight Street were all painted white, and the faithful gathered before dawn at the top of the hill in Buena Vista Park to greet the sun. The sun rose on time, and they rang bells and breathed deeply and exhaled OM, the first sound in the Universe. Then the pallbearers lifted the fifteen-foot coffin, to be filled with the artifacts of hip, and bore it down the long hill to the street. They paused to kneel at the crossroads of Haight and Ashbury and brought the coffin to rest for the moment in front of the Psychedelic Shop, which had a huge sign reading "BE FREE" in place of its famous mandala. Then the elated mourners swept the street, in preparation for the procession at noon.

At noon a huge banner was stretched across the street. It read "DEATH OF HIPPIE, FREEBIE, BIRTH OF THE FREE MAN." The coffin was carried to the Panhandle, where more newspapers, beads, fruit, cookies, posters, flowers, and buttons were added to the remains. A banner was held up reading "The Brotherhood of Free Men is Born." And, as the procession began, the crowd sang Hare Krishna, but slowly, as a dirge.

The procession moved slowly down the Panhandle towards Golden Gate Park. First came a legion of photographers, walking backwards, and then the coffin, over ten struggling pallbearers, and then a hippie laid out on a stretcher, holding a flower to his chest, and then about 200 mourners, some in elaborate costume, some shaking tambourines, some carrying babies, some dodging cameras. When it reached the park the procession turned left, now with a police escort, whose job seemed to be to keep the procession jammed onto the sidewalk. Six blocks later they turned left again, hauling the coffin up the steep hill on Frederick Street, and at the top of the hill they turned again on Masonic Street, which goes steeply downhill, to complete the circle of the Haight. The coffin picked up speed as it moved downhill, the photographers jumped to get out of the way, and the dead hippie squirmed to stay on the stretcher. And then, halfway down the steep Masonic Street sidewalk, their path was blocked.

A Cadillac had been left parked in a driveway.

The funeral procession came to a crushing halt, and the police escort —a lone cop—sauntered over and began to write out a parking ticket.

"Move the car," someone yelled. The owner walked out of the house and began to argue with the cop.

"Hassle him later," they yelled. "Move the car!"

The cop gave the man a ticket, and the owner returned to his house. The Cadillac remained in the driveway and the pallbearers were groaning.

At which point the cop consented to let the procession by-pass the car in the street.

The procession ended where it began, in the Panhandle. The hippie on the stretcher rose from the dead, looking punchy, and the banners were used to kindle a fire under the huge coffin. The flames took to it quickly and rose ten feet in the air as the crowd cheered. They danced in a circle around the burning coffin and the cameramen and, as the charred coffin crumbled and the fire died down, free men began to leap over the flames. Then the crowd gasped with horror as they saw the fire engines approach.

"The remains!" someone yelled. "Don't let them put it out!" The crowd blocked the firemen and spokesmen argued with the chief as his men readied their hoses. When the hoses were ready, the crowd parted, and the coffin disappeared in a monster cloud of spray and black smoke. The fire was out in seconds, and the firemen moved in with shovels to break apart the smouldering remains. A few diehards were still arguing with the chief, but the mourners had already begun to wander off.

Saturday, the *Chronicle* reverently reported that the Hippie was dead, but by Monday they were back in business again, with their daily quota of copy from the Haight. The banner remained strung across Haight Street for a week, as a reminder, and the Psychedelic Shop was closed and boarded up, and the parking meters were cleaned of the white paint. But the kids still panhandled and sold newspapers and lounged in the doorways, and the occasional tourist still gawked from behind the locked doors of his car. Nothing had changed. It all was the same.

But an exorcism is a subtle thing, and some of the dejection that plagued the Haight in the wake of the Summer of Love did appear to be gone. When a phalanx of fourteen cops swept down Haight Street Tuesday in a daylight raid to net runaways, the community responded with vigor and outrage and, despite threats by Police Chief Cahill, the raids were not repeated. The heat was on and the Haight kept cool.

Within a few weeks, the Switchboard was out of debt and danger, and a series of well-attended benefits brought a generous reserve of funds into the coffers of the clinic, which reopened in late October. The Straight Theatre, which was denied a dance permit by an ever-harassing city, held huge "Dance Classes" (for which permits are not needed) to the accompaniment of the Grateful Dead. And the Diggers were delivering free meat to communes and distributing 5000 copies of a twenty-page free magazine called *Free City*.

The elders now harbor hopes that San Francisco will indeed become a "free city." If any city can, it can, but it must be born, not made. The hippie was made but the community called Haight-Ashbury was born, and it was a virgin birth—an evolutionary experiment and experience. It was beautiful, I am told, in the golden age before the Human Be-In which awoke the media to the precious copy lying untapped on the south side of Golden Gate Park. "Were you here a year ago?" people ask. If you were, then you know.

But then the seekers came en masse, enticed by the media. "They came to the Haight," a handbill relates, "with a great need and a great hunger for a loving community. Many, wanting to belong, identified with the superficial aspects of what 'hippie' was. They didn't drop out but rather changed roles.

"As a result the tone of Haight-Ashbury changed. With many people coming in expecting to be fed and housed, the older community tried to fulfill their needs. Rather than asking them to do their thing, the community tried to give them what they came for. The community tried to be something it wasn't.

"The early members tried to save the community and as a result it began to die. It began to die because in the effort to save it the individuals lost themselves. Without individual selves the community started to become a shell with little within; to maintain the community feeling, meetings replaced relationships and organization replaced community.

"By the end of the summer we were forming organizations to save something that no longer existed. Community is a creative thing and saving is only a holding action. By desperate clinging, we lost."

They lost, but they learned.

Love was not all you needed, contrary to the Beatles' claim that it sustained life; now that the first adherents of the "drop out, tune in, turn on" school have rejected the concept of separation from society, radical politics has gained new converts. If the latecomers lack a history of continuous involvement, their militancy more than adequately compensates.

From the Haight:
The Politicalization of Hip

I can speak for myself, as anybody in all honesty can, but I am here like many others for some of the same obscure reasons. H-A seemed like the last hope; an outpost of humanity in a land of deodorized plastic mannequins engaged in one way or another in the computerized annihilation of the Vietnam people and the destruction of human emotion here in America.

Almost everybody here was at one time or another engaged in some form of political activity whether it be civil rights, anti-war or both. Yet long before it happened, it seemed to most of us that white middle-class America was charging down a blind alley that ended at the Army's bayonets and club swinging Oakland police defending America's military establishment against the people for whom it was created to protect. The white man had put his hope in the black man to make his revolution, and the black man answered, "Make your own, whitey, I'm through working for you."

White political activists, unable to create a base in their own communities, were tossed out of the ghettos, ignored, and abused. Peaceful demonstrations, civil disobedience, electoral politics: the tools of the brainwashed middle class that the authorities permitted them to use could change the course of the Vietnam war about as much as Senator Fulbright's speeches to a deaf Senate. But most of white America, inculcated with years and years of propaganda in their schools, were too numb and scared to admit the facts of reality.

Pacifists chained themselves to a drafted brother in a vain attempt to arouse the conscience of those who had none. The great society had whitewashed the mind and soul of the American people. They were bought off, bludgeoned, coerced, and forced to obey; and they in turn felt it their obligation to force others to obey. Psychologically America was sick. Their minds had turned into mechanical obedience machines incapable of doing anything they were not allowed to do. Those who disobeyed and rebelled were sent to the psychiatrist to be reconditioned into a state of stoic obedience.

Almost anyone over thirty-five, as Dr. Dylan said, couldn't be trusted. You knew only too well the concessions, the lies, the crimes they had committed in order to be where they were. How many times had they looked the other way, salved their conscience with a new car, or cheated and abused the ones they were supposed to love in order to alleviate their agony and escape reality? Yes, they could not be trusted, and that goes for the millions of black men whose minds are white and can be bought off with a shiny new Cadillac.

So we left, dropped out, lit up our pipes and popped our acid. There was nothing left to do. So few seemed to understand, so many were afraid of losing that airconditioned life of luxury without feeling in the wasteland of America called the suburbs.

People's minds, it seemed, had been destroyed by too many words, their values too distorted, their fears too great. We were waiting, trying to live out the time until it was all over. Until we could just forget and somehow live in a world too horrible to endure any longer. Yet we pumped the nation full of acid, pot and what have you. We created a new perspective, new forms, a new culture; a clear cut tribute to the decadence and horror of the America we refused to take part in.

We told the nation, its youth, that they were not alone in their feelings, their dissatisfaction, their agonized torment. Something was really wrong with America that could not be cured by a new anti-poverty program, a peace offensive, or wage increases.

America had become a nation of scared individuals believing that they alone were insane with desires and feelings that must be suppressed in order to conform. Conform, conform, in your heart of hearts and obey. What other choice was there? The question created us and we created a choice.

There would probably be no H-A without the war and perhaps the anti-war movement would not have reached the cold brutal turning point from disobedience and submission to rebellion and violence had there been no "hippies"; the pre-hippies, hippies, and past hippies who marched, got arrested, sang, screamed and cried; who philosophized, ignored the law and were pushing all the time.

Hippies are more than just people who walk down Haight Street with beads, bells, long hair, stoned on drugs. They are a concept, an act of rejection, a militant vanguard, a hope for the future.

You might say that some of us were waiting, waiting, to see if what has happened could ever take place. The law for most of us is the law of the men who control, dominate, and rule. It is broken every day without a thought. The only fear is that of being caught and ending up in jail.

The law is made by the rulers, for the rulers, and in their interest alone. They violate it at will in a country where the people are allowed to dissent but never actually to act to bring about real change. White middle-class America is allowed to protest the war in Vietnam, to fortify their ego, but never once will they legally be permitted to do anything that will actually alter its conduct or bring it to a halt. It seemed as if the youth of America just could not disobey their parents, their teachers, the "elected" masters; but we did, openly and defiantly, and we were the first!

To stop this war, this carnage, we must do what we are not permitted to do. We must break the law. The law we never made, but was made by people who told us they were our servants and had become our masters; our masters ruling us for their own designs and destroying our lives for their own purpose.

We have been exploited by our government and our social and economic system into working and dying for a crime that benefits only our leaders. We on Haight Street had openly refused to be used anymore to be manipulated, coerced, and destroyed as human beings. And we told the whole nation.

Yes, we are political; yes, we are revolutionaries; yes, we represent by the way we live a complete break with the American way of life. Yes, we stand for a new culture based on cooperation, love, and peace rather than competition, hate, and violence. Yes, we are certainly helping to end the wars here in America between man and man and the war there between two ways of life. Yes, there is a revolution going on in the world and a fight to the death between two social orders, two ways of living and thinking.

We have gone AWOL from the great American Army that is our society, renouncing the easy plush future that could have been ours, yes we have deserted. We had come to the conclusion that our society was corrupt, vile, and heinous, and that to obey any of its dictates, any of its concepts was to doom us eventually to a living death killing others as we died.

Yes, we are committed, dedicated people choosing between two ways of life, two social orders, two concepts. We have renounced the meaningless morals and promises of an evil society. We have abandoned it, physically, intellectually, emotionally, and economically.

But now the age of peaceful, lawful protest and dissent is over. With smashed skulls and blood white America has come to the conclusion it had sought to avoid at all cost. That we are living under a tyrannical, violent system of oppression that will stop at nothing to achieve its aims, and that if we desire to end the destruction of human life here and abroad there is no alternative but illegal and violent measures.

This is the truth our government has sought to hide and conceal. This is the truth that many of us have always known but were afraid to admit. This is the reality of America today which we must change and alter our lives accordingly or else acquiesce, bow our heads silently in submission and take our place in the great American Army set on death and destruction. And it is just this that is becoming more and more impossible for increasing numbers of Americans, and one of the many reasons is the long-haired hippies.

Newspapers and television reports of demonstrations rarely tell the full story. When the police are brutal, according to demonstrators, the media are silent, but if one demonstrator is overly militant, the odds against sympathetic treatment increase enormously. Underground reporters, on the other hand, look—and generally think—like experienced radicals; as a result, they capture the moral flavor of a demonstration more immediately than the reporter who refuses to take chances and remains behind police lines.

Oakland Induction Center: Tuesday, October 17, 1967

V. T. RONAY

Apology:

The decision to write. My first thought was to request a large blank space. Violence does not allow articulation. The negation of truth and justice by its very lack does not permit reasonable communication and information, does not transform the inertia of the masses. Then I listened to the KPFA tapes of the encounter. How curiosity-ridden the Americans are. It was only the repeated sounds of what I had seen. But despite curiosity those people not present must at least know of the events, even if they were not privileged to have known the horror.

This morning position:

It is the fate of the protected American to be witness through the news media to horror. The TV, however, does not permit the comprehension of the reality of events. I did comprehend the blood, screams and the lack of faces on the cops. The blood on the clubs. But it was not my blood. I was witness in a safer place—across the street from the Induction Center. I had horror without fear. I had no physical contact. I was not close enough to hear the clubs hitting heads. I held a camera —a legitimate protective barrier behind which many people hid—behind which is America. When the action commenced, however, I be-

Avatar, November, 1967

came oblivious to the recording device in my hand. I had no sense of relief in avoiding the violence, no gladness of escape. These were the people that make my life, my home, my community and someday my government and country. I was watching these people who are my life being tortured.

The events:

The underlying notion: From my small understanding of the plans for the morning I saw a naïveté of which we all partook. The plan called for not one mass of people but many groups. The objective was to replace those arrested and removed from the doors of the induction center with more people so that the work of the law enforcement officers would be a continuous, never ending task, thereby not letting the inductees enter the building. Whether an actual shutting down of the building was seriously aimed at, or simply a necessary and essential rallying cry is not important. A demonstration of dissent from government policy regarding the war in Vietnam was the intention, and this place was the chosen spot. Two other points of strategy besides mobility seemed to be founded on this sad naïveté. At the campus rally Monday night we were urged to turn and run when the police began the attack (not as in LA where people ran backwards, going slowly and confusedly and so being slower moving targets for the police). Also, the people in the indented doorways of the induction center sat crowded in these recesses. The naïveté of our imagination precluded any conception of the relentless, aggressive fury of the police. We did not imagine that there would be 2000 cops to 4000 people. We did not seriously imagine, in spite of repeated warnings by the leaders at the rally, the scope of the violence by the cops. The police completely sealed off the streets leading to the center. There was no possibility of regrouping and coming down other streets. The image is of canyons between buildings with bulldozers clearing away the impediments to the proceedings. As a machine mashes what it does not move so the people crouching in the doorways were not permitted to leave and were trapped and beaten and when eventually given room to arise and run, they were chased and hit by swinging clubs. We did not know what law enforcement brutality was.

The dimensions:

The first and most striking shock in the events was the disparity of size between the police and the demonstrators, mainly kids. I had never noticed how small and skinny students and non-students are. Once the police line stood against the students it was impossible to see the people. Law enforcement officers are recruited partly by size, and they are massive instruments. The average members of the community, whether male or female, do not exercise nor are they addicted to a notion of the necessity of violence. So, not only were the sizes way out of proportion, so also was the protection used. The people had only their skulls and their screams. The line of offense had the helmets, muscles, gloves and a dedication to violence. When cries of police brutality have been raised in the civil-rights actions, I inconsiderately guessed situations of good large blacks and law enforcement officers fighting it out at an only slightly unequal level, the police having more refined equipment. Likewise, I have always viewed billy clubs as instruments of pushing and poking—not in the prehistorical sense of a deadly weapon used to break bones, damage kidneys and ovaries and crush skin. I was set straight: brutal as in animal, club as in caveman. Brute—lacking the ability to reason. *Webster New World Dictionary*. And the differences were psychological as well. Please pardon the impression but it seemed as though some of the men in blue were on some kind of amphetamine. The total rigidity, however, exceeded the powers of any drug I have seen used. They wore only short sleeved shirts although it was rather chilly at 5 and 6 a.m. Many police were silent and faceless two hours before their attack. A girl attempted a very reasonable non-hostile dialogue with a law enforcement officer who did not even look at her and did not speak to her. It was as though he was in a room immersed in pitch blackness and frozen in terror. This was not ugliness. Many police are ugly. This man had no face. What this individual had been given or told is impossible to imagine. The time came for the attack and it expended itself in a short seven-minute burst down the street, sweeping the young people beyond the block in front of the induction center. A line of law enforcement officers faced us with their clubs bloody. Some ten or so highway patrolmen milled in the empty street in front of the building—smiling. Another day another dollar? The only reflection by a policeman that I saw (must give credit where due) was a law enforcement officer facing us who looked down at his club between his hands, saw the large dense mass of blood on it and attempted to rotate the club discreetly so that the blood would not be exposed to our view. In this time directly after the clearing of the street the law enforcement officers were impassively facing us, as said. But the action had occurred and now they stood feet apart, heads occasionally turning and clubs held horizontally in both hands. Most hands gloved, some holding the clubs easily and lightly, but some men gripped the long stick tightly and now pressed the wood hard across their groins. Unknown powers. I am forced to wonder what comes out in the wash.

Violence is a disease. It is contagious. Dialectic is left behind. There is a transcendence of the logos in violence, just as in beatitude. The experience commands in its own vocabulary. When the defenders of law and order break away from what they are employed to uphold there is nothing for the victims to turn back to, the protection of the citizen has been removed. The police defeated their own reason for existence. The anticipated method of police restraint was the due process of law. There was little attempt at arrest. The force was the method. Our naïveté led us to expect proper and legal arrests. People not prepared for arrests were instructed not to come to the induction center. Every participant had a phone number written on his arm. Detailed procedures for getting names of all arrested persons to the steering committee were explained.

So we must begin again. Our faith in democracy is too strong to be shaken by the departure and we shall continually struggle for it.

A slight digression: Now it is a well-known and thoroughly justifiable fact that there exists little political consciousness of the black in America. There is nothing in this country for them to cherish. They have only their black skin to fight for. And looking around this morning I saw an occasional black policeman and although I cannot recall any black demonstrators I suppose there were a few. If a comparison between the violence of Tuesday and the riots of the summer is made, it is clear the police are not nearly as concerned about the ghettos as they are about the threat presented to them Tuesday by the pale little people hoping for peace and communication and not for power. It was the white that created this immorality and I suppose it would be appropriate for us alone to be bloodied in overcoming it. But the country we are in is very very large and there will come the moment when the two races must help each other, when there will not be room or time or self-concern enough to examine pigment or its lack. I hope by then we will have understood enough of Malcolm X to know the necessity for joint power.

And a word about those who give only their sympathy to us. I was very lucky. The choice of witnessing Tuesday was taken out of my hands. *Avatar* asked me to relate what was going on and I agreed. I had not planned to risk arrest, or to spend the morning there. I prefer the style of the ride on a truck filled with a rock band as on April 15. I have been apathetic about revolutionary tactics. It's not my bag. But I warily meandered into the scene. If each of us could help someone go to a demonstration, just any old pleasantly sympathetic friend who is doing his own thing to stop for three hours, not as a participator, but just as an observer attend such an event, we will have assisted that person immeasurably. This is the way "love" will transform those unmoved people. Their step towards us will be influenced I suppose by finer more subtle methods at which advertising seems adept. There are many sheep here. Through their inaction they are wolves. Since this day I have become free to help my brother. The girl's scream rising above the entire scene at the height of its violence. The four law enforcement officers tackling and beating one short fellow who had attempted to break away from his police escort in the middle of the empty street. These are burdens for those who saw as well as for those who were not there. Make love . . . but baby the blood's in my eyes and I can't see where you are.

As one always hears the background noise of moving feet, cars, sea or wind in the trees, the background noise I have been hearing in actual auditory hallucinations at every quiet moment are the sounds of thousands of people cheering, cheering burning cards and arrests. Through coming together we shall make changes. How hard it is that citizenship must be a thing learned and not to be had by nature. But we learn this love for our country now.

The Ivy League, in popular mythology, is the last bastion of gentlemanly behavior; here, Boston Brahmins, Jewish intellectuals, and western cowboys supposedly achieve some mutual understanding and learn how to run the country. It may have worked that way once, but the formula no longer holds true. Recently, at a prep school long distinguished as a breeding ground for Harvard, Yale minister turned draft protester William Sloan Coffin was attacked for his "moderation" by well-dressed (but not less radical for being well-dressed) students.

The author of this piece is the product of such an institution. A member of one of the more prestigious Harvard final clubs and an honors student, he expresses thoughts on the war and the draft that are as disturbing as the views of the traditional "beards and kooks." Resistance to the war, like death and taxes, now transcends class lines, and even the sons of bank presidents can no longer be shielded from social issues by attending the "right" college.

The Pentagon Affair
and the Exorcism of Innocence

JONATHAN CHANDLER

This girl is no bearded protester or one of those "all-too-real college professors"—she is straight from a Norman Rockwell portrait. The eyes twinkle with the unashamed joy of youth, the blond hair is conventional and brushed, the flowered dress reaches almost to the knees. Her voice is raised in a clear soprano. "We shall not be moved," she sings. "Just like a tree standing by the water, we shall not be moved."

She is very wrong about that. A federal marshal forces his foot under her. Pushing her with his club, he yells, "You're sitting on my foot. Move!" The men of the 82nd Airborne raise their rifles in expectation. The marshal jabs again. Then a rifle butt is slammed upon her head as another glances off her shoulder. She weeps hysterically. Blood is everywhere, staining her hair, her dress, streaming down her face. The marshal drags her through the lines, and that is the last we see of her.

There is so much to learn in this America: the way a rifle butt sounds hollow, like a defective bass drum, as it strikes a bald man's head, the way a Negro soldier cries and is relieved from duty, the way television lights make you feel like an animal, acting out a behavioral-science experiment. These are immediate, personal things, and they grab you hard. But you had to be there to feel it, and while we were being "dispersed," most of you were going about your daily lives, pretending either that the war does not affect you, or that your car lights turned on in daylight constituted an act of "responsible patriotism."

No one can speak for all those who went to Washington that Saturday in October. There was no ideological unity and much disagreement about tactics. But we were unanimously clear on one point: that the government refuses to level with the American people about its military adventure in Vietnam and that it refuses to respect the views of 46% of its population, which feels that this war is a mistake. If you believe that 46% is composed of hippies, bearded weirdos, and self-styled revolutionaries, then you will not take us seriously. And over the last three years, you haven't.

What will distress you, therefore, is how very much we are alike. I shave daily, I don't attend those mythical campus LSD parties, I am embarrassed by slogans, I don't look well in mod clothes. If there had been no war, I might well have become a normal citizen, a lawyer with a clean Army record, a loyal Democrat, a content, if occasionally troubled suburbanite. Now all that is impossible. For the war is not only destroying Vietnam, it is also brutalizing our domestic lives to the point where quite ordinary citizens are beginning to speak of open resistance, of refusing the draft in large numbers, of greater disruption of government activities.

That is what Washington was all about, and that is precisely why you were not told what happened there. The media blanket events with trivialities, they focus on individuals, they distort and sometimes tell outright lies. But the communications revolution is double-edged; when events are described even as they are still in progress, the participants get a clearer view of their actions. In Washington, some of the very troops who fired tear gas pellets heard the official reports over our transistor radios. No gas had been fired by soldiers, the Army claimed, but protesters were using it for propaganda purposes. "If the government can't tell the truth about an event in its own backyard," someone shouted to the troops, "how do you expect them to tell you the truth about Vietnam?" There was no answer.

There was no response from the military at all during the day, except from the surprisingly receptive MPs. The generals waited until night, when the Pentagon took on the terrifying atmosphere of a German amphitheatre. Columns of troops defended the entrance steps, and on the mall facing the demonstrators, yet more columns reinforced the front line of marshals and MPs. The lights from the Pentagon created eerie shadows, barely softened by the glow from our campfires. The MPs could see our faces and hear our softly insistent cries of "Brother, we're not here to oppose you, it's the people who control you we've got to see." The troops were offered food, cigarettes, and conversation about issues of mutual concern. Over and over, our loudspeakers reiterated our commitment to their safety, our spokesmen apologizing for any individual acts of provocation and urging them to join us.

This passion was not without effect. Moments after it was announced that a soldier had "dropped his rifle, taken off his belt and helmet, and walked into the crowd," a soldier lacking rifle, belt, and helmet was marched into the Pentagon under what looked like an armed guard. After that incident, tours of duty were shortened, and when it was totally dark and the newspaper deadline had passed, the 82nd Airborne was substituted for the MPs.

The 82nd is a tough outfit. Many have been in Vietnam, most saw action in Detroit. A flock of young demonstrators—camped quietly for the night, committed to non-violence—would be easy targets for dispersal. Yet tear gas was readied, helmets were snapped tight. We implored the commanding officer to communicate with us, but the huge speakers on the Pentagon roof were never used. Sitting quietly, the front lines with their backs to the troops, to avoid any possible provocation, we waited for the impossible: massive government-ordered violence against several thousand middle-class citizens. Today, the sister of Malcolm X had warned, you will learn what it is to be black. Now we know.

Systematically, the marshals pushed into the middle of the line, trying to divide us. I do not exaggerate when I say that hundreds were methodically beaten in the process. When I left at midnight, unable to witness the massacre any longer, the troops had broken through, although they suffered a few unforgivable casualties at the hands of bottle-throwing fanatics who responded in kind to the government attack. As they retreated across the fields, many demonstrators were weeping, but it was impossible to tell as they stumbled toward Washington whether their tears were for their cause or for their country.

But do not be deceived. We will not be intimidated by political repression. On our most pedigreed campuses, students are militantly demanding the separation of their universities from this country's immoral war effort. We are coming together in a more perfect union, and in true democratic fashion we will insist on equal punishment for our acts of disobedience because we are all leaders. At Harvard, for example, where students sat-in against a recruiter from Dow Chemical, the nation's largest napalm producer, not one of the 400 demonstrators budged when the dean arrived to read the university regulation about expulsion.

And this should not be too difficult to understand. Albert Camus stated our position best: "I should like to be able to love my country and still love justice." It is those who respond with "My country, right or wrong" who invite this government to ignore the essential concerns of right and wrong, and it is against this possibility that we will dedicate our energies, and if necessary, our lives.

As the war became more serious, the American peace movement rapidly expanded until it seemed as though every politician—in or out of office—opposed the war. Visions of conference tables co-opted many of the disaffected, and the optimism of the negotiators further defused support for the Left. Suddenly, adults are talking about the new viability of the democratic process; if we judge by actions, however, it still looks as though the people in Washington aren't listening very closely at all.

If the Government pays no attention to us, it should not expect us to be overly enthusiastic about its activities; the most popular topic for draft-age men is how to beat the draft. Those who argue that Vietnam is merely an aberration, that "Johnson is not Hitler," are insufficiently precise. The point is precisely that this generation can only intellectually appreciate the German ovens, while we see burning napalm on the news each evening. If we choose to fill the jails or leave the country because of it, at least we are insuring that a more human spirit, though threatened and condemned, is not yet extinguished.

Resist the Draft

WAYNE HANSEN

I sit here with a pile of yesterday's speeches on my left, a jumble of questions in my head, and an ache in my heart which has little to do with any of this, except cosmically perhaps. Yesterday, October 16, I handed my draft card to Jack Mendelsohn at the Arlington Street Church and joined over three hundred other men in the same illegal act. What we all did was sanctified by the church, but I don't think that that made any of us feel any less personally responsible. Maybe it was kind of comforting to know that not everyone in the U. S. hated you for doing what you felt was right—and they do hate us, you know, they hate us with everything they've got and they call us all the shitty names they can think of like traitor and coward and anti-American and it's the biggest bunch of fucking lies, the same kind of stuff you hear from any sick and dying festering thing which hates every real and honest and courageous *living* thing around it. I can tell you one thing, no one was

Avatar, October, 1967.

more surprised than I was when I did it. When I first came into contact with the whole middle-class college scene of anti-war and Help the NEEgrows in Mississippi, I thought it was the silliest biggest cop-out ever created. I know why now and I know why I've changed. Before I saw only the appearances of the scene, in much the same way as the guy who drives through Harvard Square on Saturday night might think that a few sixteen-year-old kids who've combed their hair down over their ears are the essence of the so-called Hippy Movement. No wonder they're turned off—I'm turned off too. But what I've seen now is the fire in the center of that movement, the sun of the solar system of the anti-war, future freedom in America movement, and I recognized it in my brothers and I belonged there and nowhere else. It is a change that only those very close to me could know about, but it is an astonishing change. My hair has not turned grey and my teeth have not fallen out, my clothes are the same clothes I have always worn, but the fire inside comes out like a blast from a furnace, my eyes are akindle and my heart, my heart which has always been drawn by the truest feelings *only* is lying in the middle of Main Street, America, now screaming, now pleading, now weeping, now still and patiently awaiting the return of the deepest and truest American values, the ones on which this country was founded, the heart and soul of America. I am standing, my heart joined insepa-rably with the heart of true American reality, saying only one thing, that man has the right to freedom which is both joy and service, and that he must forever carry his highest ideals out into the world to have them stifled by stagnating societies and the entropic forces of the universe, *only* to make it absolutely necessary for him to build them all around him, to create his own world, which by the depth of its source is every-one's world. America must return to the source of its light.

Those of us who yesterday said no to the laws of this country at the same time said yes, everlastingly yes, to the spirit of America. We are the true Americans, reborn at a time when it is almost a crime to be truly American. Those creeps who drove by the church in a Cadillac waving an American flag and calling coward, why, they don't even know what it is to be an American. I say it is a crime for them to misuse such spirit, only the raggle-taggles of it is theirs, because while we burned those cards with our hands, we carried that spirit in our hearts, but while they carried that symbol in their hands, they trampled that spirit long, long ago, when they did not continually work to keep it alive. Oh, maybe they had it once, reciting the pledge of allegiance in a second-grade schoolroom or jammed in a fox hole in Italy with shells bursting over their heads, but they have died to it and it is dead in them and they are still like a branch cut from a tree whose dry leaves still rustle in the wind—they have no source of life. We might thank them for having done well once, but we cannot respect them, for they no longer do.

My brothers, how can I tell you. I walked to the Common yesterday without knowing all I would do by the end of the day. But I sat and I listened while men spoke, and there were times when I could not tell whether the voice that rose up over the crowd was Howard Zinn's voice or Ray Mungo's voice or my voice or everyone's voice united as one. I walked across the Common and to the Arlington Street Church and I could not tell if we were two thousand marching in Boston on October 16 or all of humanity on its slow, painful and joyful progression to the freedom which is its birthplace and its goal. I sat in the Arlington Street Church and I could not tell if we were the names and the bodies we are known by now or if we were Paine and Franklin, and Jefferson or Emerson, Lincoln, and Thoreau. We were all of them, all of them on our way to becoming more of them, for the knowledge that was theirs is yet for us to learn, but we are learning, the pure vision that was theirs we yet must see, but we are seeing, and the strength to manifest that vision that was theirs, must be ours also—and yet we do not have it, but we will.

The Beg-In is an idea so profoundly humiliating, so devoid of the self-advertisement that too often characterizes peace demonstrations, in short, such a good idea, that it has never been used. Now, with battlelines drawn on both sides, it seems inapplicable; millions of beggars would be required to make any impression on an Administration that systematically responds to large demonstrations with increased escalation.

"If two people march," this Berkeley Barb editorial claims, "the papers would say one half." For every Vietcong we kill, we probably claim two dead. And it is well known that some police multiply the worth of confiscated marijuana by ten, for publicity purposes. The relationship of certain ratios to contemporary events would, if we could verify them, probably tell us more about our times than the stream of "interpretive" histories that clog our bookstores and our minds.

Toward a National Beg-In:
Crawl for Peace

Do you believe the end is in sight, and that the umbrella of protection is like cotton candy in the rain? Will the President push the panic button, and get on the gold phone, to the trolls in their caves, and command them to let loose their arrows?

Or were you impressed by the results of the last peace march, and do the results of that march make your pulse pound in the dark?

The boob tube mutilates the word, and if two people march the papers would say one half. Just an arm and a leg, folks, walking down the street, and that's why it's front page news, folks.

When nothing else works, what's left to do?

Here's what. Get down on your hands and knees, and beg for the life of your little girl, or your side-kicks, or your dog. Because we've tried everything else.

That's what's behind our plea for a National Beg-In. We all know it's hopeless. The Beg-In will fail, like every sit-in and the civil-rights move-

Berkeley Barb, June 9, 1967

ment and the peace marches and everything you do in the Great Atlantic and Pacific Empire.

But this is a media-designed event. When the TV camera zooms in on you, their microphones will pick up this:

"Please, LBJ, don't kill me, don't kill my woman I beg you. We want to live. Let us live and do our thing. Please don't attack North Vietnam. Please stop killing American Boys and Vietnamese people. I'm begging you, Congress, listen, please."

And when the police come to get you and your friends, you will say to the fuzz: "Please don't take us away. We're only begging for peace, we don't want any trouble. We're begging you, please don't arrest us."

The Beg-In is designed to be the most humiliating spectacle we can put on. You must be prepared to humble yourself for all the eyes to drink in.

We will practice by crawling on our hands, knees, elbows, bellies across the mall, up the stairs, through the corridors, into the mayor's or city council's chambers, to implore them to intercede for us.

When we have learned to wail and roll our eyes for mercy, we will take our pleas to the White House. Thousands and thousands of prone suppliants will cry out in a massive Crawl For Peace and National Beg-In.

Wriggling past the monuments, through the parks, across the lawns to moan under Johnson's window, "Nooooo, please no more bombing, no more killing, please, please, please, oh, please let everyone live, Oooooooh, pleeeease."

Because there is nothing left. You're begging for your life. That's where it's at. That's the statement that must be made. Nothing else works, and begging probably won't either, at least I don't kid myself, but we have to do it. We can't sit by and let them blow up the world.

How long have we been on the brink? Can you take it anymore? Then the Beg-In is a chance for release, catharsis if you like.

Beg-In's could take place all over the United States, and if it can be done, the rest of the world.

Nothing upsets them more than the scene on Haight. And why? It threatens. And the Beg-In will threaten too.

No matter how humiliated we are by the Beg-In, they will be more confused, more ashamed, more humiliated. They won't know what to make of it. It will shake them up. If they see thousands of people crawling down the street, begging for peace, begging the press to cover the event honestly, what can they do, what can they think? They will be moved, and will call us nuts.

But we'll beg them to listen, and every time a reporter asks a question, we'll beg the leaders of the world, and the men who tend the corral.

What can you do, doctor, when the patient seems delighted and convinced that he's pure, but you know that he's on the way out?

So I'm begging you. If these arguments make any sense to you, think it over. Let's everybody get down on our hands and knees and make the Beg-In.

Now's the time, there is no time, before the engines of war grind up all the love, and powder it, and then try to market it, and push it on TV, and give it to the Vietnamese, and put a little of the instant love in the bombs, just a pinch.

But instant love doesn't work when you mix it with gunpowder.

And one other thing, when you're out there marching, wouldn't it be nice to have a little effigy of LBJ, sort of like a little doll, or better, a puppet. No, don't burn it, don't hang it, beg it for your life, and ask yourself if you let puppets pull your strings.

Please do this, we beg you.

Epilogue

In other times, one approached epilogues with a certain finality; the author at least knew his own mind well enough to draw the loose ends together for his readers. Now such confidence is presumptuous. Existential moments for a few have become existential hours for many; at no time in our memory has the mood been so full of anguish, so devoid of hope.

The last few months present a consistent history of non-communication for me. A member of a fellowship committee indicated that my candidacy would be rejected because I had edited a book about the "youth problem" and could offer no solutions. A highly placed official of the Harvard University administration admitted to me, straight-faced, that Harvard valued order and procedure more than it cherished individual lives. And one of the directors of a leading psychiatric clinic stated that it no longer bothered him to read the newspapers and realize that most of the country was probably insane. All three men are still able to cope, although the strain of dealing with what one of them called "the troubled young" is beginning to upset them more than they would like.

Because I am directly affected by this madness, it has already minimized my ability to cope, and I do not believe I am alone in this situation. By no one's decree, each of us must individually confront a system that already fulfills some of the less generous definitions of totalitarianism. The damage that this will cause—in wasted energies and lost ambition—is incalculable. Already, there are depressing trends that no one dares to report. In some departments at Harvard, many seniors have dropped their theses; what bothers the professors is that these are mostly the high-honors candidates. Lower classmen regularly interrupt lectures to debate their instructors, a phenomenon almost never witnessed at Harvard. And enough freshmen were distressed about their miseducation to appear in groups before the Dean to inform him that their situation was intolerable.

I do not write about Harvard at such length because Harvard is in any way "underground" or subversive; on the contrary, it is still as staid as one might expect. But "staid" these days means radical as opposed to revolutionary. The underground has surfaced—it is everywhere. If underground means hostility to authority and a denial of traditional assumptions about life, literature, and politics, then it has now been legitimized by what used to be considered the Establishment. The underground newspapers are the flimsiest manifestation of such sentiments; they are perhaps only the first tangible beginning of a disaffection so radical that it will frighten America as much as the black revolt.

What is hard to explain to aging cynics is that these people mean it; they are not just acting out some classic ritual dance of rebellion. If these notes—articulate and incoherent mutterings from an underground as visible as our long-haired youth—are dismissed as the usual whines of "cussers and doubters," then we no longer take each other seriously. And if that happens, those who argue that the times never change, that parents and children have always fought, that the system has always been unjust, and that *Realpolitik* is the rule in personal affairs as in international relations, may find themselves so isolated from reality that their state may as well be called pure fantasy.